The Complete Idiot's Guide to Dealing with In-Laws Reference Card

Checklist for Building Great Relationships with In-Laws

_____ 1. Don't be afraid to speak up if your in-laws' behavior conflicts with your values or beliefs.

_____ 2. Be proactive: Create your own goals—don't fall victim to the past. If you come from an abusive, dysfunctional family, you are not destined to pass on that behavior to the next generations—and you don't have to accept it from your in-laws.

_____ 3. Decide what kind of family you want. Then work with your in-laws to create it.

_____ 4. Develop a capacity for self-awareness. Take a few steps back from the situation and think about your own thoughts, feelings, moods, and actions.

_____ 5. Fight embedded tendencies and change your interactions with your in-laws.

_____ 6. Remember that the way you treat any one of your in-laws affects every relationship in the family.

_____ 7. Do things that build trust among your in-laws, such as being kind, apologizing, keeping promises, and forgiving.

_____ 8. Be a friend. Spend time with your in-laws and take an interest in their work, hobbies, ideas, and experiences. Knowing them better will make for fewer problems.

_____ 9. Listen carefully and try to put yourself in your in-laws' position.

_____ 10. Use constructive ways to settle problems and differences of opinion among your in-laws.

_____ 11. Think win/win: Find ways for everyone to come out ahead.

_____ 12 Synergize: Come up with a solution that is more than the sum of its parts.

_____ 13. Schedule time with your in-laws. Make it qual... ...doing things together that everyone enjoys.

_____ 14. To keep your relationship with your in-laws ... believe in each other.

alpha books

Checklist for Dealing with Difficult In-Laws

If your in-laws...	Don't...	Instead...
Hate you.	Hate them in return.	Try to forge bonds through common interests and kindness.
Ignore you.	Assume that your in-laws know how you feel.	Explain how you feel in a straight-forward manner. Keep your cool.
Make a mistake based on ignorance of your culture.	Be overly offended.	Educate them about your heritage.
Pit you against your spouse or another in-law.	Bad-mouth the offending in-law.	Call a family meeting and explain your position.
Spoil the children.	Be accusatory or judgemental.	Consider the long-range effect. Is this issue worth the battle?
Disparage your success or the success of your children.	Hurl a cake in their direction.	Exaggerate the negativity to point out the error of their ways. Then sit back and smile.
Put your children to a loyalty test with your spouse.	Let it go.	Form an alliance. Be firm and clear that such behavior can't continue.
Sexually, physically, emotionally abuse a vulnerable in-law or child.	Ignore it.	Gather your evidence and then call authorities to report the abuse.

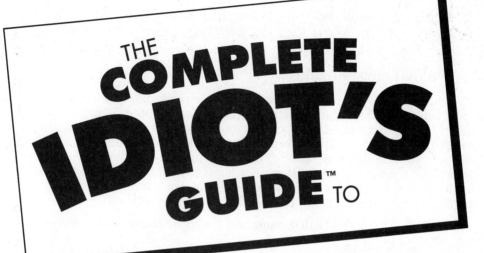

THE

COMPLETE
IDIOT'S
GUIDE™ TO

Dealing with
In-Laws

by Dr. Laurie Rozakis

alpha
books

A Division of Macmillan General Reference
A Simon and Schuster Macmillan Company
1633 Broadway, New York, NY 10019-6785

This book is for my wonderful father-in-law, Nick Rozakis, and my delight-ful mother-in-law, Marie Rozakis, with much love. I have truly been blessed; you are very special people.

©1998 by Laurie Rozakis

THE COMPLETE IDIOT'S GUIDE name and design are trademarks of Macmillan, Inc.

International Standard Book Number: 0-02-862107-7
Library of Congress Catalog Card Number: 97-80975

00 99 98   4 3 2 1

Interpretation of the printing code: the rightmost number of the first series of numbers is the year of the book's printing; the rightmost number of the second series of numbers is the number of the book's printing. For example, a printing code of 98-1 shows that the first printing occurred in 1998.

Printed in the United States of America

Alpha Development Team

Publisher
Kathy Nebenhaus

Executive Editor
Gary M. Krebs

Managing Editor
Bob Shuman

Marketing Brand Manager
Felice Primeau

Senior Editor
Nancy Mikhail

Development Editors
Phil Kitchel
Jennifer Perillo
Amy Zavatto

Editorial Assistant
Maureen Horn

Production Team

Production Editor
Linda Seifert

Cover Designer
Mike Freeland

Designer
Glenn Larsen

Photo Editor
Richard H. Fox

Illustrator
Jody P. Schaeffer

Indexer
Nadia Ibrahim

Production Team
Angela Calvert
Kim Cofer
Mary Hunt

Contents at a Glance

Contents

Part 4: And Baby Makes Power Play 205

18 Sexpectations 207

19 Kidding Around with the In-Laws 217

20 Baby Talk 229

Foreword

First things first. If you're a friend of Woody Allen, please make sure to get him a copy of this book. It is written with such wisdom and humor that I know, if he reads it, he'll discover all sorts of ways to warm the heart of his bitter mother-in-law, Mia Farrow. Now think about it. If this book could guide wild Woody into mad Mia's arms (or at least get them to shake hands), imagine how it could improve your in-law relationships. Dr. Laurie Rozakis does a masterful job of offering common-sense solutions to in-law problems that range from simple slights to cosmic catastrophes. You can apply her tips to in-law struggles that are as old as the Bible ("My geeky brother-in-law wants to sleep with me") and as new as 1998 ("My geeky brother-in-law keeps propositioning me by e-mail").

For 10 years as an advice columnist based at the *Chicago Sun-Times*, I've been well aware that few readers' woes are as troubling and exasperating as those involving in-laws. Just consider these letters, none of which were sealed with a kiss:

A son-in-law writes that his father-in-law always wants to take him hunting: "He'll say to me, 'Let's go kill some dinner!'and I feel like saying to him, 'Let's shoot you in the foot so we don't have to go!'"

A mother-in-law complains that her daughter-in-law expects 30 hours of babysitting a week: "My son's wife said, 'Why'd you become a grandmother if you didn't want grand-children?' I felt like saying, 'You selfish nutcase! I didn't apply to be a grandmother. You made me one!'"

A daughter-in-law complains: "My husband and I have been married for 11 years, but my mother-in-law still displays photos of his ex-girlfriends all over her house. Isn't it time for her to put away the prom picture with good old Mindy?"

Sometimes, I can give advice to readers based on experience. I am the loyal son of a veteran mother-in-law. I am the devoted husband of a loving daughter-in-law, and I try to be a loving son-in-law to her parents. Of course, I've also been called a meddlesome brother-in-law, and since I have three young daughters, I suspect that someday I'll be a suspicious, annoying, impossible father-in-law.

Actually, I have long been a student of the in-law game. I am the grandson of four people who, in their lives, served as fathers- and mothers-in-law for a combined 203 years. So I've seen fierce combat, great love, and sharp comebacks. All of that has come in handy as I've tried to write pithy answers to readers' letters.

For instance, one woman wrote to me saying that she and her husband take his mother out for dinner and a drive each Sunday. "My mother-in-law sits in the front seat, next to her son, and I'm alone in the back. Is that proper?" I told the young woman: "Assuming your mother is healthy enough to climb into the back seat, that's where she belongs. If your husband doesn't agree, suggest that you drive and he sit in back with his mother. Then drop them both off for Sunday dinner and drive home alone. They'll find their way."

Then there was the man who wrote: "Every time my mother-in-law visits, she snoops around the house asking questions: How much does this cost? How much does that cost?' It's like she's appraising everything we have. How can I respond?"

I advised: "Next time your mother-in-law asks, 'How much does this cost?' politely respond, 'I'm sorry, it's not for sale.'"

These answers work fine as entertainment in a newspaper advice column. But obviously, in-law relationships are more complicated and need more detailed attention. That's why I plan to start suggesting this book to readers seeking solutions to in-law dilemmas. Dr. Rozakis offers just the right mix of moxie and heart, with direct, bite-sized, non-confrontational tips. She also provides scores of anecdotes, jokes, statistics, and historical asides, all of which serve to remind us that we're not alone—the in-law parade marches by most every house in the world. There's a measure of comfort in that.

Who knows? Perhaps someday, this book will lead Soon-Yi to say the words, "Mom, thank you for welcoming Woody as a son."

Jeff Zaslow, *Chicago Sun-Times* advice columnist

Introduction

In-laws.

The very word strikes terror in the even the most stout-hearted.

In-laws.

Ever feel the urge to emulate the Romans and simply throw your relatives into the rushing waters? If so, you've got plenty of company.

In-laws.

We can choose our friends but not our family. And therein lies the problem.

A bunch of my in-laws, 1996.

What You'll Learn in This Book

In *The Complete Idiot's Guide to Dealing with In-Laws*, I'll tell you how to cope with some of the most common—and distressing—problems you're likely to encounter with your in-laws. Today, being an in-law is more difficult than ever before, with divorce, nontraditional families, blended families, and step-parents, step-children, and step-everyone else.

This book will help you understand the stages that everyone goes through when they become an in-law...or acquire some new ones. It will help you learn powerful strategies for dealing with the different types of in-laws you're likely to acquire, including scatterbrains, powerbrokers, and competitors. You'll see how to cope with the well-meaning and not-so-well-meaning cranks in your family, too.

Being a good in-law takes a lot of hard work, but it's well worth the effort. Whether you're dealing with your mother-in-law, father-in-law, sister-in-law, brother-in-law, or ex-in-law, each person in your extended family has the potential to enrich your life—or make it miserable.

Remember how you cried when you discovered that Mary Martin was flying with strings? Remember how shattered you felt when the New York Jets went 1–15? Remember how you felt when your hair began to thin—just as your middle began to plump? Well, your in-laws can drive you round the bend, too.

I can't promise you that if you marry into a large family (or acquire one through everyone else's marriage, intermarriage, and rampant reproduction) you'll experience heaven on earth (that's a pint of rocky road, a down comforter, and a Ginger Rogers-Fred Astaire movie), but I *can* guarantee that by the time you finish this book, you'll have the tools you need to deal with even the most difficult in-laws.

This book is divided into five parts that take you through the process of developing healthy and fulfilling relationships with your in-laws. You'll learn how to make a good first impression on your in-laws, how to agree on mutually acceptable names for each other, and how to accept each other's differences. Most of all, you'll finish this book better equipped to create the kind of family that everyone wants—and deserves. Here's what you'll find in the five parts of this book:

Part 1: In-Laws and Outlaws teaches you the ground rules for establishing a healthy relationship among in-laws. First, I'll teach you some of the key issues you'll encounter as you blend your family with your beloved's clan. Then I'll show you how to get off on the right foot by making a great first impression with your in-laws. Along the way, we'll solve some of the immediate problems you'll face with your in-laws—especially the issue of what to call them!

Part 2: Trouble in Paradise shows you how to plan your wedding, so you can make sure that rice is the only thing that's thrown on your special day. Then we'll focus on the two most common problems that you'll encounter with your in-laws: Your mother-in-law and your father-in-law. Just so no one feels slighted, I cover issues that arise with sisters- and brothers-in-law, too.

Part 3: In-Law and Order covers the two main conflicts among in-laws: Money and power. If your in-laws are like everyone else's, the arguments in your family range from the distribution of material goods to wrangles over turf issues. In this section, you'll learn how to use conflict to bring your family closer together.

Part 4: And Baby Makes Power Play focuses on the key issues that probably obsess your in-laws: Your sex life, reproductive plans, and child-rearing practices. In this section, I give you the questions *and* the answers so you'll be armed for these assaults.

Part 5: Circumstance-in-Law describes the curve balls that life lobs at us and our in-laws. In this section, you'll learn effective techniques for dealing with some of the most serious problems that confront in-laws, including chronic illness, abuse, addiction, aged in-laws, divorce, and widowhood.

More for Your Money!

In addition to all the explanations and teaching, this book contains other types of information to make it even easier for you to learn how to get along well with your in-laws and create healthy families. Here's how you can recognize these features:

It's All Relative

These are interesting, useful bits of background information that give you even more of an "inside edge" when it comes to dealing with your in-laws. You could skip these tidbits, but you won't want to because they're much too tasty!

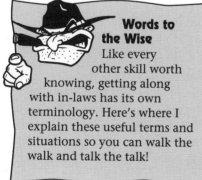

Words to the Wise

Like every other skill worth knowing, getting along with in-laws has its own terminology. Here's where I explain these useful terms and situations so you can walk the walk and talk the talk!

Don't Go There

These warnings help you stay on track. They can make it easier for you to avoid the little goofs—and the major pitfalls—that can sink families.

Family Matters

Use these hints to make it easier and more enjoyable to get along with your in-laws.

Part 1
In-Laws and Outlaws

When Hank Aaron was up to bat for the first time in his major league career, the catcher for the opposing team tried to rattle him by saying, "Hey, kid, you're holding your bat all wrong. You should hold it with the label up so you can read it."

The young rookie for the Milwaukee Braves, who later went on to become the greatest home-run hitter of all time, was not at a loss for words. He simply replied, "I didn't come up here to read."

You *know* why you're up at bat, but that doesn't mean that everyone else does. Becoming an in-law has never been easy, and it's getting more challenging as families change shape faster than Oprah gains and loses weight.

In this section, you'll learn the ground rules for establishing a healthy relationship among in-laws. First, I'll teach you some of the key issues you'll encounter as you blend your family with your beloved's clan. Then I'll show you how to get off on the right foot by making a great first impression with your in-laws. Along the way, we'll solve some of the immediate problems you'll face with your in-laws—especially the issue of what to call them!

Chapter 1

Married to a Mob

In This Chapter

➤ Define "in-laws"

➤ Discover why in-laws are important

➤ Shake your family tree

Deep in the Tennessee hills, a farmer's mule kicked his mother-in-law to death. An enormous crowd of men turned out for the funeral. The minister, examining the crowd outside the church, commented to a farmer friend, "This old lady must have been mighty popular. Just look how many people left work to come to her funeral."

"They're not here for the funeral," replied the friend. "They're here to buy the mule."

As George Burns once said, happiness is having a large, loving, caring, close-knit family—in another city. In this chapter, you'll define "in-laws" and explore the role of your spouse's family in your life. I'll help you sort your in-laws so you can figure out *who* you're going to have to deal with in your spouse's clan, whether you're just married, remarried, or long-married. You'll be amazed (and probably terrified) to discover how many in-laws you really have. (Hint: In nearly all cases, a mother-in-law and a father-in-law are just the tip of the family tree.)

This chapter also helps you to discover that you're not the only one who believes that everyone else's family handles its problems logically—it's only *your* in-laws who are crazy, aggravating, overemotional, uptight, and a few fries short of a Happy Meal.

Monkeys in the Family Tree

Let's start with a little family survey to see how your in-laws stack up against the competition. Here are five possible family situations. Circle the letter of the answer that best describes *your* in-laws.

1. Your in-laws find a stranger in their backyard so they…

    a. ask the intruder to identify himself. Your in-laws *always* identify people in their yard before shooting at them.

    b. check the alarm system to make sure the family jewels are locked in the safe, give the French poodle "Snookums" a Valium, and grab a nine-iron for protection.

    c. invite him in for a little nosh, maybe a brisket, some noodles, and a cheesecake or two. Hey, even robbers get hungry.

    d. look up from *The American Farmer*, nod at each other, and send Killer the 300-pound Doberman to deal with it.

2. It's holiday time, so your in-laws…

    a. purchase a nice centerpiece prepared by a taxidermist.

    b. make reservations at that understated new French place on the Upper East Side.

    c. go to Miami. Remember: Spring ahead, fall back, and winter in Miami.

    d. gather their 200 closest cousins and set out the Jell-O salads, white bread, and milk.

3. Your in-laws see a car broken down on the side of the road, so they…

    a. use pantyhose and duct tape to tow it to Twitchell's Rent-a-Wreck.

    b. have the chauffeur deal with it. These issues can be *so* messy.

    c. see if the driver is married. So what if he's short? He can stand on his wallet.

    d. rebuild the car from top to bottom in 15 minutes.

4. Your in-laws are unfailingly polite: they always:

   a. provide an alibi to the police for family members, rarely fish coins out of public toilets, and always offer to bait your hook.

   b. tip the doorman at Christmas. What *was* his name again?

   c. try not to make noise while they're listening into your phone conversations.

   d. offer you the first look at the new JC Penney winter catalog.

5. Your in-laws always:

   a. dim their headlights for approaching vehicles, even if the gun is loaded and the deer is in sight.

   b. leave and never say good-bye.

   c. say good-bye and never leave.

   d. call before they visit.

Score Yourself

➤ **Mainly A's** At the movies, your in-laws talk to characters on the screen, even though tests have proven they can't hear you. Better run for cover.

➤ **Mainly B's** Your father-in-law, Warren Henry Clark Francis XVIII, wears plaid pants on *and* off the golf course. Your mother-in-law, Eleanor, puts on pearls and chiffon to play bridge. Of course, you'll never be good enough for their darling child. Fortunately, there's a fat trust fund.

➤ **Mainly C's** So what if she *is* Mrs. Portnoy? She's still a helluva cook. And a little guilt never hurt anyone.

➤ **Mainly D's** How many times *has* your father-in-law told you about the ribbons his pig won at the 1975 State Fair?

It's All Relative

Throughout history, arranged unions were the accepted form of marriage almost everywhere in the world. By the 20th century, arranged marriages in Western societies were deader than Elvis (sorry, folks), but they still persist in India and parts of Africa today. Of course, arranged marriages would still be the norm in America if more parents had their way.

What's an In-Law?

Okay, so now you know that some in-laws are, um, more *inbred* than others, but we still haven't defined what makes someone an *in-law*. You know an in-law isn't a breath mint, floor wax, or the nifty high-impact polymer used in storage containers. What *is* an in-law? Where do you draw the line between family and non-family?

Are in-laws just the immediate kinfolk on your spouse's side (that is, parents) or do you have to include all of your spouse's assorted brothers, sisters, aunts, uncles, and grandparents who usually surface only at weddings, funerals, or tailgate parties? And what about ex-spouses? Once the divorce papers are signed, do these relatives become non-in-laws?

Where do you draw the line between who's in and who's out when the will is read and the California onion dip gets passed around? Take the following quiz to see who *you* consider to be a legitimate in-law.

> **Words to the Wise**
>
> The term *same sex spousal equivalent* is a nice way to cover all the bases when it comes to identifying someone living with someone else of the same sex. The term is more specific than "companion," but less in-your-face than "lover." "Significant other" is also in the running.

Put a check mark next to each of the following categories that you consider an in-law. (Don't worry if they're not part of *your* family yet. This is the nineties—they'll join soon enough.)

____ 1. Mother-in-law

____ 2. Father-in-law

____ 3. Stepmother-in-law

____ 4. Stepfather-in-law

____ 5. The mother of your same sex spousal equivalent

____ 6. The father of your same sex spousal equivalent

____ 7. The parents of your stepbrothers

____ 8. The parents of your stepsisters

____ 9. Spouse's grandmother

____ 10. Spouse's grandfather

____ 11. Brother(s)-in-law

____ 12. Sister(s)-in-law

____ 13. Son(s)-in-law

____ 14. Daughter(s)-in-law

____ **15.** Spouse's aunts

____ **16.** Spouse's uncles

____ **17.** Spouse's cousins

____ **18.** Spouse's former mates, if children were involved

(No credit for any pets your spouse may have acquired in a previous relationship, even if they *do* eat from the table.)

You should have checked all twenty categories. "What!" you yelp. "*All* these people are in-laws?" Yes, they are. According to the argument my husband and I had last night (the argument that I won), each and every person on this list is considered an in-law today.

And what's more, you're likely to have more than one entry in each category. For example, because my father-in-law has three former wives and one current wife, I have four mothers-in-law. Fortunately, I really like three of them very much.

Here's how I define an in-law: An in-law is someone who...

➤ has a blood tie to you or your spouse, however tenuous it may be;

➤ has become a de facto member of your spouse's family by reason of charm, need, or longevity;

➤ you're going to face at important family functions, such as Thanksgiving, the opening of a new Bloomingdales, or the first day of hunting season.

Swimming in the Gene Pool

Even though we grant in-law status to a whole stack of people, not all in-laws are created equal. Like chickens, some in-laws rank higher than other in-laws in the pecking order. This is reflected in the official leave policies of many large corporations. Here is a policy from a major corporation that states the amount of time an employee is allocated when a specific relative shuffles off this mortal coil:

> **Family Matters**
> Any offspring your spouse has produced from previous relationships is considered a *child*, not an *in-law*. Any offspring your spouse has produced from an extramarital encounter (whether or not you have killed your spouse in the meantime) is also a *child*.

> **Family Matters**
> What do we do with the long-time family friends who are called "Aunt" and "Uncle" as a sign of respect? I've dubbed these folks "faux in-laws." Feel free to use this term in your family as appropriate.

> **Words to the Wise**
> Another definition of *family* is "any group of persons closely related by blood or kinship, as parents, children, uncles, aunts, and cousins."

Up to three working days may be allowed, one being the day of the funeral, without loss of pay, for cases of death in the immediate family. Immediate family for purposes of this policy includes: Spouse, child, parents, parents-in-law, brother, sister, grandparents, grandchildren, son-in-law, and daughter-in-law. Only the day of the funeral may be granted as a day without loss of pay in the case of other relatives. Exceptions will be considered on an individual basis.

This Ain't the Brady Bunch

In the movies, Danny DeVito and Arnold Schwartzenegger can wake up and discover they're twins. In real life, families are just as surprising—and convoluted. With half of all marriages ending in divorce, in just a few years former in-laws can start stacking up like empty pop bottles.

It's not unheard of today for Daddy to skip out with the au pair, get a face-lift, and start a whole new family. Then Mom takes up with her Fen Shui master and goes to La La Land to find her navel and herself. Thank goodness someone invented those "Hello My Name is _____" stickers; they're great for identifying the players at family dinners. As far as modern families are concerned, name stickers are the best invention since DNA typing.

When I was growing up in the 1950s and 1960s, I didn't know any couples who had divorced. Oh, I knew a lot of really miserable couples cohabiting in separate bedrooms with the kids serving as the demilitarized zone. I knew too many families split by strife and silence—but they were all what passed for "intact." And in public, at least, they seemed reasonably nuclear. That was before the explosion.

Now, the nuclear family is as rare as a pork chop at a bar mitzvah. Today's families are hyperextended, scaffolded on an intricate—and often precarious—framework of in-laws, ex-laws, and outlaws. Nontraditional households are increasingly common, with strengths and weaknesses all their own. Check out these statistics on the changing face of the American family:

➤ Single mothers, single fathers, blended families, and grandparent caregivers account for 49 percent of households in the country today.

➤ One in three American families with children under 18 is headed by a single parent.

➤ An estimated 3.4 children in the U.S. live in a household headed by a grandparent.

We've gone from the nuclear families in *Father Knows Best* and *Leave It to Beaver* in the fifties to the divorced single mother of *One Day at a Time* in the seventies. Ten years later came the single corporate working mother who hired a single live-in house cleaning dad in *Who's the Boss*. In the nineties, Hollywood just threw up its hands about the state of the American family, resulting in the no-parent home in "Party of Five." And hey, let's not even get into *Soap*. Now that's a family!

Gaze a few years into the future and chances are you'll find that the family has continued to evolve in strange and wondrous new ways. What does this mean for you? There are sure to be more in-laws on *your* horizon!

It's All Relative

The Canadian divorce laws don't take into account the extended family of Canadian Asians. At divorce, the couple is supposed to split its assets equally, but the situation isn't that simple in extended households. In Asian culture, the parents-in-law usually live with married sons, not daughters, because a daughter is "given away" in marriage and thus is no longer a part of her parents' family. Since most parents-in-law do not contribute to household expenses, they can often amass substantial wealth at the expense of their daughter-in-law. As a result, an Asian Canadian female often finds her rights abrogated during divorce.

A Real Cast of Characters

Here's a "typical" contemporary family: Lin and Ralph. Lin's father has two children from a previous marriage. Then he married again and had another child. When that marriage collapsed, he separated and married a woman with two daughters. A few years later, he divorced her and moved in with a younger woman who has a daughter of her own. They've been together for more than a decade now. Then we come to Lin's mother, who came out of the closet and declared she was gay when Lin was in high school. She lives with her partner out West somewhere—and we haven't even gotten to Ralph's side.

Can't tell the players in this family without a scorecard? *Your* family is probably even more convoluted than this one. Why not make your own scorecard to help you know who you have to deal with? Here's how.

Start with a *pedigree chart*, a list of you and your relatives. Here is an example of a branch from the pedigree chart of the world's original dysfunctional family, the British Royals. The homicidal Tudors shown here are descended from whole dynasties of warmongering Plantagenets. In turn, they produced mounds of gibbering Stuarts and mad Hanoverians. There are more bones in *this* closet than in the Colonel's trash bin. Let's start with Henry VIII, the Big Daddy of Divorce. He ended up with a slew of ex-wives and in-laws, as this pedigree chart shows:

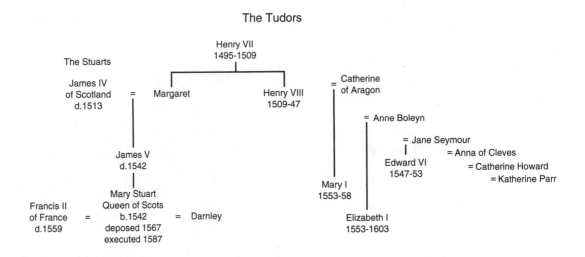

The Tudors

Henry VII
1495-1509

The Stuarts

James IV
of Scotland = Margaret   Henry VIII
d.1513   1509-47

= Catherine
of Aragon

= Anne Boleyn

= Jane Seymour

= Anna of Cleves

Edward VI   = Catherine Howard
1547-53
= Katherine Parr

James V
d.1542

Mary I
1553-58

Mary Stuart
Queen of Scots
Francis II   b.1542
of France   =   deposed 1567   = Darnley   Elizabeth I
d.1559   executed 1587   1553-1603

Those Wacky Windsors

Then we come to Henry's far-flung kinfolk, the Windsors. The in-laws in this family have never been particularly friendly; "frosty" is a charitable way to describe their relationships with each other. The Queen never got chummy with any of her daughters-in-law, neither toe-sucking Fergie nor noble Diana. Queenie was chilly toward Princess Anne's ex, Mark Phillips, as well.

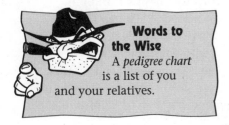

Words to the Wise

A *pedigree chart* is a list of you and your relatives.

The disastrous relationship between Diana and her in-laws has received the most attention. Diana was never exactly thick with her in-laws, Queen Elizabeth and Prince Philip. Their insensitivity to her problems was extraordinary. Diana even appeared on television to discuss her strife with her in-laws: "Well, maybe I was the first person ever to be in this family who ever had a depression or who was ever openly tearful," she said in a famous interview.

The Windsors

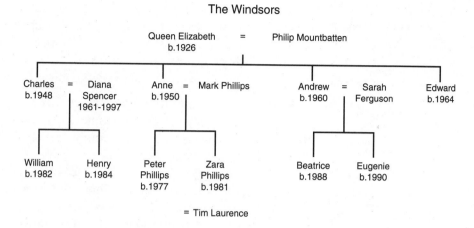

Shake, Rattle, and Roll

To keep the players straight for now and future generations, take a few minutes to construct your family tree—even if it has more than a few nuts in it. Use the following blank genealogical chart to record in-laws, outlaws, and ex-laws. Write in the names of everyone you consider related to you by blood or marriage.

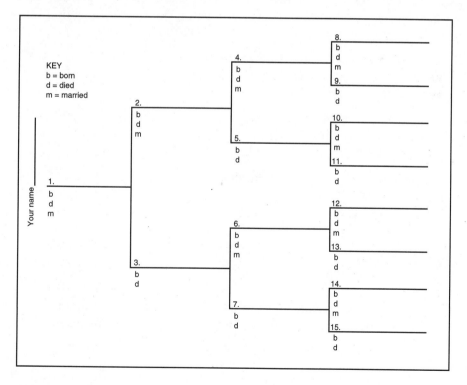

Family Matters
There's some great software available that can make it easy to chart your in-laws and discover who's who in your family.

Don't Go There
Be careful if you decide to share your family chart with others. An unscrupulous person could use information on it to obtain fraudulent financial records and credit. Information such as mother's maiden name is often required for establishing credit.

In addition to keeping the players straight, creating a family chart is a great way to start building strong bonds with your in-laws, or help repair those bonds if they have become frayed. Showing a genuine interest in your in-laws' family heritage can help you create enormous goodwill.

I started a pedigree chart for the Rozakis clan 16 years ago when my son was born. Even though my in-laws and I have always enjoyed genuine affection, I found that recording the Rozakis family genealogical chart gave my father-in-law and me even greater respect for each other. He admired my efforts; I admired his prodigious memory and efforts to gather information for me. He even contacted family members in Greece to fill in some missing entries!

If you really get interested in tracing your extended family, you can find genealogical records in libraries, archives, houses of worship, cemeteries, courthouses, and other facilities. Here are some useful sources you can use to find information about your extended family:

"Where to Write for Vital Records," a pamphlet issued by the U.S. Government (Consumer Information Center, P.O. Box 100, Pueblo, CO 81002).

National Archives and Records Administration
8th and Pennsylvania Avenue, NW
Washington, DC 20408

National Genealogical Society
4527 Seventeenth Street North
Arlington, VA 22207-2363

Afro-American Historical and Genealogical Society
P.O. Box 73086
Washington, DC 20056

We Are Family

No other social group is as loved, hated, bragged about, imposed upon, lied about, worshipped, concealed, ignored, or elevated as the family. Family can double our fun or devastate our holidays—not to mention our lives. That's because relatives…

➤ Link us to the past

➤ Fashion our identities

➤ Steer us into the future

While you may be tempted to scream, "Take my family—please!" you know that you're bound to your family with bonds of steel. That's why it's so important to learn how to deal with your in-laws effectively.

Frequent Flier Families

In the past, extended families were united by the need for survival. As a result, family members focused on a common challenge, usually poverty, a hostile environment, or malevolent neighbors. Belonging to a family gave its members a keen sense of pride, safety, and continuity. There was a shared sense of purpose.

Today, however, most families are scattered to the four corners of the globe. The challenge for survival has changed. We're no longer pitted against the elements. Rather, we now struggle for economic success, respect, and freedom from substance abuse and crime.

The Grass Is Always Greener

Unfortunately, our models for family success are about as realistic as Pamela Anderson's body. "Leave It to Beaver," "Father Knows Best," "The Waltons," and "The Cosby Show" teach us that everyone means well and nearly all problems can be resolved in 30 minutes (minus commercials). Parodies of family life such as "The Simpsons" and "Married with Children" are just as cockamamie. Even "realistic" shows like "Roseanne" ultimately cop out: How many families have their problems solved by winning the lottery?

We have been seduced into thinking that everyone else's in-laws are perfect. Other families can handle their problems easily; why can't we? No matter how nutty your family may seem, rest assured that it's normal. That doesn't necessarily make it easier to cope with in-law conflict, however. You'll learn ways to deal with family conflict in the chapters that follow.

The Least You Need to Know

➤ In-laws are people related to you by marriage. They are also people who are considered part of the family.

➤ Our in-laws link us to the past, help create our identities, and steer us into the future.

➤ Trace your family tree to learn who's who and build bonds with your in-laws.

➤ You think *you* got in-law problems? You ain't read nothing yet!

Chapter 2

So, What's the Problem?

In This Chapter

➤ Find out *why* it's important to get along with your in-laws

➤ Discover the most common sources of friction among in-laws

The poor farm boy married the rich girl from town and now he had to deal with his disapproving mother-in-law. Her dire predictions about his worthless future seemed born out when he couldn't make a living selling men's clothing. To further complicate matters, the young couple couldn't afford to buy their own home, so they moved in with the bride's mother—where they stayed for the next 33 years!

Even when the couple finally moved from Independence, Missouri to Kansas City, and later to the White House, Harry Truman's mother-in-law, Madge Gates Wallace, was still there. "It was very hard on my father," Truman's daughter Margaret said years later. "He made it his business to get along because he loved my mother."

And you think *your* in-laws are difficult? "Bet your bootie they are," you say, "but it can't be *my* fault," you swear. "After all, I'm a good mother-in-law, father-in-law, daughter-in-law, son-in-law, brother-in-law, sister-in-law." Pick one. Hmmm…

In this chapter, you'll first discover why it's so vital to get along with your in-laws. Then you'll see what difficult situations you're most likely to encounter when you become an in-law. Next, I'll help you discover what role *you* play in creating warfare with your in-laws. Finally, it's time to find out how well you get along with your in-laws by taking my simple "In-Law Survival Test" (patent pending).

Take No Prisoners

Even though only about 20 percent of all married couples live with their parents-in-law today, relations between in-laws haven't changed that much since the days of Harry Truman and his mother-in-law. In fact, even when generations of in-laws don't live together, phone, fax, and FedEx often make it seem that way. Planes, trains, and automobiles sometimes make it all-too-easy for the in-laws to visit. And visit. And visit.

Getting along with your in-laws isn't essential for a happy marriage. We all know couples who have horrendous in-law relationships but successful, fulfilling marriages. Even though they've gotten stuck with in-laws from the dark side, these couples have managed to stay together and even prosper.

Don't Go There
Trouble with your in-laws is usually a sign that you and your spouse need to build a stronger family unit on your own. That has to come before anything else.

Nonetheless, being on good terms with your in-laws can greatly help your marriage as well as your overall happiness. That's because a strong relationship with your in-laws provides solid marital support. Regular everyday life heaps enormous stress on every marriage; crisis increases the tension. Under normal circumstances, a strong support system is useful. Under crisis situations, it's essential.

It's All Relative
The percentage of people who get along with both sides of the family increases as people move through their forties, fifties, and sixties. As people mature, some of the in-law issues they dealt with when they first got married often work out.

Here are the top 10 most common problems people have with their in-laws. Put a check mark next to each problem that you have faced with *your* in-laws.

Top Five Causes of Conflicts with In-Laws

____ 1. **Going to the Chapel and We're Gonna Get Married**

"Here I was at age 33 and my in-laws were dictating what kind of wedding I was having. They picked out the caterer, the florist, the band, and the photographer. When I complained, my husband said, 'Let them alone. After all, I'm their only child.' My husband and I paid the bill for the entire affair and the only thing I got to pick out was my dress. And that's only because it was my mother's dress!"

Sound like your life? If so, check out Chapter 7.

____ 2. **The Other Woman in Your Marriage**

Lena's career as a systems analyst is thriving. So are her two children. Her marriage, however, is not in such good shape. Her husband, Dennis, has been involved with another woman throughout the 10 years of their marriage—as well as before. Even in Lena and Dennis' wedding picture, the Other Woman is clutching Dennis' hand, as if she were the bride. Her name is Mildred. She is Dennis' mother.

Does this scenario fit your situation? Get the inside skinny on this in-law problem in Chapter 8.

____ 3. **Deep Freeze**

Soon after Lou and Annabel were married, Annabel's father started treating Lou like the Creature from the Black Lagoon. "I felt about as welcome as hemorrhoids," Lou said. "Annabel's father referred to me in that peculiar form of address known as third-person invisible: 'Would he like any more mashed potatoes? 'Is he still married to our daughter'?"

Do you have a father-in-law like this? Not to worry. I show you ways to deal with daddy-in-law in Chapter 9.

____ 4. **Culture Clash**

Nick, born and raised in North Carolina, married Kim, who spent her childhood in Cambodia. Soon after the wedding, Nick ate dinner with Kim's parents. They sat on the floor, Cambodian style. Nick saw Kim's elderly uncle pick up the small bowl next to his plate and drink from it. Nick did the same, gulping down all the drink. "Good?" asked Kim's mother. "Yes," Nick answered, and Kim's mother refilled the bowl. Again Nick drained it; again Kim's mother filled it. This continued until Nick felt like a balloon at the Macy's Thanksgiving day parade. "If this continues, I'm going to float out of here," he thought. Nick didn't realize that when Cambodians empty their bowl or clean their plates, it's a signal to their host that they want more. Kim might have told Nick this, but she was too busy helping her mother to notice his plight.

Are you concerned about cultural differences with your in-laws? See Chapter 10.

> **Family Matters**
> Draining your glass and cleaning your plate have different meanings in different cultures. Jordanians leave a small amount of food on their plate to be polite; Filipinos and Egyptians leave a tidbit to show that their host has provided well. Thai people leave a morsel to show they are finished or that the food was delicious; but to an Indonesian, leaving food on your plate is impolite.

_____ 5. **Sloppy Seconds**

"I married Sam after a brief courtship," said Marcia. "He was already divorced from his first wife, Linda. Unfortunately, everyone in the family loved Saint Linda. Her picture still hangs over the mantel in my parents-in-law's house; nothing I can do is as good as what Linda did. She even taught Sam's little sister to ride a bike!"

Are you coming in a distant second to the first spouse? See Chapter 12 for ways to deal with this common source of friction with in-laws.

Five More Danger Zones

Haven't found your family's hot buttons yet? Not to worry! To paraphrase a famous Russian writer with in-law problems, all happy families are the same, but every unhappy family is unhappy in its own way. Here are five more ways that in-laws make each other's lives miserable. Check the ones that apply to you.

_____ 1. **Holiday Horror**

"I think I'm Gumby," Lisa said. "Both sets of parents want us to spend the holidays with them—every holiday. Do I get frequent-flier miles for aggravation? And what about letting us start our own holiday traditions?" Are you being s-t-r-e-t-c-h-e-d between families by holiday demands? See Chapter 14 for effective strategies for setting limits.

_____ 2. **Bungee Gifts**

Joyce, a talented amateur painter, worked in a dentist's office to put her husband Justin through law school. Joyce's parents gave her $10,000 for art lessons so she could develop her talents. Before Joyce could start her lessons, however, Justin's tuition bill came due. Because the couple had agreed that their top priority was having Justin finish his professional training, Joyce used the $10,000 for his tuition. Joyce's parents hit the roof. "That money was for your training, not his!" they screamed. "But the money was a gift," Joyce replied. "The word 'gift' means no strings attached." Apparently Joyce's parents were reading a different dictionary.

Does this sound like your family? If so, check out Chapter 16.

_____ 3. **Baby Talk**

Greta's in-laws were from the "old school": The only good grandchild was a male child. After all, who else was going to carry on the family name? It wasn't until Greta produced a son that she—and her daughters—were fully welcomed into the family. "To this day," Greta complains bitterly, "my in-laws shower attention on my son and ignore my daughters."

In Part 4, I deal with the issue of in-laws and grandchildren.

_____ 4. **And Baby Makes...Complications**

Every time Felice's mother-in-law came to visit, she turned up the heat so "the baby wouldn't get a chill"; the baby got prickly heat but the plants never looked better. Barry's mother-in-law was horrified that he (a man!) was entrusted with such complex tasks as diapering and feeding. That's not to say that some in-laws really do know best, but whose baby is it anyway? Judging from the behavior of some in-laws, the issue is up for grabs.

Part 4 covers dealing with child-rearing and in-laws.

_____ 5. **Tied for Life**

Here's my friend Terri's problem with her in-laws: "My husband's 16-year-old daughter Emily wants to drop her dad's last name. When my husband and his ex were divorced, his ex went back to her maiden name. My husband is very upset about this and doesn't know what to do. We live across the country from them so communication is hard. Now my husband's parents have gotten involved. It's tearing our relationship up." No matter what the legal papers say; as long as a child is involved, there's no such thing as an ex-in-law.

I cover this situation in Part 5 and give you strategies for dealing with it.

It's All Relative

In general, men are more likely to get along better with both their mothers and their mothers-in-law than women are.

Pushing All the Buttons

It's not just that Bob's mother-in-law looks like James Cagney. It isn't even that after 20 years of marriage she refers to Bob as "What's His Name." (The formal title—"That Man Who Married My Daughter"—is reserved for big family gatherings.) Bob can even overlook the fact that his mother-in-law thinks his career in sales is a front for drug dealing and sends his wife—her daughter—money to help her "until What's His Name finally gets on his feet."

No, what really yanks Bob's chain is that his mother-in-law calls his daughter "Roberta Sue" even though her name is "Nicole Ann." "Where does my mother-in-law come off renaming my child?" he once demanded. "I haven't renamed the old bat—though I have been sorely tempted."

This is a clear-cut case of mother-in-law as sinner and son- and daughter-in-laws as saints. Or is it? Rarely are relationships between in-laws as simplistic as they appear on first blush. You know that it takes two to tango, balance the checkbook, and spin out the family dynamic.

For example, why doesn't Bob's wife, daughter of the shrew, speak to her mother about her over-the-top behavior?

It's All Relative

In a recent poll, 32 percent of those surveyed said they get along better with their own mother than with their mother-in-law. Only 6 percent of all people surveyed said they get along better with their mother-in-law than with their own mother.

All in the Family

When in-laws say:	They actually mean:
"Is this dinner?"	"This is really *food*, isn't it?"
"Mmm, it sure is yummy."	"I'd rather eat No-Frills doggy chow than this swill."
"Did you use a recipe?"	"No one could make anything this bad with help."
"Oh, what a lovely blouse!"	"A chimpanzee could put an outfit together better than you."
"Did you redecorate?"	"Have you ever heard of a vacuum and dust cloth?"
"It's so nice of you to invite us to dinner."	"Next time, we eat out. It's our treat."

Ever feel like you don't speak the same language as your in-laws? The words make sense on their own, but the sentences don't add up? If so, you're not alone. How well *do* you get along with your in-laws? Put a check mark next to each sentence that describes your interactions with your in-laws.

_____ 1. When my in-laws step into the room, I start sweating like Dan Quayle at a spelling bee or Mike Tyson at a NOW rally.

_____ 2. I still haven't recovered from the first time I met my in-laws. Calling it "disastrous" is charitable.

____ 3. Everything would be fine if my in-laws weren't as thick as a plank—and about as interesting.

____ 4. My father-in-law calls me "cement head." I take it as an endearment. After all, it's better than what he *used* to call me.

____ 5. I always try to be late for any social engagement that involves my in-laws because they make me so crazy.

____ 6. I'd rather chew ground glass than spend an evening alone with my in-laws.

____ 7. I love my parents-in-law. My brother-in-law the skin head is an entirely different matter, however.

____ 8. My husband and I fight when my in-laws are around. We fight when *his* in-laws are around, too. *All* the in-laws drive us crazy.

____ 9. I still call my mother-in-law "Um, er" because I've never resolved the name issue.

____10. I complain to my friends about my in-laws constantly. That's okay; they all complain about their in-laws, too.

Score Yourself

10–8 check marks	It could be worse. I'm not sure how, but work with me here.
7–5 check marks	Hang on; help is on the way.
4–3 check marks	At least the plumbing is working this week.
2–0 check marks	You must have my in-laws. Give them back.

Peace in Our Time?

Earlier in this chapter, you learned the main reasons why in-laws clash. "I seem to fight with my in-laws about everything," my friend Shari told me recently. After we spoke about the fights, Shari came to see that her problems with her in-laws had tenacious roots. Let's delve more deeply into the situation to find the underlying sources of conflict with in-laws.

How many of these underlying causes can you recognize in your relationship with your in-laws?

➤ **Lack of love**—You just don't like each other. And maybe you never will.

➤ **Fear of rejection**—Will they shove me away?

Family Matters
When you say your in-laws drive you crazy, what you're really dealing with are the personalities of the people involved. Often, the roles we play are scripted for us long before we arrive on the scene. These are often the roles we assume in childhood and play into adulthood, polishing and perfecting them whether they fit our current situation or not.

➤ **Low self-concept**—Am I good enough for their family?

➤ **The urge to control**—Who must always be right?

➤ **Poor communication**—Do I feel like no one is really listening to me?

➤ **Unresolved anger**—Are people holding grudges… and holding them and holding them?

➤ **Misplaced anger**—What is *really* bothering us?

➤ **Disagreements over roles**—Do we see things from radically different perspectives?

➤ **Fear of differences**—Is race, religion, or culture causing rifts in our relationship?

➤ **Jealousy**—Are my in-laws envious of each other's good fortune?

The Least You Need to Know

➤ Getting along with your in-laws can greatly help your marriage as well as your overall happiness.

➤ There are 10 common reasons why in-laws clash: Lack of love, fear of rejection, low self-image, the urge to control, poor communication, unresolved and misplaced anger, disagreements over roles, fear of differences, and jealousy.

➤ You can't change someone else; you can only change yourself. Start building better relationships with your in-laws by recognizing your role in the conflict.

Guilty Until
Proven Innocent

An attorney was sitting in his office late one night when Satan appeared before him. The Devil told the lawyer, "I have a proposition for you. You can win every case you try, for the rest of your life. Your clients will adore you, your colleagues will stand in awe of you, and you will make embarrassing sums of money. All I want in exchange is your soul, your wife's soul, your children's souls, the souls of your parents, grandparents, parents-in-law, and other in-laws." The lawyer thought about this for a moment, then asked, "So, what's the catch?"

Today, lawyer bashing is almost as common a pastime as zinging one to post office clerks, politicians...and in-laws. Hey, we all know that in-laws cause *all* the problems that we can't attribute to rapacious lawyers, tightly wrapped postal clerks, and slimy politicians. While we're at it, let's not forget comic books, rock 'n' roll, and junk food.

Here, you'll look at the in-law situation from another point of view. Some people *do* have in-laws from hell who deserve to be conked on the head with a shovel and buried in the backyard. There's just no way around it. But far more common, the relationship with your in-laws is a two-way street—you get what you give. In this chapter, you'll discover what role *you* play in the family circus. Then you'll learn why conflicts with your in-laws can be so painful.

Truth or Dare

You've explored the reasons why you clash with your in-laws. You and I know that *you're* the perfect in-law…it's all *their* fault. Maybe it is—and maybe it isn't.

What role do you play in conflicts with your in-laws? Take this easy quiz to see. Circle the answer that best describes your reaction to each situation.

The Simple In-Law Survival Test

1. Your pillar-of-the community-father-in-law decides to chuck his job, divorce your mother-in-law, and become a charter fisherman in Barbados. What do you do?

    a. Make sure he understands the full implications of his midlife crisis and harebrained scheme.

    b. Decide to stowaway on his boat. Hey, only a fool turns down a free vacation.

    c. Serve as a mediator between your in-laws and the rest of the family, who are convinced that Pops is a few cans short of a six-pack.

    d. Try to talk some sense into the salty dog; maybe he'll agree to a two-week cruise instead.

    e. Stalk off in a huff. Who is he to get all the attention when you're having a hard time at work this month?

2. Your mother-in-law and sister-in-law are on the outs yet again. What do you do?

    a. Tell them that they're still acting like nincompoops and isn't it time they just grew up?

    b. Screen the calls on your answering machine so you don't have to deal with either nitwit.

    c. Let them use you as a sounding board. Call all the other relatives (on both sides) so they know which side to take in the argument.

    d. Arrange a lunch so the two sides can come together and talk out their differences. You even pick up the check.

    e. End up getting blamed for the problem…as usual.

3. Your daughter-in-law once again asks you to baby-sit. However, that night you have a date with a well-preserved college prof you met at an AARP meeting. What do you do?

    a. Tell your daughter-in-law to stop being so cheap and hire a baby-sitter once in a while. Do you look like Mary Poppins?

    b. Agree to baby-sit but cancel at the last minute.

    c. Reschedule your date and baby-sit, but tell your son that his wife is taking advantage of you.

    d. Find another reliable person to baby-sit for your grandchildren that night.

    e. Baby-sit. After all, when did you ever get a break?

4. Your husband's cousin, a brain surgeon, leaves his wife for his office assistant, a bleached blond young enough to be his daughter. The moment the doctor's divorce is final, he and the bimbo move in together. The family is fuming but decide to pay a visit to the unrepentant couple. What do you do?

    a. Inform the doctor that someone as well-educated as he is should know better; the sex will give him a coronary. Tell the tramp that she's making a fool of herself.

    b. Explain that you're learning to speak Serbo-Croatian and keep your head-phones on the whole day.

    c. Make kissy-face while you're there, but be sure the following day to tell everyone in the family that the strumpet had black roots and your cousin was wearing lifts in his shoes.

    d. Sit at a strategic place so your aunt and uncle can't pelt their Son the Doctor with the dinner rolls.

    e. Sympathize with the doctor's main squeeze: It's not her fault that she's his blond shoulder candy.

5. Your sister is marrying a man whose religious background is very different from your family's beliefs. Everyone in your family, except you, opposes the marriage. What do you do?

    a. First, see if you can get The Infidel to convert to your religion. If he won't, tell your sister she's making a huge mistake.

    b. Give your sister a kiss and head for the mall. After all, it *is* Supersaver Sunday.

    c. Get on the horn and make sure that everyone in the family knows the scoop. Otherwise, how can they make an informed decision on the issue?

d. Put out some chips and dip, gather the clan, and try to work this mess out.

e. Cozy up to your sister's fiancé because you know how lousy he must feel. After all, you're the one everybody's usually picking on.

It's All Relative

Winston Churchill's beloved wife Clementine learned early on that she had married not just her husband but also his strong-willed mother as well. When Clementine and Winston returned from their honeymoon, the couple discovered that Lady Randolph Churchill had completely redecorated their new home in a much more elaborate style than Clementine liked.

6. Your brother-in-law is in financial trouble yet again, and once more puts the touch on you and your husband. What do you do?

a. Help him this last time if he will agree to the rules you set down. He has to quit gambling, get a second job, and stop being such a big sport.

b. Blow him off. Let the loan sharks break his legs.

c. Lend him the money he needs, but let everyone in the family know you are the Sainted Sister-in-Law.

d. Go over his financial records, lend him what he needs, and put him in touch with a social service agency that helps people untangle their finances.

e. Feel pity for little ol' you. After all, you're always the one everyone hits up for a loan.

7. You and your spouse have broken the bank buying the house of your dreams. For the furniture alone you'll be in hock until the cows come home. You invite the whole family to visit House Beautiful. At the party, your sister-in-law's three-year old colors the designer kitchen wallpaper with all 36 Crayolas. What do you do?

a. Go postal! Bellow at your brother and sister-in-law for being lousy parents, demand they pay for new wallpaper, and give the little tyrant a smack on the seat of her pants for good measure.

b. Lock yourself in the bathroom and have a good cry.

c. Freeze a smile on your face and accept your brother and sister-in-law's apologies. The next day, make sure everyone in the family knows how badly you have been treated.

    d. Choke back your tears and work out a reasonable settlement. Maybe you split the cost of the new wallpaper.

    e. Realize you had it coming to you for not giving the three-year old something constructive to do during the party.

8. Your brother-in-law decides to become your sister-in-law. Understandably, the family is less than thrilled with Carl's decision to become Carla. What do you do?

    a. Tell Carl that he'll be an ugly girl and he should leave all his organs intact.

    b. Live and let live. After all, it's Carl's life to live as he sees fit.

    c. See if you can sell the "before" and "after" pictures to the tabloids.

    d. Make sure that Carl has gotten the counseling he needs, and then try to get the rest of the family to see the situation from his point of view.

    e. Find yourself blamed for not being more understanding of the family's turmoil.

9. Your father-in-law, a widower, has been diagnosed with Alzheimer's disease. He lives in another state, near your married sister-in-law. The other siblings are scattered to the four corners of the globe. What do you do?

    a. Do your research, decide on your father-in-law's new living arrangements, and assign financial responsibilities to the rest of the family. Then you give every-one their orders. Hey, *someone's* got to take charge.

    b. Visit your father-in-law but stay out of the planning. After all, he's your father-in-law, not your father, so it's not your place to butt in.

    c. Call your in-laws and see where everyone stands on the issue. Offer your own solution, too.

    d. Investigate the options and try to work out a solution that leaves everyone satisfied.

    e. Nobody wants your opinion anyway, so send a card and keep a low profile.

10. While your sister is out of town on a business trip, you accidentally stumble on your brother-in-law in a liplock with the chippie next door. They don't see you. What do you do?

    a. Give your brother-in-law-the-louse time to get home, confront him, and threaten to tell your sister if he doesn't break off the affair immediately.

    b. Ignore the incident. After all, he might have been giving her mouth-to-mouth resuscitation.

c. Rush home and call your husband, parents-in-law, parents, and the rest of the free world to ask for advice.

d. Privately suggest to your brother-in-law that he get some counseling for his sex addiction.

e. Decide that it serves your sister right. After all, Daddy always loved her best.

Know Thyself

Are you a foot soldier in the family battles—or a general? Tally up the number of A's, B's, C's, D's, and E's you circled. Then use the following key to see where you fit in the equation.

➤ **A lot of A's** You're a real pit bull, Fido, always ready to jump in where angels fear to tread. Your motto? "Might makes right." You know how to make others dance to your tune—or pay the piper. You're convinced that your way is the right way. While you're usually right, others quake in fear when you come barreling in to take charge of a family crisis.

➤ **A lot of B's** What color is the sky on your planet, bunky? You sail merrily above the fray, stopping in every now and again for a reality check. You don't mind having a few yuks with the clan, but family fights are so dreary you just check out. Oh, your body is still anchored to the sofa, but your mind is somewhere in the stratosphere. So what if you're unreliable? No one's perfect.

➤ **A lot of C's** Thank goodness for auto dial and e-mail; it makes it so much easier for you to keep your nose in everyone else's business! If you ran a newspaper, your motto would be "All the news that fits we print." You're so plugged into the action that you could foment a family revolution in less time than it takes to nuke a bagel.

➤ **A lot of D's** You're the family Voice of Reason, the mediator, the one with the level head. Some in-law or the other is always calling in the middle of the night to plunge you into another crisis. You know how to keep the kinfolk from coming to blows when everyone chooses sides and takes up arms. While it's gratifying to be the family savior, you're starting to pop Tums like they were M & Ms.

Don't Go There
Beware of pigeon-holing your in-laws into these categories. These family roles are as fluid as Elvis Presley's hips, which means that people can switch roles with the situation.

➤ **A lot of E's** Been in more hot water than the shellfish at a clambake? Always singing "Nobody loves me, everybody hates me, think I'll eat some worms?" You're the family scapegoat, the perennial victim. No matter what you do, it's never the right thing. By now you've learned to just give up, because you can't win anyway.

Role Playing

Life would be a whole lot easier if you could shove this list under your obnoxious in-law's nose and say, "See, see, that's what you do to me. It makes me crazy. Stop it now!" Unfortunately, even if they see the light, chances are good that nothing will change.

Don't beat your head against the wall trying to get your in-laws to act the way you want. All you'll get for your efforts are a sore head and a dented door. You heard it here first: You can't change anyone else; you can only change yourself. Good communication often helps, but in the end, you have to come to terms with your reaction to the situation—and then deal with it. That's what you'll learn in this book.

Heaven on Earth

Mother to daughter: "Your boyfriend is such a jerk that I would be delighted to be his mother-in-law."

To hear mother-in-law jokes, you would think there is a natural animosity between people and their in-laws. There usually is—and maybe there should be, especially when your children abandon you and get married. You love and feed and tolerate the little idiots for years. And then they leave you for some stranger they like better.

What about that guy who married your daughter? We all know what he *really* wants from her. As parents, it's our job to protect her from guys like that. But once your daughter gets married, attitudes shift. The same parents who had been warning her to be careful out there start craving grandchildren and demanding sudden pregnancy. What they once warned her against they soon come to demand. Congratulations on your wedding. Now get in the sack and get to work.

Lucky in Love

But even before the grandchild impulse takes hold, there are natural pressures involved in a relationship with in-laws that can work against smooth relations. After all, it's not natural to welcome the loss of a kid's attention and its subsequent refocusing on somebody else's kid.

However, there are *some* families that do welcome in-laws with open arms and hearts. I am fortunate to have wonderful, supportive in-laws. My father-in-law Nick Rozakis has always been there for us. From the day we announced our engagement, he has always been a bulwark of common sense, generosity, and support. My mother-in-law Marie Rozakis is also a gem. Warm, loving, and kind, she is one special lady. I've got some great brothers-in-law and sisters-in-law, too.

I Love You, You Love Me, This Is Not Reality

Not everyone can be lucky enough to marry into Barney's family or the Rozakis clan. The rest of us have to be content with the Queen of Mean as a mother-in-law or a potato-head brother-in-law. But even if you *have* married into the Brady Bunch, there are bound to be tensions with your in-laws.

And few things put more strain on a marriage than conflicts with in-laws. Three-quarters of all married couples have problems with their in-laws, according to *Prevention* magazine.

Unfortunately, most in-laws don't know the maxim: "Differences don't give us the freedom to judge other people." Where there are differences, there are potential problems, which often surface as criticisms.

One reason criticism from in-laws can be so hurtful is that we don't expect them to be enemies. They are family. We count on them to be on our side. We hope they will build us up, not tear us down. The late Hubert Humphrey once observed that "behind every successful man stands a surprised mother-in-law." Fortunately, it doesn't have to be that way. "Mom," "Dad," "Son," "Daughter,"—regardless of lineage—can be supportive.

Read on to find out how to resolve some of the most common problems that in-laws can create for you, your spouse, your children, and your kin.

The Least You Need to Know

➤ Honestly assess how you contribute to the uproar.

➤ Recognize that there are natural stresses built into the in-law situation that you can never control.

➤ Realize that you can't change someone else; you can only change yourself. Start building better relationships with your in-laws by recognizing your role in the conflict.

Chapter 4

Ground Rules

In This Chapter

➤ See what makes a rotten parent-in-law

➤ Find out what makes a rotten son- or daughter-in-law

➤ Learn the basic techniques for getting along with your in-laws

---

Are you normal? Check out these facts about people to find out. Did you know that...

➤ 40 percent of women have hurled footwear at a man

➤ Only 30 percent of us can flare our nostrils

➤ 14 percent of us eat the watermelon seeds

➤ When nobody else is around, 47 percent of us drink straight from the carton

➤ Four out of five of us have suffered from hemorrhoids

➤ 39 percent of us peek in our host's bathroom cabinet. 17 percent of us have been caught by the host

➤ 44 percent of us reuse aluminum foil

➤ 20 percent of women consider their parents to be their best friends

➤ 42 percent of people polled in O-Cedar's national cleaning survey would rather visit their in-laws than scrub their tubs

Now, that last point either means that nearly half the people in this country like their in-laws or nearly half the people in this country really hate cleaning their tubs. How can you become part of the former group rather than the latter bunch? That's what this chapter is all about!

Reality Bites

Fiction:

Smiling Grandma, every hair in place, proudly carries the golden turkey to the elegantly set table. Meanwhile, Grandpa, carving knife at the ready, basks in the glow of his happy family. His face is shining with joy. The generations delight in each other's company, in-laws happily passing the peas and praising the mashed potatoes.

Fact:

Grandma is furious because she's been stuck in the kitchen again while her selfish daughter-in-law (who should work less and take better care of her son) went to the mall. Grandpa is indeed aglow, but his ruddy color is due to the scotch he's been guzzling all afternoon. No one would trust him with a carving knife. Louie is furious because his brother-in-law Irving is driving a new Beemer and all *he* has is a 10-year-old Chevy. Chris is wondering if this is the right moment to come out of the closet, but everyone on Marty's side is homophobic. The teenage grandchildren are chugging beer in the garage while Aunt Alice once again criticizes Louie's wife for having six kids. Anthony and Trish have filed for divorce. Cousin Nicky has hated his in-laws since the day they met. The feeling is mutual.

Reality check:

People around the world dream of family harmony. They also dream of winning the lottery, attaining washboard abs overnight, and actually finding something worth watching on prime-time television. Unfortunately, there are some situations you just can't win.

➤ You're more likely to get struck by lightning *eight times* than win the lottery.

➤ The only thing on my body that gets flatter every day is my chest.

➤ TV? Forgetaboutit. Every time I find a show I like, it gets canceled.

Fortunately, there *are* situations you can resolve. These are the situations that matter: Conflicts with your in-laws. I can teach you the techniques you need to deal with the in-laws who drive you crazy. Let's start with a look at what makes a horrendous parent-in-law.

Twelve No-Fail Steps to Being a Terrible Parent-In-Law

Soon after they were married, David and his wife Jennifer went to have Sunday dinner with David's parents. As David's mother heaped his plate with roast beef, Jennifer said, "Rita, David has cut back on red meat."

"Jennifer," her mother-in-law answered sharply, "I've known my son longer than you have. Therefore, I understand him better and know what he likes better than you do!"

"Would you stop butting into their lives, Rita," David's father Joe said. "Besides, you could afford to cut down on the food yourself."

"Mommy's a fatty! Mommy's a blimp!" David's brother yelled.

All in all, a typical Sunday dinner at David's house.

With luck, your family situation isn't as dicey as this one is. Nonetheless, nearly all families face problems with their in-laws. Listen up, mother-in-law and father-in-law. Here are my 12 easy steps for making the problems with your in-laws much worse than they already are. (Note: You can use these steps at any point in your son or daughter's marriage. They are guaranteed to make a bad situation much worse.)

1. Don't waste any time; try to disrupt the marriage long before the walk down the aisle. When your son or daughter announces the engagement, throw a temper tantrum about how you are losing your child to a real chowderhead. Pull out your hair, moan a lot, and bang your head against the nearest wall. Try this wail: "My baby! My precious baby! How can you marry this jerk? This is the thanks I get for all my sacrifices?" Don't forget to mention how you changed all his or her dirty diapers.

2. If all else fails, fake a heart attack or threaten to cut your child out of the will. Drastic measures are encouraged.

3. If the fools persist and actually do get married, be sure to telephone them on their honeymoon night. (My mother really did this; I kid you not.) Then keep up the pressure: Call at least three times a day, always at inconvenient times such as 6:00 A.M., 6:00 P.M., and midnight. Always refuse to talk to your son-in-law or daughter-in-law; talk only to *your* child.

4. Criticize your child's spouse any chance you get. Here are some ideas for getting under your daughter-in-law's skin: Attack her cooking, housekeeping, or parenting skills. For a son-in-law: Go for his inability to earn a living, do home repairs, or dress well. Note: This is much more effective if you repeat your comments at the top of your lungs to anyone who will listen.

5. Compete with your son- or daughter-in-law's parents for the couple's attention. Be sure that the "kids" spend every holiday with you. Run down the in-laws at every possible chance.

6. Get as much information about the couple's sex life as you can. Offer frequent advice about specific details such as positions and frequency. Hey, who knows better than a parent?

7. Be sure to nag your son- and/or daughter-in-law to have a child. After all, all your friends have grandbabies and it's only fair that you have a few, too. If the couple really does produce a child, nag them to either a) have more, or b) stop their reckless reproduction. Don't they know there's a world problem with over-population?

8. Be sure to show up your son- or daughter-in-law as often as you can. Handy parents-in-laws take note: If you're a Bob Vila groupie, do some home repairs so your son-in-law looks like he's instructionally impaired.

9. No matter how small the slight, don't let it go by. *Never* forgive and forget.

10. Always assume the worst of your son- or daughter-in-law. For example, if your child doesn't call you on a regular basis, assume that your child's spouse is responsible.

11. Try a little sabotage. Give your daughter-in-law your son's favorite recipe, but leave out a key ingredient or change the cooking time so the dish burns. Why should you be shown up by that little twit who stole your baby boy?

12. If the marriage gets a little rocky, fan the flames. Be sure to say "I told you so" and bring up various slights you received at the hand of your son- or daughter-in-law.

Bonus hint: Always use your child as a go-between when you have problems with your son- or daughter-in-law. This stirs up a lot of trouble really fast.

Twelve No-Fail Steps to Being a Terrible Son- or Daughter-In-Law

Since I'm an equal-opportunity advice-giver, I also offer the following ways for sons- and daughters-in-law to destroy any hope of getting along with their in-laws. Hey, two can play this game. Why leave all the fun to the older generation?

1. Never include your in-laws in the wedding plans, even if they are paying for part or all of the festivities. Hey, forking over the moolah is their job as parents, isn't it? Why should you have to consult their wishes?

2. If your in-laws persist in trying to invite some guests of their own to the wedding, feel free to throw your own temper tantrum. Another great technique is to issue an

ultimatum to your spouse-to-be, along the lines of "It's either them or me. You have to choose now."

3. If the marriage does go off, try to ignore your parents-in-law. This is easier to accomplish if you never call them by any name. If you ignore them, maybe they'll pack up their tents and sneak away. Don't forget to ignore your brothers- and sisters-in-law, too.

4. Criticize your parents-in-law, brothers- and sisters-in-law, and assorted in-laws to your spouse at any and all opportunities. Push the buttons with words like *lazy, fat, uneducated,* or *cheap*. Try to hit all the sore points that have bothered your spouse about his or her parents and siblings for years. Be sure to tell your parents and siblings about how lousy your in-laws are, too. And don't forget to have everyone pass along your negative comments to your in-laws. That way, everyone can get in on the turmoil.

5. Don't forget to tag all the bases. To accomplish this, complain to your in-laws about your spouse constantly. See how much trouble you can stir up *this* way.

6. If your parents-in-law call the house, never let them talk to their son or daughter. Hey, they had the first 20 or so years with your beloved. They deserve more?

7. Ask your parents-in-laws and other in-laws for money. Ask early and often. And never, never show gratitude.

8. If you have children, give them a name that you know your in-laws will hate because it offends their religion, heritage, or customs. Refuse to compromise on this point: You get to choose the baby's first name and the middle name, too.

9. Demand that your parents-in-law baby-sit. Be sure not to give any notice: Remember, your parents-in-law have nothing better to do anyway. And destroy any bonds your parents-in-law form with their grandchildren. Hey, they screwed up your spouse, didn't they? Why should they do it again with *your* children?

10. When your in-laws baby-sit, criticize the way they take care of your child. Hint: Be sure to stock the house with food they either detest or cannot eat because of dietary restrictions. If they want to eat, they can bring their own food.

11. Remind your spouse how much better your parents are than your parents-in-law. Hold all grudges as long as possible. Hint: You might want to jot down real and imagined slights to help you remember all of them. Then show the list to your in-laws to make sure they understand how rotten they are.

12. Exclude your parents-in-law from every important event in your life. Withhold all important family information; always let them hear about key events from a third party. It's none of their business if you're moving to Guam, expecting triplets, or not joining them for Thanksgiving dinner.

Bonus hint: Never acknowledge any thoughtful gestures from your parents-in-law. Try not to recognize their achievements, either. After all, it's your *turn* to shine.

See a common thread here? Each of these tongue-in-cheek "suggestions"...

➤ tears down your in-laws.

➤ shows a lack of consideration.

➤ creates trouble in the family.

➤ demonstrates unrealistic expectations.

➤ is dishonest and unfair.

➤ does not respect boundaries.

Basic Training

Your in-laws are a crucial part of your spouse's life. This makes them a crucial part of your life as well. No one ever said it was easy to balance your needs with the needs of others—especially the needs of an entire new family. Hey, if it was *that* easy to link two (or more!) families and create instant bliss, this book would be a whole lot shorter. But creating family harmony is possible—and it's very much worth the effort.

You realize it won't be easy to build bridges—and rebuild some that have been burnt—but you also realize that it's a valuable way to spend your time. The return you get on your investment will last the rest of your married life. Here are some ideas to get you started. Later in the book, I'll show you ways to implement each of these techniques to suit your specific needs and situation.

1. **Work with your spouse.**

   This is the key rule, numero uno, the whole enchilada. In this book, I'll be giving you lots of suggestions and techniques for dealing with your in-laws. But as my wonderful husband reminded me last night, dealing effectively with in-laws all starts with *first* working conflicts through with your spouse. Remember, you're in this together.

   Never put your spouse in a situation where he or she has to choose between you and a relative. If you do so, you're putting your spouse in a nearly impossible bind. Instead, try to understand the bond your spouse has with his or her grandparents, parents, and siblings. If possible, try to support that relationship. Even if your spouse has parents from hell, they are his or her parents.

2. Set boundaries and limits.

No candy before mealtime for the kids? No loans for in-laws? With your spouse, decide what's important and what's not. For example, we let our kids eat anything they want anytime. Want ice cream ten minutes before dinner? Fine by me…as long as you eat a reasonable dinner. But we're really, really picky about school work. I don't think it has dawned on my kids yet that there is a grade below "A." Working as a team, set your family values. Then communicate your values to your in-laws. *All* of your values and *all* of your in-laws.

> **Family Matters**
> A happy marriage is *not* like football; there are no successful end-runs in this game. *Never* go behind your spouse's back when you deal with in-laws. And don't tolerate it if your spouse does.

Speaking of boundaries, don't make promises that you can't keep. Remember Neville Chamberlain, Hitler, and Poland? In an attempt to achieve "peace in our time," British politico Neville Chamberlain gave Poland to Hitler as part of the British appeasement policy. Remember how well *that* worked? Hitler just kept right on seizing chunks of Europe. Placating people to keep the peace rarely solves the problem—especially if your in-laws are tyrants.

3. Enforce the boundaries and limits.

Without being as inflexible as a teenager, stick to your guns. For example, if you don't want drop-in company, tell your in-laws that you'd prefer that they call before they show up at your doorstep. If they ignore you, don't answer the door the next time they just happen to drop-by. Even if they do have a lemon meringue pie.

4. Communicate directly.

Whenever possible, avoid communicating through a third party. Don't ask your spouse to talk to his sister about something she did that hurt your feelings. Talk to your sister-in-law directly.

> **Don't Go There**
> Don't confuse listening and responding. You're not obligated to do something just because your in-laws want you to, but you *should* acknowledge their input. People get pushy when they feel you're turning them down without really listening, so they tend to scream louder. Maybe then you'll hear them!

If something bothers you, address it as soon as possible. Sometimes it's a genuine problem; other times, it might be a misunderstanding. Tori married into a family whose members had been born in Germany. Every time a family member went into the kitchen, he or she shut the door—often leaving Tori out. For years, she stewed over the situation. Finally, she got up the courage to ask her mother-in-law why she closed the kitchen door. "Why, to keep in the heat," she answered. "We always did that in Germany." Closing the kitchen door had nothing to do with Tori. A cultural misunderstanding had caused years of distress for her—which neither her in-laws nor she ever realized.

5. **Know yourself.**

Shakespeare said it a zillion years ago, and the advice still holds today: Don't try to remake yourself into the person your in-laws want. For example, what if they're looking for little Susie Homemaker and you're a high-powered corporate attorney? You're under no obligation on your day off to bake Swedish rye bread and churn your own butter. Get a manicure and call for some take-out instead.

6. **Get with the program.**

Not every father-in-law lives to snake out your kitchen sink; not every mother-in-law dreams of baking cookies with her grandchildren. This is the nineties, bunky; Pops is more likely to be surfing the 'Net and Granny's probably rollerblading. Put away the stereotypes and adjust your thinking to the reality of the situation. Don't expect what people can't deliver.

> **Family Matters**
> Think of your in-laws as a potential resource to expand your support network. You can accomplish this by approaching your in-laws the same way you would any potential friend. Respect them, be interested in them, and listen to them.

7. **Learn to cool off.**

I tend to jump in where angels fear to tread. It's always headfirst, too. Fortunately, my husband is far more levelheaded. Many times, the best thing to do is nothing. Time heals many wounds—and wounds many heels.

While we're at it, play nice. Spare your in-laws the insults and character attacks. For example, Jack's father-in-law once called his son a knee-jerk liberal. "I had it on the tip of my tongue to call him a "bloody fascist," Jack said. "Fortunately, I bit my tongue—even though he really *is* a fascist."

8. **Be mature.**

Your parents have to love you; it's in the contract. But your in-laws don't. Accept the fact that your in-laws aren't your parents and won't follow the same rules. Try to think "different"—not "better" or "worse." To make this work, give in on small points and negotiate the key issues.

> **Family Matters**
> When the going get tough, the tough often stay neutral. Even if the situation has gone Bosnian, try to be civil if you can't be silent. Switzerland has the right idea; patient restraint. No one held a caucus and made you the family spokesperson.

Learn to see the situation from your in-law's point of view. And even if you don't agree, act like a big person. For example, I hate pork. I never eat it; I rarely cook it. Nonetheless, for years my mother-in-law would make a pork roast when we came to her ßhouse for dinner. After wallowing in more pork than Congress produces, I came to see that she was trying to please her poor pork-deprived son. Big deal: I learned to have a salad before we ate at her house. My husband porked up in peace and the only one to suffer was Babe, the poor porker.

> **Family Matters**
> You and your spouse are more powerful than you think. You're adults; you're a family unit. You can control visits, holiday celebrations, and access to grandchildren. Don't assume that you're powerless. No one can push you around if you don't let them.

9. **Be kind.**

    Even if you have to grit your teeth, try to say something nice. And if you really can't say anything nice, shut up and smile.

10. **Keep your sense of humor.**

    A very dear friend tells this story: "When I was pregnant with my first child, my father-in-law bought me a special gift: My very own funeral plot. 'Why a funeral plot?' I asked him. 'Well,' he replied, 'you might not make it through the birth and I thought you should be prepared.'" I probably would have slugged the codger upside his head; my friend, in contrast, laughed and thanked him for his gift. P.S. She and all her children are fine.

The Least You Need to Know

➤ Without too much work, any in-law can make a bad situation even worse. With just a little more effort, however, you can become friends with your in-laws—or at least friendly.

➤ Work with your spouse to set and enforce boundaries and limits.

➤ Communicate directly and keep your temper.

➤ Be mature, kind, and self-aware.

➤ Above all, keep your sense of humor.

Chapter 5

First Contact

In This Chapter

➤ See *why* first impressions can make or break your relationship with your in-laws

➤ Get in on the ground floor

➤ Learn how to make a good first impression on prospective in-laws

Driving home from work one day, a man stopped to watch a local Little League baseball game that was being played in a park near my home. As he sat down behind the bench on the first-baseline, he asked one of the boys what the score was.

"We're behind 14 to nothing," he answered with a smile.

"Really," the man said. "I have to say you don't look very discouraged."

"Discouraged?" the boy asked with a puzzled look on his face. "Why should we be discouraged? We haven't been up to bat yet."

Hope springs eternal, the poets say—and well it should. Otherwise, why would we exercise, redecorate, or flirt? It pays to be hopeful, whether it's your first up to bat at Little League baseball or your first up to bat at Big League in-laws.

Don't Go There
Among the most frequently cited reasons for a poor first impression are bad hygiene and perceived rudeness. So wash and be nice.

The first time you meet your in-laws, you have a chance to get the relationship off on the right foot—and so do they. That crucial first meeting can give you a jump on happiness, or set the relationship back for years. That's why it's so important that your first meeting with your in-laws goes smoothly. In this chapter, I'll teach you some ways to make sure that when you get up to bat in the in-law game, you hit a home run!

Saturday Night Fever

Picture this scene: It's the first time you're picking up your girlfriend at her house. Even though you've only been dating a short time, she seems to be The One you want to spend eternity with. You quickly wipe your clammy hand on your jeans before you shake hands with your beloved's father. So what if he's glowering like a bull under a red flag? So what if he's bigger than the national debt—and just as out of control? "I have a gun and a shovel and no one will miss you," he growls. "Try anything with my precious daughter and you're a dead man."

Meanwhile, your beloved's mother looks like she just escaped from the stake at Salem. Nonetheless, you make a stab at conviviality with this witty suck-up: "You're looking particularly lovely tonight, Mrs. Cleaver." She shoots you a look that would curdle milk. Dad releases the safety on the .45. You dive for cover under the sofa.

Ever been here? And you lived to tell the tale?

First-Night Jitters

That first meeting with the in-laws usually takes place long before anyone thinks seriously of walking down the aisle. In most cases, you meet your prospective in-laws for the first time when you and your intended are still dating. First contact usually takes place so early in the relationship that neither party really believes that this is It.

Here are two reasons why it's so important that you always kiss up to your date's parents, siblings, and assorted kinfolk.

> ➤ **First impressions are made fast.** Studies have shown that most people form an impression of someone in less than five minutes. It usually takes longer to get a burger than it does to form a first impression. That being the case, you don't have a lot of wiggle room to impress someone with your strength of character.

> ➤ **First impressions can be lasting impressions.** Most people are stubborn (as you surely know already). They may call it *resolute, steadfast, unwavering,* but it's really

just plain ornery. They don't like to be proven wrong. This can work in your favor if you've created a good first impression. If things went well, you can glide on that goodwill for years. But what happens if your first meeting with the prospective in-laws was a clunker? It might take you years to convince your "resolute" mother-in-law that you're really not an ax murderer, a cross-dresser, or a Donny Osmond fan.

Face Off

That being the case, it's vital that you make a great first impression on potential in-laws. Below are 10 proven tips to make that process less painful.

Ten Tips for Making a Good Impression on Prospective In-Laws

1. **Dress for success.**

   Guys, put on clean underwear. I know this is tough because some of you are very attached to your undies, but work with me here. How can you tell it's time to change your dainties?

   ➤ When your boxers have turned the color of a dead whale and developed new holes so large that you're not sure which ones were originally intended for your legs.

   ➤ When your BVDs are down to eight loosely connected underwear molecules and have to be handled with tweezers.

   Women, the Morticia Addams look, classic as it may be, doesn't cut it in the Heartland. Ditto for the Spice Girls. Difficult as it may seem, even RuPaul may be a little over the edge for some folks. Consult the following chart for some role models to emulate when you meet the in-laws for the first time:

Yes	No
Debbie Gibson	Debbie Does Dallas
Oprah	Orca (the Killer Whale)
Mary Queen of Scots	Typhoid Mary
Betty Crocker	Joe Cocker
Madonna (classic style)	Madonna (zesty Italian)

2. **Leave the motorcycle home.**

   Your vehicle sends a potent message.

Don't Go There
Don't park in the family's driveway or block the driveway so that no one else can get in or out. That spot is usually reserved for someone who lives there, pays the bills, and is just itching to find something wrong with you.

3. **No curbside service.**

   If you're picking up your date, get out of the car. Walk up to the house. Ring the bell. Go the whole nine yards. And ditch the outmoded sexual stereotypes: women as well as men are allowed to drive on dates today.

4. **Remember your manners.**

   A little consideration goes a long way to making a good impression. You know the basics:

   ➤ Say please and thank you.

   ➤ Don't make any strange noises.

   ➤ Put the seat down.

5. **Be yourself.**

   President Calvin Coolidge once invited friends from his hometown to dine at the White House. Worried about their table manners, the guests decided to do everything that Coolidge did. This strategy succeeded, until coffee was served. The president poured his coffee into the saucer. The guests did the same. Coolidge added sugar and cream. His guests did, too. Then Coolidge bent over and put his saucer on the floor for the cat.

   What's the moral of the story? Pick one:

   a. Never have dinner with Calvin Coolidge. (Not a big problem, since he's dead.)

   b. Before you eat, always check the plates for cat hairs.

   c. Order tea, not coffee.

   d. Be yourself.

   The envelope, please. The answer is—d! You got that one. Now, I'm not advocating that you do what comes naturally, (pleeze, spare us *that*), but I am saying that you shouldn't pretend to be someone (or something) that you're not. Use your company manners, but stay true to yourself. After all, that's why that beautiful man or woman by your side fell in love with you in the first place.

6. **If you're coming for a visit, bring a hostess gift.**

   When we were dating, my husband-to-be beat my mother into submission with frequent gifts of elaborate desserts. Although she railed that the lemon meringue was runny, the Linzer tortes dry, and the seven-layer cakes a layer short, she ate every crumb. Afterward, she was even civil to him. This was a major accomplishment, because she was trying to staple my feet to the carpet so I would live with her forever.

7. Treat the sibs well. Hey, you never know.

Before he dated Diana, Prince Charles dallied with her older sister. Shy Di was the little kid hiding behind the 12th-century armor while Chuck was making time with Lady Sarah. But when the smoke cleared, it was the little sister who got the nod and became the Princess.

8. Don't share your favorite pick-up lines with your girlfriend's father or brother or boyfriend's mother or sister.

Resist the urge to share even the good lines like "Hi, the voices in my head told me to come talk to you" and "Yo. You'll do."

9. Wear your Scout uniform.

Flashing your honor society pin is going a little too far, however.

10. Avoid controversial topics.

This is not the time to debate the issue of land mines in Bosnia, the situation on the West Bank, or the relative merits of "I Can't Believe It's Not Butter."

Family Matters
Making eye contact can greatly improve your chances of creating a good first impression.

Family Matters
What can you do if you get trapped in a sticky conversation? For example, what happens if someone asks you to name the human race's single greatest achievement? If you're backed into a corner, go with something safe like "democracy," the "polio vaccine," or "frozen pizza."

The "remote control" is *not* a good choice.

Don't Go There
When in doubt, avoid these three topics: Sex, politics, and religion.

Body Talk

We like to flap our jaws and rearrange a lot of air molecules, but sometimes the real message is hidden behind the words—in nonverbal communication. Reading someone's *body language*, a form of nonverbal communication, can often tell you how he or she is responding to you. This is a great technique to use with prospective in-laws, who are unlikely to come straight out and declare, "Helen, I like this one" or "Lou, I think we have a stinker on our hands here."

Words to the Wise

Body language is a form of non-verbal communication. Body language includes such gestures and movements as nodding, crossing your arms and legs, tapping your foot, jiggling your leg, and looking someone in the eye.

Take this quick quiz. Match each gesture or movement with its meaning. Write the letter of the correct answer in the space provided. You will use some letters more than once.

Meaning

a. agreement and interest

b. defensiveness, distance, and resistance

c. boredom

d. you've outstayed your welcome

e. lack of understanding

Body Language

_____ 1. leaning forward and facing a person squarely

_____ 2. blank stares

_____ 3. tightly crossed legs

_____ 4. looking at a watch

_____ 5. nodding

_____ 6. tapping a foot

_____ 7. looking someone in the eye

_____ 8. arms crossed

_____ 9. drumming fingers on the table

_____ 10. taking a swing at your head with a six-foot zucchini

Answers

1. a   6. c

2. e or c   7. a

3. b   8. b

4. d   9. c

5. a   10. d

The Dating Game

And what about you, parents of the lucky couple? You're the in-laws-to-be. What can you do to make that first meeting easier for everyone?

For starters, you can screen out duds. Why waste all the time and energy getting to know someone who will fade out of your life faster than soap on a rope or a Nehru jacket?

To make it easier for you to separate the winners from the losers, I've prepared this handy "Application for Permission to Date My Daughter." Feel free to make copies and have all prospective applicants complete a form before they take your Buffy or Bitsy out on the town.

Application for Permission to Date My Daughter

Name _____ Date of Birth _____

Home Address _____

_____

Social Security Number _____

Driver's License Number _____

1. Do you own a van?

    _____ Yes*   _____ No

2. Do you have your own apartment?

    _____ Yes*   _____ No

* If you answered *Yes* to either of these questions, do not complete the form and immediately leave the premises.

****

Answer the following questions by filling in the blanks. Please answer freely. All answers will be considered confidential and will be used only as necessary.

1. A woman's place is in the _____.

2. When I meet a girl, the first thing I notice about her is her _____.
   (Note: If answer to question #2 begins with either a "T" or "A," discontinue application.)

3. The one thing I hope this application doesn't ask me about is

    _____

4. If I were ever shot, the last place I would want to be wounded on my body is in the

    _____

continues

---

continued

5. If I were ever beaten, the last bone I would want to have broken is my _____

6. Name of church or synagogue _____

7. Average yearly attendance _____

8. What do you want to be *if* we let you grow up? _____

_____

9. My nickname is_____

10. In 50 words or less, what does the word *no* mean to you? _____

_____

_____

I swear that all the information I have supplied is true to the best of my knowledge, under penalty of death or dismemberment.

_____

Applicant's signature

Note: This application will be considered incomplete and thereby automatically rejected unless it is accompanied by a detailed financial disclosure statement and a complete medical history.

DO NOT WRITE BELOW THIS LINE. FOR PARENTAL USE ONLY.

****

Appearance: _____ Brad Pitt

_____ The Fonz

_____ Ross Perot

_____ Evolution's missing link

_____ What passes today for normal

Intelligence: _____ Carl Sagan

_____ David Letterman

_____ Beavis and Butthead

_____ Potted plant

_____ Accepted   _____ Rejected

Pretty Please

There's still one more potent ploy in my bag of tricks. It's an oldie but a real goody. I guarantee it will endear you to even the most hard-hearted in-laws to be. Best of all, it will help make your marriage and your future relationship with your in-laws much more solid. And here it is…

Fellas, before you start planning the nuptials, ask your fiancee's parents permission to marry their daughter. That's right, go in and say, "Sir/Ma'am, I love your wonderful daughter Ellen Lou. She loves me. We would like to get married. May I please have your permission to marry your daughter?"

"What!" you yelp. "What is this? The Dark Ages?" No, it's not. We live in the Information Age, the era of the Electronic Revolution, the cusp of the twenty-first century. More information has been produced in the last 50 years than in the previous 5,000, the amount of information doubles every five years, and even the dog has its own laptop. But the more things change, the more they stay the same. Otherwise, how can we explain the lasting appeal of Pez, Pop-Tarts, and TV dinners?

But what happens if your beloved's parents turn you down flatter than three-day old soda pop? In that case, try to find out why you've been axed and work out the problem. I know this seems as old-fashioned as home-cooking, but research shows that 80 percent of the marriages that fall apart within the first year don't have parental approval. Another study showed that 70 percent of couples who divorced in the first year named in-law problems as a big factor. Starting off on the right foot can help make your marriage last.

It's All Relative

One daily edition of the *New York Times* contains more information than an educated sixteenth-century person assimilated in his or her entire lifetime.

Food Fight

Back in the old days (when cars were larger than TVs and only people of the female persuasion wore earrings) it was common for the groom's parents to hold a dinner to meet their future in-laws. When "the kids" announced their engagement, the groom's mother got on the (rotary) phone and called the bride's mother to set up a formal first encounter. Even if the in-laws had already met, this dinner was a done deal.

Today, we're more casual about life in general and weddings in particular. As a result, many couples set up their own first encounters. This is made easier by the fact that many couples live together before they tie the knot, so they have a place in which to cook and entertain. While it's certainly acceptable (and maybe even preferable) to meet everyone on neutral ground such as a restaurant, you know that nothing says lovin' like something from the oven.

There are also couples who don't meet their in-laws until they are married. As a result, the first meal encounter takes place *after* the nuptials. This often happens when one branch of the family couldn't make the wedding because they were busy saving the whales, splitting the atom, or serving time.

In either case, it takes more courage to cook that first meal for your in-laws or in-laws-to-be than it does to stick your head in a lion's mouth or wear spandex after age 30. Not to worry: help is on the way.

1. First, stay away from lions. Leave that to the Lion King.

2. You never heard of a girdle?

3. Don't worry about cooking that first meal. It's a piece of cake!

Here's how to make sure that the first meal doesn't turn into a Last Supper.

Four-Star Mom

Part of the problem with first meal fright is your spouse's feeling about his or her family's cooking. Unless your in-laws have never applied heat to food, your beloved will adore the food that emerged from the family kitchen. So what if your mother-in-law burns corn flakes? So what if your father-in-law once made a martini with chicken soup? (My father actually did this, but that's another story.)

The flavors of home leave an indelible mark on a spouse's psyche. I make bread from scratch, brownies that win first prize in the country fair, and a killer pot roast. Nonetheless, my husband still has a soft spot in his skull for Chicken in a Biscuit crackers and Snackin' Cakes, the foods of his youth. I could make this up?

Don't Go There
Catsup is *not* a vegetable—no matter what former President Reagan said.

And what if your spouse has a Super Mom? She held down a job, cleaned the house, carpooled to soccer, and made her own sauce (from the tomatoes and basil she grew in the lower forty).

And your father-in-law? He's Grill Master Supreme. The man flips burgers better than Ronald McDonald. Your familiar cry, "The take-out is here, honey," isn't going to cut the mustard with these in-laws, kiddo. Neither will your usual dinner of Frosted Flakes tarted up with raisins (that's the fruit course).

Hostess with the Mostest

So, to further good relations with your in-laws, I hereby offer a few tips for the perfect in-law meal. It won't leave your in-laws reaching for the Mylanta or thinking you're an idiot incapable of boiling water. Here are my guidelines:

1. **Attempt the impossible.**

   "Have you lost your brains, Rozakis?" you shout. "*I'm* going to make lobster thermidor or prime rib with Yorkshire pudding? Why can't I stick with my usual Franks a Lot?" No dice, you kitchen phobic. What you want is something really special, something that shows you care enough to cook the very best. With a new set of in-laws, you have to chuck the ketchup and start dicing some herbs.

2. **Don't cheap out.**

   Use the very best ingredients. It's pretty hard to goof up $22 a pound lobster. You'd be surprised how careful you get when the meal costs the same amount as the annual gross national product of a small Latin American country.

3. **Get big name food.**

   This is not the time for *scrod*. Go for *shrimp*. Avoid *chuck*; you want *T-bone, sirloin,* or *prime rib*. Then refer to the food by name, as in "I know how much you like ostrich and buffalo kebobs."

4. **Play nice.**

   Check to see what allergies and food restrictions your parents-in-laws have. Inducing cardiac arrest in your in-laws does not make a good first impression.

5. **Garnish.**

   Parsley and plastic flags are always appropriate, but don't overlook the cunning little bamboo umbrellas that go in wussy drinks, turnips carved to resemble Barbra Streisand, and pipe-cleaner animals. These little accessories divert attention from the blood-red parts of the pork roast or the black bits in the string beans. If all else fails and your food is totally inedible, your in-laws will be so busy picking out the doodads that they'll never get around to actually eating.

Family Matters
What if you really can't cook at all? In that case, make a dish from Guam, Sri Lanka, or Antarctica. No one will know if it tastes the way it should. After all, how many people eat porcupine on a regular basis? (Note: This won't work if your in-laws are from Guam, Sri Lanka, or Antarctica.)

6. **Blame it on the bossa nova.**

   If worst comes to worst, pretend that you're a politician and point fingers. Chicken undercooked? Just can't trust that new oven. Soufflé collapsed? That's what happens during earthquakes. Figs not fresh? What trouble we're having with tariffs lately.

In Case of Emergency...

➤ Serve more wine. Good wine. (If they don't drink alcohol, try some designer water. So what if they think you're profligate?)

➤ Turn on the football game. People will think it's Thanksgiving and expect lousy food.

➤ If you have a friend/relative that's known as a great cook, call and ask questions and for advice. After all, that's what friends are for!

➤ If you have a friend who owes you a favor and bakes a great strawberry-rhubarb pie, have your buddy get baking and bring it over well before the in-law arrival (and of course take the credit for this fabulous sugary delight).

   Remember: Dessert can change a bad dinner into an acceptable dinner. That's because it's the last thing they'll eat, so it's the first thing they'll remember.

Don't Go There
Fancy doesn't necessarily impress. For instance, if your in-laws are off-the-boat Southern Italians, nix on the chicken cordon bleu. If they're not adventurous, a first dinner is not the time to force curried sugar cane and goat on them.

➤ Serve more of everything. At least no one will go hungry—if the food is edible.

➤ Show the wedding videos. Your in-laws will be too distracted by Aunt Mildred's strip tease to remember that they came to your house to eat. (No video? Try the wedding picture proofs. In a pinch, a Little Mermaid coloring book might do the trick.)

➤ Announce that you're pregnant. What if you're a man? Get take-out.

As you cower under the kitchen counter, keep in mind that it's only a meal. Even if it's an unmitigated disaster from (watery) soup to (wormy) nuts, remember that it's still only a meal. You'll do better next time. Besides, in-laws rarely die from undercooked endive or burned fennel.

It's All Relative

If you're cooking a special dinner for a retro kind of guy (the kind who drives a Chevy, wears his pants well below his ample belly, and adores Bosco), be sure to include something from each of the four major male food groups: Meat, fried, beer, and red.

The Least You Need to Know

➤ First impressions count, especially when it comes to in-laws.

➤ Men, ask permission to marry your beloved. If permission is denied, find out why and work out the problems.

➤ Host a formal event to meet the in-laws. Serve food that you have cooked with your own hands.

Chapter 6

The Name Game

In This Chapter

➤ Find out what to do when you don't know what to call your parents-in-law

➤ See how to other people solve this problem

➤ Learn how to agree on mutually acceptable names for your parents-in-law

Remember what Juliet said to Romeo:

> What's in a name? That which we call a rose
> By any other name would smell as sweet...

Juliet got the poetry right, but she wasn't up to speed on the importance of names—and look what happened to *her*. Now, I'm not suggesting that calling your parents-in-law by the wrong names will result in a tragedy of Shakespearean proportions, but let's not fool ourselves here. Names sure *do* matter, whether we're dealing with teenage lovers or prospective in-laws. What you decide to call your parents-in-law can be a crucial factor in determining whether the relationship will be comfortable or awkward.

How can you figure out what to call your parents-in-law? That's what this chapter is all about. First, you'll see how others approach this thorny situation. Along the way, I'll show you how people from widely different backgrounds decide on the correct comfortable form of address for their parents-in-law and other in-laws. Finally, I'll give you some suggestions about selecting names that you can tailor to your individual parent-in-law situation. That way, you won't have to spend the next 50 years referring to your parents-in-law as "Uh" and "Um."

Has It Come to This?

A grasshopper walked into a bar and the bartender said, "Hey, we got a drink named after you!"

The grasshopper said, "You got a drink named Bob?"

When you figure out that your main squeeze is really the one who sets your heart a flutter, you're going to have to settle the top 10 major relationship issues. Here they are, in reverse order:

10. Coke or Pepsi?

9. Matching tattoos or matching nose rings?

8. Who opens mail addressed to "Occupant"?

7. Who gets in the shower first in the morning?

6. Who gets the big closet?

5. Toothpaste with whiteners or tartar control?

4. Who takes out the trash?

3. Who gets the newer car (or the only car)?

2. Which way does the toilet paper roll?

And the number one biggest issue to settle before the nuptials…

1. What are you going to call your parents-in-law?

Not to scare you, but in some relationships, what to call the parents-in-law might even be *the* major issue. That's because it carries such emotional overtones and has such long-range repercussions. In fact, deciding what to call the parents-in-law can set the tone for the entire relationship that follow.

For example, your mother-in-law is not likely to appreciate "Hatchet Face"; it's only the rare son-in-law who tolerates being called "Meathead" by his father-in-law.

Most of us aren't comfortable calling our mother-in-law "Mom"; after all, we already have one "Mom" (and one is usually more than enough). Besides, what happens if you do call your mother-in-law "Mom" and both "Moms" are in the room at the same time? Do you end up with Mom #1 and Mom #2? Who gets to be the Alpha Mom?

Here's an example of what can happen when the issue *isn't* resolved...

Hello, I Love You, Won't You Tell Me Your Name?

Sarah and Bill were cleaning up after the party when they realized that Bill's mother had left her book behind. "She's going to want to read this on the bus," Sarah said. "If I run, maybe I can catch her before the bus comes." Sarah grabbed her jacket and dashed out the door.

As she turned the corner, Sarah saw her mother-in-law heading for the bus stop. Sarah quickened her pace, but her mother-in-law was moving even faster. "Damn those senior aerobics," she thought. As Sarah picked up the speed, her mother-in-law kicked it up a notch. "It's almost as though she's trying to out-run me," Sarah thought, red-faced and panting.

Finally Sarah had enough. "Millie!" she called out to get her mother-in-law's attention. Her mother-in-law stopped. A moment passed and she turned around to face her daughter-in-law. "I was wondering when you'd finally decide what to call me," she said. "Millie is fine with me."

Pretty silly, eh? Unfortunately, it's fairly typical. Like so many newlyweds, Sarah and Bill had never figured out what to call each other's parents. The issue dragged on so long that it finally took on a life of its own, like the meatloaf in the back of the refrigerator or the rumor about alligators in the New York City sewers.

If you haven't settled on names for your parents-in-law, you'll notice the situation becoming increasingly tense. No one wants to be the one to say what everyone knows: You never address your parents-in-law directly. Everyone else in the family will tiptoe around the issue. Worst of all, if you don't establish a name for

Don't Go There
When we deal with someone who doesn't address us by our correct name or who calls us by a name we don't like, we feel devalued, discounted, and insulted.

Words to the Wise
Triangulation—When a third party gets sucked into helping two people communicate with each other.

your mother-in-law or father-in-law, you're all too likely to end up talking to your in-laws through other people—or most tragically, not at all.

True Confessions

I was telling my mother this story when it dawned on me that *she* had never decided what to call her parents-in-law, my paternal grandparents. My mother had no clue about how to resolve the issue and my grandmother was enjoying my mother's misery too much to throw her a life preserver. The issue was finally settled when my mother gave birth to darling me. Fortunately, my parents were married less than two years when the stork arrived with its bundle of joy. My timely solution to the name problem shows that even from a tender age I had a knack with relationship issues!

I was a very early talker (bet that's a real shocker, Gentle Reader). My grandmother was German, so under normal circumstances I would have called her by the German word for grandmother, "Oma." But that name was already taken, because *her* mother, my great-grandmother, was still alive and cooking (German grandmothers rarely kick, but they always cook). My grandmother's name was "Paula," so I named her by creating an entirely new word. To do so, I combined the first letter of her name—"P"—with the German word for grandmother—"Oma." Voila! My grandmother became "Poma" and that's what everyone in my family called her for nearly 40 years. (Flush with success, I also named my grandfather. His name was "Ludwig," so I named him "Nook." Thankfully for all involved, the origin of that name has not survived in family legend.)

It's All Relative

I didn't realize it at age two, but when I combined two words to create a new word, I wasn't doing anything linguistically that hadn't been done before. These combined words are called *portmanteau words*, from the British word for "suitcase." British writer Lewis Carroll (the pen name of Charles Ludwig Dodgson) created a number of portmanteau words in his masterpiece *Alice in Wonderland,* including the word "smog" (a combination of *smoke* and *fog*). Los Angeles residents thank him often.

Now, my laudable accomplishments aside, should the naming of parents-in-laws rest in the tender hands of toddlers? Maybe, but what happens if the couple never has children? Or, if the parents-in-law have no desire to be called by dopey names? Since neither situation is uncommon, you'd better read on.

Reach Out and Touch Someone

Thanks to the wonders of the World Wide Web, I was able to ask a lot of married people around the world how they decided on a name for their various in-laws. Almost no one had an easy time of it. Some had sweated more than Joey Buttafuoco crashing a prom; others got off more easily. But almost no one got off scot-free. Here's a sample response from my close friend Liz Smith Flynn who lives across the country. Her mother was Japanese; her father, American.

> My husband Mike met my mother only once, so for most of their conversation that particular question went a-begging. He called her "Mrs. Smith." I called Mike's mother "Louise" the few times I called her anything; I tried to call his grandmother "Susan" once, but that was too much, so I called her "Mrs. Dehm" mostly.

> And thinking back, I think my father called my grandmother "Sato-san"—not unusual in Japanese society, actually. And since she spoke no English and he no Japanese, it really wasn't relevant.

Here's the good news: Talking about what to call your parents-in-law is a good place for you and your future in-laws to begin building a healthy relationship. In many instances, this conversation can show how open both sides are to bringing two families together into one. A willingness to discuss the issue of names can be a harbinger of a close relationship among in-laws; an unwillingness to talk about names, in contrast, might forecast a chilly future.

Don't Go There
Some European-born Jews now living in America call their parents-in-law by the Yiddish words "shviger" (mother-in-law) and "shver" (father-in-law). Other Jews, however, consider these terms insulting. My advice? Never assume; always ask.

Fright Night

So why is the issue of what to call your parents-in-law touchier than a teenager in love? Here are the top five reasons:

1. **Fear of rejection.**

   "I thought that if I called my mother-in-law by her first name, she would think that I was disrespectful," one woman told me. "That would really put the kabosh on our relationship," she concluded. Does this sound familiar? Is this fear standing in your way of deciding what to call your parents-in-law?

2. **Fear of looking foolish.**

"What if my mother-in-law didn't want to be called 'Mom'?" Angela said. "I'd really feel like a jerk then." No one wants to embarrass themselves with their in-laws, especially early in the relationship. Better to save the bloopers for the later years when you've built up some credit.

3. **Fear of offending.**

When's the last time you used this handy little ditty?

Sticks and stones
May break my bones
But names can never hurt me.

Yes, they can. As a matter of fact, names can hurt more than sticks and stones hurled together. Names have always carried power. Among some Native American tribes, for example, there is a widespread feeling of danger in disclosing one's name, because this will enable an enemy to use magic to work some deadly injury to the person. The ancient Greeks were especially careful to disguise or reverse uncomplimentary names.

It's All Relative

Among the New Guinea Sea Dyaks, people related to each other by marriage never say each other's names, lest they call down the wrath of God.

4. **Fear of making a cultural gaffe.**

As Liz's story illustrates, names are often culturally determined. When people from different cultures marry, they are often unsure of customs, especially those surrounding such a sensitive issue as names.

It's All Relative

Among the African Caffres, a wife is forbidden to say the name of her mother-in-law; a husband cannot say the name of his father-in-law.

5. **Fear of seeming disloyal.**

Some people have no trouble calling their parents-in-law "Mom" and "Dad." They just said it felt natural. A few people even argued that it might be perceived as a compliment to their own parents.

However, a much larger group of people felt that calling their parents-in-law by the names they used for their own parents was an act of treachery, akin to refusing to listen to Dad's war stories (so what if he never got out of Hoboken?).

"What would my father say if I called my father-in-law 'Dad'?" a friend revealed. No one wants to hurt someone they love. Is this what's preventing *you* from settling the name issue with your parents-in-law?

Generation Gap

And before you think I'm slighting the parents-in-law when it comes to the name game, the opposite situation does not appear to pose a dilemma: Members of the older generation rarely have a problem calling their son- or daughter-in-law by his or her first name. And the "kids" almost never take offense at being addressed by their first names. As a result, the issue of what to call the son- or daughter-in-law almost never arises. In part, this is cultural: It is far more appropriate for an older person to call a younger one by his or her first name than the opposite way around. Nevertheless, problems occasionally arise when formal introductions need to be made.

"My mother-in-law always introduces me as her 'daughter,'" Beth complained. "I'm not her daughter; I'm her daughter-in-law. Besides, this always creates confusion, especially among acquaintances who know that my parents-in-law don't have any daughters." Even though the older woman believes that her method of introducing her daughter-in-law is a compliment, the younger woman does not perceive it that way. Instead, she takes great offense at what she perceives as over-familiarity.

Introductions such as this reflect desires and expectations. The parents-in-law want to be accepted and loved as parents. This is especially true in families that have children of only one gender or in cases where parents-in-law fear losing their own children to the son or daughter's new family.

How can you solve this aspect of the problem? Communicate! Gently but firmly, let your parents-in-law know that while you appreciate their gesture, you would prefer to be identified by the term "daughter-in-law" or "son-in-law." Under no circumstances make

Don't Go There
Siblings may even feel jealous to hear their parents addressed as "Mom" or "Dad" by their new sister- or brother-in-law. This is especially true when the child has a shaky relationship with his or her parents or is going through a traditional breaking-away period, such as leaving for college.

your spouse do your dirty work; you have to handle this yourself. (That's not to say, however, that your spouse can't do other dirty work, like mopping the kitchen floor, scooping up after the pooch, and worst of all, balancing the checkbook.)

Covering All the Bases

A little boy was overheard talking to himself as he strode through his backyard, baseball cap in place and toting the ball and bat. "I'm the greatest baseball player in the world," he said proudly. Then he tossed the ball in the air, swung and missed. Undaunted, he picked up the ball, threw it into the air and said to himself, "I'm the greatest baseball player ever!" He swung at the ball again, and again he missed. He paused a moment to examine the bat and ball carefully. Then once again he threw the ball into the air and said, "I'm the greatest baseball player who ever lived."

He swung the bat hard and again missed the ball.

"Wow!" he exclaimed. "What a pitcher!"

You can call your parents-in-laws whatever you want behind their backs, but to their faces you've got to come up with a name that satisfies everyone. This is especially true if you're not especially close to your parents-in-laws. After all, if they like you, you've got a little leeway when it comes to the name game. Even if they're not thrilled with your choice of address, they'll overlook it in their general joy that sonny boy has married you rather than that tramp down the street. But if the relationship is as cold as Pluto, the name better help bring about a thaw.

One Size Doesn't Fit All

Many other cultures have solved the issue far more neatly than we have by simply assigning traditional names to relatives. The Cheyenne, for example, have a different way of saying some relatives' names if you are speaking *to* them or speaking *about* them. Here are some examples of the form used when speaking *to* your relatives.

Title	Relative
namê_éme (or namshim)	father-in-law
né_ke'éehe	mother-in-law
néxahe	son-in-law or daughter-in-law

The Fulani tribe of Africa is equally explicit in its naming customs for in-laws. Parents-in-law and children-in-law address each other as *guna*, but it is usual for a woman to address her father-in-law as *takurundi* (father of the house) and her mother-in-law as *makurindi* (mother of the house). Elder brothers-in-law or sisters-in-law are classed as parents-in-law, and so addressed as *guna*. Younger brothers-in-law or sisters-in-law are addressed as *nyini*.

In some Chinese families, the members themselves may not address each other by their first names and must call each other by their family relationship, such as "Sister" or "Brother."

Don't Call Me Mom!

So, short of joining the Cheyenne tribe in North America or the Fulani tribe of Africa, what's a son- or daughter-in-law to do? Follow my suggestions for naming your parents-in-law, that's what. And here they are...

1. **Come right out and ask your mother-in-law and father-in-law what they want to be called.** I know, I'm suggesting something radical here, like eating less if you want to lose weight or not baking in the sun if you're over 30 (over 50 if you live in Miami or Los Angeles).

   Talking about the name issue right up front allows everyone to air their feelings and knocks stress down to manageable levels. But talking about something that's as loaded as a frat boy on Saturday night is easier said than done. Hey, I've been there and, I'm ashamed to say, *not* done that. So...

2. **Follow the lead of the rest of the family.** Obviously, this is only going to work if there's another daughter-in-law or son-in-law and the issue of names has already been settled to *everyone's* satisfaction. With the name game, one size *does not* fit all, so you have to be mighty careful you don't get sucked into calling your parents-in-law something that doesn't fit in your comfort zone.

   If you're the first to get married, there's no lead to follow. As the head weenie at the roast, you have to blaze new ground. In that case, see suggestion #1.

Don't Go There
Americans pride themselves on their informality, but people from Asia and most other places in the world do not see this as a virtue. Instead, informality often equals disrespect. Younger people should be especially careful to address older people by their titles or as custom dictates.

Family Matters
Because parents-in-law probably experienced the same problem early in their marriage, it is usually easier for them to raise the question by saying, "What would you like to call me?" and then offering suggestions such as "I would prefer to be called..." And if they don't, remember this when *you're* the parent-in-law and show some mercy to your daughter- or son-in-law by offering suggested names.

3. **Use their first names.** My sister has a delightful mother-in-law, a lively and intelligent woman whose company I greatly enjoy. Her first name is Mera, and that's what my sister calls her. It works for them.

4. **Invent a name.** Sometimes you're just not comfortable using your parent-in-law's first name, even if that's what they have indicated they want you to call them. In this case, you might want to consider inventing a name for your parent-in-law. Of course, the name must be mutually agreeable to all parties.

   For example, my mother's first name is Erna. For some reason that I can no longer remember (if there ever *was* a reason in the first place), my husband and several other sons-in-law call my mother "Oin," a mangled variation of Erna. She appears to like it because it's special and sets her apart from all the other Ernas in the world. All two of them.

   We've done the same thing for my father-in-law. His name is Louis, but everyone calls him by his middle name, Nick, which he prefers. I don't call him by either name. Instead, we made up the name Nas, the first part of a juicy Greek curse he uses to amuse us. The first few words of this useful imprecation are "Nas a fahn a..." (Here's the entire curse in translation, in case you ever need it: "May the red goats eat out your stomach lining and the white mice, too.") So my father-in-law has become Old Nas; my husband, Young Nas. Again, he likes it because it's as special as he is.

Family Matters
People in second marriages often feel more comfortable calling their parents-in-law by their first names rather than as "Mom" or "Dad."

5. **Go with the classics: *Mom* and *Dad*.** In many areas of the country and in many families, the preferred term of address for a mother-in-law is "Mom" and "Dad" for a father-in-law. Variations include "Mama" and "Pop." If everyone is comfortable with this naming system, it might be the way out of the problem for you.

6. **Try the formal route: Mother.** Some people have solved the issue by calling a father-in-law "Father [first name]" and a mother-in-law "Mother [first name]." For example, you could have "Father Bill" and "Mother Hillary." This works nicely if your in-laws happen to be the President and the First Lady or the kind of people who still wear hats and eat sitting down.

7. **Go South.** And in case you think that most Americans are dolts when it comes to naming their parents-in-law, let me tell you the ingenious way Southerners solved the problem. In the South, you call older people by their first name with *Miss* or *Mister* in front of it. Thus, if your mother-in-law's first name is "Sarah," you'd call

her "Miss Sarah." If your father-in-law's name is Lou, he becomes "Mister Lou." You can't go wrong with this, because adding "Miss" or "Mister" is a sign of great respect. (Unless, of course, your in-laws fought on the Northern side during the War Between the States. Then you'd better regroup.)

8. **Don't recycle.** I know we all want to do our part to help the environment, but asking your significant other to recycle cute pet names used by previous spouses to refer to the parents-in-law is not the way to go. Better to adopt a water buffalo in Cambodia or plant a tree in the rain forest. Unless they have a very good sense of humor or are unusually self-confident, people in second marriages are likely to be very upset about calling their parents-in-law by the pet name used by the previous spouse. In these instances, start from scratch.

Family Matters
Hopelessly stuck on the name issue? Don't panic. As time passes, the issue of what to call your parents-in-law becomes less important if the relationship is good.

The Least You Need to Know

➤ What to call the parents-in-law is a *major* issue in many relationships—*the* major issue in some marriages.

➤ Talking about what to call your parents-in-law can help you and your future in-laws start building a good relationship.

➤ Best method: Ask them what they want to be called.

➤ *Never* leave the issue unresolved.

Part 2
Trouble in Paradise

It was a dark and stormy night. A drunk left a bar and decided to take a short-cut through a graveyard. The drunk failed to see an empty grave and fell into it. He tried to climb out of it, but the grave was too deep and the rain had turned the dirt to mud, making the walls too slippery to climb. The drunk finally gave up and decided to spend the night in the grave.

A little while later, another drunk left the bar and decided to take the same shortcut through the graveyard. He, too, fell into that open grave and tried to climb out but couldn't. The first drunk watched silently as his fellow lush staggered around the grave.

At last, the first drunk stood up, tapped the second drunk on the shoulder, and said, "Buddy, you'll never get out."

Seconds later, he did.

See, almost anything *is* possible *if you set your mind to it (or get scared enough). In this section, you'll learn how to plan your wedding, so you can make sure that rice is the only thing that's thrown on your special day. Then we'll focus on the two most common problems that you'll encounter with your in-laws: Your mother-in-law and your father-in-law. Just so no one feels slighted, I cover issues with sisters- and brothers-in-law, too. Hey, we all know that no one has a monopoly when it comes to causing trouble in the family.*

Follow the steps I describe here (and stay out of bars and graveyards), and you won't get stuck in a hole with your in-laws.

Chapter 7

Wedding Bell Blues...Or How to Make Sure That the Rice Is the Only Thing That Gets Thrown

In This Chapter

➤ Learn why weddings cause such tension among in-laws

➤ Explore social, cultural, and religious differences

➤ Discover methods to make the day go as smoothly as possible

There was a fella with a parrot that swore like a sailor, a real pistol. The parrot could swear for five minutes straight, without repeating itself. However, the parrot's owner was a quiet, conservative type and the bird's foul mouth was driving him crazy.

One day, the parrot's blue streak got to be too much for its owner, so the guy locked the bird in a kitchen cabinet. Enraged, the bird clawed and scratched the wood. When the man finally released the bird, our fowl friend cut loose with a stream of vulgarities that would make a long-distance trucker blush.

At that point, the man was so angry that he threw the bird into the freezer. For the first few seconds there was a terrible din. The parrot kicked, clawed, and thrashed. Then the room suddenly got very quiet. At first the man just waited, but soon he got worried. What if the parrot was hurt?

Panicked, the man opened the freezer door. The parrot calmly climbed onto the man's arms and said, "Awfully sorry about the trouble I gave you. I'll do my best to improve my vocabulary from now on."

The man was astonished at the bird's transformation. Then the parrot said, "By the way, what did the chicken do?"

Are you feeling like the chicken, bunky? Does it seem like you've been frozen out of your own wedding plans? If so, you're not alone. That's what this chapter is all about.

With their lovely gowns, scrumptious food, and lively dancing, weddings are billed as joyous occasions. People are supposed to look forward to them. Yet it's inevitable that the major players—the happy couple and their parents-in-law—feel a sinking feeling in the pit of their stomachs when the word "wedding" is mentioned. In this chapter, I'm going to show you how many of the problems associated with in-laws and weddings can be reduced.

First, you'll learn why weddings are such emotional—and important—events concerning your future dealings with your in-laws. Then, you'll take a look at some of the most common reasons why weddings can draw in-laws apart. Finally, I'll give you some suggestions for making your wedding an occasion to forge bonds with your in-laws while getting a picture perfect day.

Going to the Chapel and We're Going Have a Big Fight

Linda Ferris, a successful real estate broker, was justly proud of her skill as a negotiator. She knew how to find a way for everyone to come out ahead—or think they had. "I'm an expert at creating 'win/win' situations," she told me. That was *before* she and her fiancé Jay started to plan their wedding, however. Then she became an expert at clenching her fists, gnashing her teeth, and pulling out her hair.

"My family is quiet," Linda said. "We're not flashy people. We wanted a small wedding in a garden, maybe 50–75 people, a strolling violinist, a cake decorated with fresh fruit. My in-laws wanted the social event of the season—catering hall, 300 people, an orchestra the size of Cleveland, and enough food to feed a third-world nation. I was waiting for them to demand fireworks and Elvis impersonators parachuting from helicopters. Well, I got the fireworks all right when I tried to stand my ground. 'When am I going to have another chance to dance at my son's wedding?' Jay's mother whined. Before we even marched down the aisle, I was ready to rearrange her bridgework."

Ideally, by the time you're ready to get married, you've gotten your in-laws to bless your union, you've decided whether to call your mother-in-law "Mom" or "Mrs. Snodgrass, Ma'am" and you've stocked up on snack foods so everyone should feel welcome.

But if getting along with your in-laws was *that* easy, the national debt would be paid, hell would be frozen over, and we'd all be ducking to avoid the flying pigs.

When your side and your beloved's side disagree over the wedding plans, guess who's caught in the middle? It's not the milkman, Cubby. Why all the fuss and feathers? Like Linda, you probably understand your parents' feelings but you also want to accommodate your in-laws-to-be. Like Jay, you love your bride, but you don't want to feel disloyal to your own mommy and daddy. And we haven't even brought in the sisters and brothers yet.

It's All Relative

The legal age for marriage with parental consent ranges from 12 for women and 14 for men in some states to 16 for women and 18 for men in other states. The required age for marriage without parental consent varies from 16 to 21 for women to 18 to 21 for men. Remember this the next time your teenager acts up. After all, a quickie marriage might be easier to arrange than a stay in the convent.

When you're planning a wedding, the decisions come faster than bills after Christmas. Tap a keg or carve a capon? Canned vows or homemade ones? Still photos or videos? Rabbi, priest, minister, judge, or Uncle Duke of the Church of the Large Donation? Then there's the entertainment. Can we convince 80-year-old Aunt Venus to do her belly dance or are we stuck with Uncle Sid and his accordion?

Weddings are especially great because they provide so many ways for your in-laws to get their feelings hurt. Been there, done that, got the T-shirt? Or are you soon going there? Put a checkmark next to each decision that has caused tension for you, your beloved, or your in-laws during wedding preparations.

Decisions, Decisions

_____ 1. Who gets invited? Does either side get more guests?

_____ 2. Which parents and in-laws get listed on the invitation?

_____ 3. Who gets top billing on the invitation?

_____ 4. What role will your sisters, brothers, and sisters-and brothers-in-law play in the preparations and actual ceremony?

_____ 5. Which side gives the rehearsal dinner?

_____ 6. Who will be the bridesmaids? The ushers? Flower children? Ring bearer? Are we talking in-laws or friends?

_____ 7. Who picks the music?

_____ 8. Do you have to wear a wedding dress of your mother-in-law's choosing or can you select your own outfit?

_____ 9. Where will the out-of-town in-laws stay during the festivities?

_____10. Who walks whom down the aisle?

And the number one stress buster: Who pays for the wedding? Making these decisions often leads to the first face-to-face struggle between in-laws. The outcome of the struggle and how people behave during it can set the tone of the relationship for years to come.

Make My Day

Words to the Wise
Serial monogamy is the newly created term for repeated marriages or long-term relationships.

Question: What's a mother-in-law's place in the wedding?

Answer: To wear beige and keep her mouth shut.

Think back on your wedding (any one will do). A perfect day? A horror show? Are we having selective amnesia? If so, take the following quiz to put your memories into words. Check the description that best fits your wedding day.

My wedding was...

_____ like playing leapfrog with a unicorn.

_____ as enjoyable as root canal without anesthesia.

_____ not unlike an IRS audit.

_____ great fun until Aunt Hortensia threw the first punch.

_____ best not remembered.

_____ an epic disaster on the scale of the Hindenberg, the Titanic, or *Airport*.

_____ completely out of my control. Who was getting hitched here—me or my mother-in-law?

_____ the greatest day of my life.

If you checked the last choice, let me tell you straight out of the gate that you're in the minority. Most couples remember at least one terrible moment during their wedding, when one set of in-laws insulted the other set over the flowers, cake, booze, location, or food. And often, the pain of that moment can linger for years.

Whose Wedding Is It Anyway?

A wedding is ostensibly for the bride and groom, but the two sets of parents and siblings often make self-serving suggestions and even unreasonable demands. The stew of everyone's expectations, wishes, and demands can make for a real Mylanta moment. It's a sucker bet that something is going to go awry and someone is going to pitch a fit.

In part, it's because a wedding is a transition in the lives of all those involved, and any transition stirs up strong emotions. Besides the excitement and anticipation, comes fear and probably more than a dash of terror. Parents feel a sense of loss ("My baby! My baby is leaving home!") along with their joy.

At the same time, unresolved feelings often bubble to the surface. Perhaps your parents-in-law had horrendous weddings; perhaps they got off on the wrong foot with their own in-laws as a result. Hurt feelings aren't the sole realm of your parents-in-law, however: a sister or brother-in-law might have just as much trouble dealing with your nuptials because of what happened at *theirs*. Be forewarned: In these cases, your in-laws are likely to view the wedding as a chance to rectify old wounds. You're likely to be the one caught in the cross fire as they press to get what *they* want at the wedding, not necessarily what the bride and groom want.

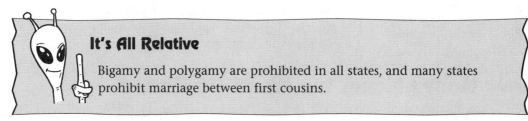

It's All Relative

Bigamy and polygamy are prohibited in all states, and many states prohibit marriage between first cousins.

There's usually a hidden agenda and it's always the same: Who has the power? Who will make the decisions in the family: His side or her side? Who gets the final say?

Ring Ding

Some parents start turning the screws even before the engagement. The pressure may start with the engagement ring (or lack thereof). Here's my friend Chrissy's story:

> When I got engaged to Greg, I couldn't get the kind of ring I wanted—I had to wear his grandmother's ring. Now, I'm not one to refuse a free diamond, but I wasn't

even allowed to change the setting! The ring was really out-of-date and looked terrible on my hand. But family tradition demanded that it be kept in pristine condition so I could pass it down to *my* son or daughter. That way, I guess, the ring could make them as miserable as it had made me.

Other friends told me stories of having their mother-in-law pick out their engagement ring ("Of course you'll use my jeweler, sweetie") or even counsel them not to get an engagement ring at all. ("Sonny boy is still paying off his college loans. Don't you want him to get out of debt before you start demanding fancy jewelry?")

A few couples refuse to be bullied but the majority of people give in to the pressure to keep the peace. Often, they're young and unused to dealing with these pressures. Later, they often regret their decision. "My mother-in-law wanted me to get the same shape and size ring as all the other daughters-in-law so there wouldn't be any competition," said one woman. "I gave in because I didn't want to be seen as a troublemaker. I didn't like the ring when I got it. I still don't like it, years later. In retrospect, I should have stood my ground."

Family Matters
It was the accepted practice in Babylon 4,000 years ago that for a month after the wedding, the bride's father would supply his son-in-law with all the mead he could drink. Mead is a honey beer, and because the calendar was lunar based, this period was called the "honey month"—or what we know today as the "honeymoon."

Hindsight is 20-20; it's always easy to look back and know what we *should* have done. As someone who gave in a lot more than she should have while planning her wedding and has regretted it ever since, here's my advice: Stand your ground from the very beginning. There's no call to be snippy, but the sooner you make your wishes known, the easier it will be to set appropriate limits and boundaries as you plan the rest of the wedding festivities.

~~Love~~ Money Makes the World Go Round

Money, as you are already doubtlessly aware, represents forces and values far beyond a mere summing-up of one's liquid material worth or simple purchasing power. Money, especially in our ostensibly classless, proudly democratic, and ferociously free-market society, symbolizes pride. It represents freedom. It serves as an obsession, measure of self-worth, and Holy Grail all rolled into one. Plus, if you have lots and lots of it, restaurant owners are nicer to you and you usually get your way—especially when it comes to planning your kid's wedding. It's the cynic's golden rule, folks: The one with the gold rules.

Weddings are more sensitive than a teenager with acne because they're not only a public declaration of a couple's love, but also an open show of the bride's social status. Even if the bride and groom are paying the tab themselves, the scope of the wedding reflects on the in-laws. Trust me: You don't want to be in the firing range when the parents-in-law play "Can you top this?" with the finances.

Money Business

Because planning the wedding is linked to financial issues, those who foot the bill often have the ultimate say in what type of wedding it will be. Some families will amiably negotiate the amount of money they have to spend and try to decide fairly who will pay for what. Others, in contrast, use money as a weapon to get their way. "I'm paying for it and I'm going to get what I want!" one father told his son-in-law to be.

In the good old days, when Spencer Tracy was the *Father of the Bride* and Elizabeth Taylor the adoring, darling daughter, the family of the bride arranged the wedding and paid for it. Even the language of weddings—"Giving the bride away"—placed the responsibility squarely on *her* family's wallet. The groom was responsible for the liquor, transportation, and photography.

Fortunately for all involved (especially for those of you who have 10 unmarried daughters or just one child in college), this tradition is being shattered faster than Communism. Today, more and more couples split the expenses according to who can afford what. As a result, resentment can arise when the bride's parents get stuck footing the whole bill when they were expecting the groom's parents to fork over their fair share.

Hey, Big Spender

Think that's all that can go wrong when money issues come up? Think again. Here are some other problems that can arise over the wedding expense:

➤ One side overspending to impress their friends and neighbors.

➤ Parents-in-law resenting the expense because they feel the marriage won't last.

➤ One set of in-laws thinking the other set is cheaper than a 2,000 pound canary; the other side overspending to counter that impression.

➤ The bride and groom being left in a hole by well-meaning but profligate parents—or fiscally irresponsible ones.

Culture Clash

Arina, born in Afghanistan, was excited about her brother's upcoming wedding to Mina, a young woman from India. Arina didn't have time to talk to her brother and Mina about the wedding. In keeping with her own Afghani tradition, Mina wore a white dress, a symbol of luck and happiness for the wedding couple.

That morning, Arina showed up at Mina's house to help her prepare for the wedding. When Mina saw Arina, she started to tremble and her faced turned ashen. Mina's other relatives acted equally upset when they saw Arina. Some turned away; others were openly hostile. "What have I done wrong?" Arina wondered. Before the wedding, Mina's aunt took Arina aside and explained that wearing white to an Indian wedding is a very bad omen. It is thought to bring back luck, even death, to the couple. Only a bitter enemy would wear white to a wedding.

Don't Go There

Don't wear black or white to a Chinese wedding, for both colors are associated with death.

Arina thought she was honoring the wedding couple by wearing white; the bride and her family took her outfit as a sign of the worst possible ill-wishes. Cultural differences can wreck havoc at weddings. Sometimes, even the best intentions are misinterpreted due to differences in region, background, and heritage. Here's another example:

The Hawthorne family sent out invitations for the forthcoming wedding of their daughter Carol to Guatemalan-born Ernesto Colon. Since the Colon family lives in California and the wedding was to be held in Florida, the Hawthornes enclosed maps to the catering hall and information about hotels in the area. They listed the names, rates, and amenities at three different hotels. They also suggested that guests make their reservations as soon as possible, because hotel space was limited.

The Colon family was so outraged when they received their invitations that they refused to go to the wedding.

The Hawthornes believed they were being considerate by including hotel information. To the Colons, however, the family of the bride should have welcomed the groom's family into their home, no matter how crowded they might be. The Colons interpreted the information about hotel reservations as rejection. After all, the Colons had traveled across the country to attend their son's wedding; weren't they at least entitled to simple hospitality?

It's All Relative

In pre-Revolutionary China, arranged marriages were the norm. It was common for a bride and groom to meet for the first time on their wedding day.

Once they discovered the reason for the misunderstanding, the Hawthornes felt embarrassed. They did not change their plans, however, because having strangers as house guests was not part of *their* cultural heritage. In an effort to maintain a semblance of family relations, the Colons finally decided to attend the wedding and stay in a motel, but their feelings were not soothed. Relations between the Hawthornes and Colons were never good.

Religion is another potential minefield when it comes to weddings. Parents and parents-in-law often react violently when their children marry outside their faith. Bad feelings often spill over to sisters- and brothers-in-law, too. Read on.

Strangers to the Tribe

Families often feel threatened by a religious outsider. Some in-laws react by observing traditions more strongly than ever; others, in contrast, go for a frontal assault. I know of two women who refused to attend their sons' weddings because they were interfaith marriages. In-laws of all religions can feel endangered by outsiders trying to crash the family gates.

Nonetheless, from the time of Ruth the Moabite, who chose to cling to her Jewish mother-in-law ("Whither thou goest…thy people shall be my people"), interfaith marriage has been an especially thorny battle for Jewish people. Many Jews feel surrounded by forces chipping away at the tribe. To some Jews, the melting pot has become a meltdown as intermarriage is accomplishing what centuries of oppression could not.

It's All Relative

Since 1985, more than half of all Jews have married outside their religion; and of that half, only 25 percent are raising their children Jewish.

Come Together, Right Now

How can you bring in-laws closer together when religious differences threaten to make the wedding as incendiary as Krakatoa? First of all, show your in-laws that you're willing to learn more about their religion. For example, read up on Passover; learn more about Easter; find out who Buddha is. Then, invite your in-laws to learn more about your belief system. This doesn't mean that you should abandon your faith; quite the contrary. It *does* mean that education and openness can dispel stereotypes and fear. If your in-laws are unreceptive to your overtures, make sure they understand that you're not trying to sway their beliefs. I cover this issue in depth in Chapter 11, "Vive la Difference!"

Take the Middle Ground

Note to atheists/agnostics/nonpracticing believers: What happens if you're not religious—but your in-laws are? This can be a very difficult situation, especially when you're planning the wedding. My friend Peggy, for example, was born into a Catholic family but never attends church or follows the rituals. She considers herself an agnostic. Her husband, in contrast, comes from a very devout Catholic family. Here's what she said about her experiences:

> My fiancé and I wish to be married outdoors in a civil ceremony, but his very, very Catholic parents are going ballistic about it. I want a nonreligious or nondenominational ceremony, but I'm afraid I'm going to cave in to the pressure of family—and regret it later. I've chosen to compromise and have a minister, but still do the outdoor route. Still, this isn't sitting well (it's the aisle to the altar or the road to hell as far as they're concerned), but they're happier than if it were a judge.

Family Matters
Recognize that you are marrying not just your honey but his or her entire family as well.

This is a fairly common situation. If it happens to you, I'd suggest that you go Peggy's route—compromise. Find some middle ground that everyone can accept, so that the in-law relationship gets off to a smooth start. It's worth the effort.

Bridge Across Troubled Waters

You're no idiot. You know that starting out as a couple is more difficult than mastering underwater fire prevention or barefoot aluminum dancing. As the wedding approaches, you're still feeling each other out (and *up*) and trying to be on your best behavior. You're simultaneously thrilled to discover all that your partner is...and crushed to discover all that he or she is not.

So while you're traveling the emotional interstate with your honey, why not build some bridges with your prospective in-laws at the same time? Start with the rehearsal dinner.

The rehearsal dinner is a great time to meet everyone, create good feelings, and begin your wedding celebration. The groom's parents usually host the dinner, but as with many wedding traditions, this is no longer a strict rule. Sometimes the bride and groom will host the dinner themselves. Other times, it will be hosted jointly by several people. Think of the rehearsal dinner as a dry run for the Big Day.

Party Hearty

Your rehearsal dinner can be a formal lunch at a restaurant, a clam bake on a beach, or a picnic in your backyard. Some restaurants have private rooms, which are nice for setting up a table of hors d'oeuvres so people can walk around and mingle before dinner. This can force the in-laws to get to know each other because there's no easy escape. If you want to separate the landlubbers from the shipshape, try renting a boat for the day and serving greasy salami sandwiches and warm beer.

Invite everyone who will take part in the wedding ceremony. Here's your guest list for the rehearsal dinner:

1. The wedding party

2. Spouses or dates of all adult attendants

3. Parents and grandparents of the bride and groom

4. Priest, rabbi, minister, or whoever is officiating

5. The musicians or soloist, if he or she is a close friend or family

> **Family Matters**
> It's not required that you send out invitations for your rehearsal dinner, but if you have time, it's a good idea. The invitation will tell people exactly where the rehearsal will be held, what time to be at the rehearsal and where and when the dinner will be held. If you do send out invitations, the general rule is that they should be less formal than your wedding invitation.

6. If you are having small children in the wedding, the parents of the children should be invited, but many times the children will not attend the dinner in order to get to bed early and avoid driving everyone crazy.

7. You can always invite other family members who are not part of the ceremony

8. Ditto on out-of-town guests

Make sure that everyone is introduced to each other, either through formal introductions ("going around the table") or informally ("mixing and mingling"). It's also a good idea to thank your parents and future parents-in-law and propose a toast at the rehearsal dinner to say "thank you" for all their love, support, and help for the wedding.

Play Nice, Kids

How else can you help bring the in-laws together over the wedding preparations while getting the wedding you want? Here are some ideas:

1. For the bride and groom...

   ➤ This is your wedding. If you have strong convictions on a specific issue, say so—or forever hold your peace.

   ➤ Establish your identity as a couple by sticking together and making joint decisions.

➤ If you *are* paying the entire cost of the wedding, you can theoretically have things exactly the way you want. But be careful what you wish for...you may get it. Instead of being a big baby, consider giving in on small issues to establish good relations with your in-laws from the get-go.

➤ If you are *not* footing the bill, be prepared to compromise on significant issues.

➤ No matter who pays for the wedding, the wedding couple ought to discuss and decide on such important issues as the day, time, religious or secular service, customs, location, guest list, music, and so on.

➤ Under no circumstances act as the negotiator between the two sets of parents. Even if you are the chief negotiator for the UN, it's not your job to arrange peace in our time among the in-laws. It is your job to get married.

2. For the parents, parents-in-law, sisters-in-law, and brothers-in-law...

➤ Remember that this is your child's or child-in-law's marriage, not yours.

➤ Be there to help the bride and groom have the day *they* wish to have, not the day *you* think they should have.

➤ Even if you are paying for the entire wedding, be sure to consider the other set of parents involved.

➤ Respect other people's customs and culture, even if they are radically different from your own.

➤ Understand that you don't have to love this stranger who has stolen your child. All we're asking for here is a little respect. Ditto for the other set of parents-in-law and all their relatives.

3. For everyone...

➤ Try to have face-to-face meetings from the very start to allow both sets of parents to state their piece and make their demands.

➤ Nip problems in the bud. Don't let differences become disagreements become cause for nuclear disarmament.

➤ Try not to prejudge, even if you get stuck with some prospective in-laws who got into the gene pool while the lifeguard wasn't watching.

➤ See your parents-in-law as people, individuals with their own tastes and back stories. Don't just view them as his parents or her folks.

➤ Different is not necessarily bad, just different. (Unless it involves hard-boiled eggs, Cool Whip, and a hula hoop. Then it's very bad.) Try to make allowances for differences and to reach compromises.

➤ Realize that everyone has an equal stake at making this marriage work. Even if you think that your son-in-law isn't the sharpest knife in the drawer. Even if you think your daughter-in-law is so dense that light bends around her. You want the kids to be happy.

➤ You can be brutally honest with yourself, but don't be so quick to spread that honesty around. Voice your concerns and then sit back. When in doubt, keep your mouth shut.

➤ Be aware that something is going to go wrong. Uncle Fenster will dance with a lampshade on his head (even if he has to bring it with him). Aunt Daisy will get potted and sing "Moonlight Bay" at the top of her lungs. There's no way around it.

> **Don't Go There**
> The answer to "How do I look in this outfit" is never "Fat." This is especially true for (a) an altered wedding dress and (b) any tuxedo picked up five minutes before the wedding.

➤ Realize that you're tense, frustrated, nerves on edge. You're likely to overreact at least once during the planning or party.

➤ Manners were invented to smooth the way over difficult social situations. If at all possible, follow the traditional wedding rules. These strict protocol edicts can help forestall explosions.

➤ Keep your sense of humor. If you and your beloved can laugh at some of the absurdity, you'll be able to defuse some of the tension.

➤ A little tolerance buys a lot of goodwill.

➤ Use common sense.

➤ Good luck.

It's All Relative

Any palm readers out there? If so, the "marriage line" is the line under the little finger which begins outside of the palm and extends inward to the palm. The marriage line not only indicates marriage, but all forms of romantic relations including relations with lovers and friends. Commonly, it is said that one marriage line indicates one marriage and two lines indicate two marriages. If there are several marriage lines but none with any clarity, it suggests a late marriage.

The Least You Need to Know

➤ Recognize that all in-laws bring their emotional baggage to the wedding preparations and ceremony. This colors their actions and reactions.

➤ Cultural and religious differences can cause explosions.

➤ If possible, have both sides plan the wedding together to forestall later problems.

➤ Stand fast on big issues; give in on the little ones.

Chapter 8

Mommy-In-Law Dearest

In This Chapter

➤ See what strife mothers-in-law can cause

➤ Learn ways to deal with these problems

➤ Find out how to state your concerns frankly but nonjudgmentally

➤ Discover why it's important to forgive—if not forget

➤ Understand that it takes years to build trust

Getting along with your mother-in-law is a very important issue in most marriages. Mother-in-law problems can even destroy a marriage. As a result, I'm going to be serious in this chapter. But first, one last joke before I retreat into solemnity. Stop me if you've heard this one:

> Hank was amazed at the length of the funeral procession going down Main Street. Watching for awhile, he observed that the cortege consisted entirely of men and that it was led by a man holding a Doberman pincher on a leash. When his curiosity got the better of him, he walked up to the man at the front of the line. "Excuse me for interrupting you in your time of grief," said Hank politely, "but I've never seen such a funeral procession. Would you mind telling me who it's for?"

It's for my mother-in-law," explained the mourner. Tightening the leash, he gestured down at the dog and said, "My Doberman here killed her."

"Gee, that's terrible," commiserated Hank. But...hmmmm...is there any way you might lend me your dog for a day or so?"

The bereaved son-in-law pointed his thumb over his shoulder and answered, "Get in line."

There's no doubt that mothers-in-law have gotten a bum rap, right up there with Donny Osmond, the Mets, and Brussels sprouts. In some households, mother-in-law bashing has even become a blood sport. This chapter is designed to help you avoid being either the basher or the bashee—or getting caught somewhere in the middle. I'll teach you how to establish a good relationship with your mother-in-law. And, if you're on the other side of the fence, I'll help you learn ways to get along more smoothly with your daughter- or son-in-law.

First, you'll find out why it's important to get along with your mother-in-law. Then, I'll survey some of the most common causes of conflicts between mothers-in-law and their married children. Along the way, I'll give you strategies for coping with these problems. Finally, you'll learn what to do if all else fails and your mother-in-law remains as weird as Michael Jackson, as blazing as a jack-o'-lantern, or as hostile as Jack the Ripper.

It's All Relative

The common houseplant with long, razor-sharp leaves is called "mother-in-law's tongue." How much you want to bet the botanist didn't cotton to *his* mother-in-law?

Take My Mother-In-Law, Please

The classic tension between couples and their respective mothers-in-law has resulted in misery, mania, and even mayhem. The strife is so commonplace that it has resulted in some great jokes. (So what if I promised in the beginning of the chapter to be solemn? I lied.) Here are a few of my favorite yuks. How many of these chestnuts apply to *your* mother-in-law situation?

➤ *Question:* What's the definition of mixed emotions?

Answer: Watching your mother-in-law back off a cliff in your brand new Mercedes.

➤ *Question*: Is it possible to kill your mother-in-law with a newspaper?

Answer: Yes, if you wrap an anvil in it.

➤ A pharmacist tells a customer, "In order to buy arsenic you need a legal prescription. A picture of your mother-in-law just isn't enough."

➤ First cannibal: "I really hate my mother-in-law."

Second cannibal: "Okay, so just eat the vegetables."

➤ One day a husband was late coming from work and his wife was nervous.

"Oh, I just know he's having an affair with some woman," she said to her mother.

"Why do you always think the worst?" her mother replied, "Maybe he's just in some kind of accident."

It's All Relative

In British and Australian slang, "mother-in-law" is a drink, a mixture of stout and bitter. So which part is more insulting: "stout" or "bitter"?

All joking aside, according to researchers at Utah State University, nearly 60 percent of all marriages suffer from tension with mothers-in-law, normally between the daughter-in-law and her husband's mother. Every daughter-in-law I know has had at least a little trench warfare with her mother-in-law; every mother-in-law I know has complained about her daughter-in-law on occasion. Neither are sainted mothers-in-law and daughters-in-law immune from a random tiff, misunderstanding, or mud wrestle. I even hear about mother-in-law issues from strangers, as the following strange encounter illustrates.

Throw Mama from the Train

Waiting for a movie to start, I couldn't help overhearing the conversation going on in front of me. (Actually, I leaned forward to hear better.) Each woman was complaining about her mother-in-law.

"My husband's mother started criticizing me at my wedding 20 years ago and she never stopped," the first woman said. Complained the second, "My mother-in-law thinks her son—my husband—is her personal handyman. She calls at least once a week, insisting he come over right away and fix this or that. When is he going to fix all the broken stuff in *our* house?" The third woman? Here's what she said, "My mother-in-law stops by all the time, expecting us to drop what we're doing and entertain her. And my husband does."

I knew their complaints weren't unusual. It seems that the nagging, meddling mother-in-law has become a stereotype. Unfortunately, it's often with good cause. Managing a healthy relationship with your mother-in-law can be as difficult as sitting through a

Don't Go There
Clashes with your mother-in-law may actually intensify as you get older. A newly married young woman may not be very confident about her own opinions, and if she has a mother-in-law who says things ought to be done this way, it's harder to challenge her. But by the time a woman is middle-aged, she's normally a well-established adult who has her own strong opinions and feels more confident. As a result, she's more likely to confront her mother-in-law head-on. Ouch.

Brady Bunch marathon, staying awake while reading *War and Peace,* or finding a taxi when it's raining. Or all three rolled into one.

Why so many misunderstandings between mothers-in-law and their daughters- and sons-in-law? Often, it's a matter of mothers not wanting to let go. The mother may not recognize her son as being an adult, and so she continues to treat him like a kid, even after he gets married and has a family of his own. Since all's fair in love and war, mothers can get equally attached to their daughters and make life heck on earth for their sons-in-law. See, guys, you thought you were home free. Think again.

Collision Course

Obviously, collisions with your mother-in-law are not good, no matter what their causes. When you and your mother-in-law are on bad terms, the tension takes a big toll on everyone within firing range. (And thanks to technology, the firing range goes from here to Pluto.) Who can get caught in the fallout?

➤ Your spouse and children may feel they are caught in the middle and resent being forced to choose sides. That's because they usually *are* caught in the middle and they usually *do* have to take sides.

➤ Constant criticism, contention, and combat are as much fun as an ingrown toenail. What about the opposite reaction—the cold war? Stony silence does not make for a pleasant afternoon (or a pleasant life).

➤ Your physical health may even suffer from the constant stress with your mother-in-law.

➤ In extreme cases, the marriage can be imperiled as spouses, feeling the need to take sides, are pulled apart from each other.

Words to the Wise
Mothers-in-law have inspired such terror that there's even a word for it: *pentheraphobia* (fear of your mother-in-law).

Mother-in-law battles can poison family life. What starts out as a relatively simple feud between you and your mother-in-law can spill over to the entire family. As a result, family get-togethers become strained. Before you even realize what's happening, your husband, kids, father-in-law, and other relatives are also drawn into the battle.

Although it isn't necessary to become best friends with your mother-in-law, it *is* important to be on good terms with her. What follows are some common complaints about mothers-in-law and suggestions for making peace.

Mothering Heights

"I can't do anything without my mother-in-law second-guessing me," Marjorie said. "She sees me wearing a pink dress and tells me I would look thinner in black. I put a sweater on my son and she insists he needs his winter coat. If I cook with butter, she gives me a lecture about cholesterol. She's always telling me what to do. I'm nearly 40 years old and she treats me like I'm a child. Besides, I have my own mother to nag me. I certainly don't need another nagmeister."

Does this description fit your mother-in-law? Does she offer unsolicited advice on any and all problems, even things that she has had no experience with at all? Does she see herself as an expert on everything from the Elbonia currency to zebra breeding? If so, you may have the "know-it-all" mother-in-law dilemma.

These mothers-in-law share the following characteristics:

➤ They think they know more than you do. Much more.

➤ As a result, they offer "recommendations." A lot of them.

➤ They don't respect the laws of time and space.

Therefore, they offer their advice anywhere: In your home, in their home, at family gatherings, shopping malls, political rallies—you name it.

➤ Their voices usually carry from here to Guam. They like to give *everyone* the benefit of their unsolicited advice.

➤ They actually believe they are helping you.

➤ They usually have a need to control. Sort of like a combination of Catherine the Great, Atilla the Hun, and Roseanne.

It's All Relative

The traditional Navaho Indian mother-in-law wore bell earrings to make her whereabouts known so that her son-in-law could avoid her. Some of today's mothers-in-law, however, are as covert as a Stealth bomber—and just as deadly. I should know; my husband has one.

What makes this situation especially tricky is the sobering fact that these buttinsky mothers-in-law sometimes really do know more than you do. In more instances than we might want to admit, their advice is solid. After all, they have had years of experience coping with the problems that face newlyweds: Settling money issues, furnishing a home, allocating responsibilities fairly, applying heat to food. In addition, they have often dealt with the problems of marriage veterans: Being the second wife, dealing with step-children, and balancing a career and marriage. So you interfering mothers-in-law, don't give up hope yet. We can reach an amicable compromise here. I promise. First, let's hear from my friend Elizabeth:

> Elizabeth's mother-in-law went beyond giving unsolicited advice and actually interfered. "Our two daughters spent the weekend with my mother-in-law while my husband and I went out of town," she explained. "Grandma has the tendency to spoil our kids, and they already have plenty of toys, so we specifically told her to not buy anything for them that weekend. When we got back Sunday night, the first thing our daughters did was show us the new doll house Grandma bought them. I was so mad I could barely speak."

What could Elizabeth do in this situation? What can *you* do when your mother-in-law criticizes you or interferes with your family structure? How can you discourage unwanted suggestions without having a big confrontation? Try the following three methods or select the ones that best suit your situation, style, and mother-in-law. Each method will leave you *and* your mother-in-law feeling well-treated.

It's All Relative

Does it really surprise anyone that Mother-in-Law's Day occurs less than one week before Halloween?

Plan Ahead

Family Matters
Don't fret if you're not fast on your feet when it comes to witty repartee. When you're dealing with an irate or intrusive mother-in-law, you don't get any points for the snappy comeback. You're better off waiting until everyone has cooled off to initiate a dialogue.

Okay, so maybe you don't do your Christmas/Hanukkah shopping in August and perhaps you don't have a million dollars put away for your retirement, but some of us obsessive-compulsive types have had great success by planning ahead when it comes to dealing with a meddling mother-in-law. Here's how.

Before she arrives to offer her, uh, *helpful* hints and otherwise run your life, review her most recent comments that rubbed you the wrong way. Was it her criticism about your cooking? Did any of her zingers at your parenting skills hit home? Were you offended at her jab at your (too successful/ not successful enough) career?

Once you list the criticisms, focus on the issues that bothered you the most. At the same time, however, realize that no complaint is too small to consider if it stuck in your craw. Did your mother-in-law nail you for dirty potholders? Did you rate a sneer for a smudged window? If it bothered you enough to remember it resentfully, include it on your list.

Now, consider proper responses. Play the script over in your head, writing the ideal dialogue as you go. Anticipating the types of remarks your mother-in-law might make and how you could respond helps you in five important ways. Visualizing the encounter can...

1. show you where you're being oversensitive—and where you're right on the mark.

2. help you judge if your mother-in-law is genuinely trying to be helpful—or if she has some not-so-selfless motives.

3. guide you to keep your temper in check when she next offers advice that you find hurtful.

4. help prepare a response that acknowledges her side of the issue as well as yours.

5. build better a relationship with your mother-in-law.

Being on red alert with a mother-in-law attack empowers you by giving you the upper hand. This may not reduce *her* stealth attacks but it *will* cut your resentment and help you deal with the issues it raises.

> **Don't Go There**
> Visualizing an unpleasant scene with your mother-in-law and replaying the dialogue does not mean that you should work yourself up into a lather, however. Stay cool.

Terms of Endearment

My husband and I are young, both in our early twenties. We have a six-month-old daughter, whom we adore. My problem concerns my mother-in-law. She used to have a lot of control over our lives when we were younger. In fact, we all got along great until my daughter came along. My mother-in-law had hoped that we would all continue to be "close" (in other words, she would be in control) after my daughter was born. My husband and I are trying to establish our own, independent lives as adults, and she is making it very difficult. She constantly complains she doesn't get to see the baby often enough. This is creating a lot of strain in my marriage. How can we politely let her know that we love her, but that things are different now because we are "grown up?" We tried talking to her once but she was extremely offended.

Even though your mother-in-law may not be a ray of sunshine, let's assume her motives are pure. By doing so, you've created a "win-win" situation rather than a "take-no-prisoners" one.

The growth of children into adulthood can be very hard for some parents. But this is a necessary evolution, and one that parents must encourage, rather than hinder. Regretfully, some mothers-in-law don't realized how important it is for new parents to create their family unit.

If you're in this situation and have already tried talking to your mother-in-law, perhaps you could confide in someone your mother-in-law respects, and ask him or her to enlighten her. She may be extremely offended, but until she can let you be grown-ups in charge of your own family, she may not be a welcome part of your lives.

Family Matters

Any time you need to hash something out with an in-law (especially your mother-in-law), arrange to have the talk in a neutral setting: At the park, in a restaurant, during a walk around the neighborhood. If possible, try to settle differences while you're both doing something enjoyable.

Don't Go There

Police in Los Angeles had some luck with a robbery suspect who just couldn't control himself during a lineup. When detectives asked each man to repeat the words, "Give me all your money or I'll shoot," the man shouted, "That's not what I said!" The moral of the story? Watch what you say when you explain your feelings to your in-laws, especially your mother-in-law. Make sure you don't reveal too much.

Even if you don't appreciate her choice of words, you can still thank your mother-in-law for her concern. Reassure her that you will ask for her input if and when you feel you are at a dead end. You might say, "Endora, I care for you ("love" might be stretching it) and I appreciate your concern. But the best way for us to be close is for you to let me do things my own way." Make it clear that you still want her to be involved with your family, but it has to be on your terms, not hers.

Talk Soup

Now comes the cherry on the cupcake, the prize in the box of Crackerjacks: Communication. I left this method for last because while it's usually the most effective, it can also be the most difficult. That's why you need help. And who better to call on than your spouse? After all, it *is* his or her mother.

You and your spouse should talk to your mother-in-law, as a couple, and make your concerns clear. Set aside a time and place to talk when everyone involved feels relaxed. If this is impossible, go for the least stressful situations. Don't confront your mother-in-law at a wedding, funeral, or big sale day at the mall. At least stack the deck in everyone's favor.

Fight the urge to run down a list of your mother-in-law's annoying traits. Instead, start with something positive, such as, "Mom, I know you mean well, but it really bothered me when (pick one) you ignored my instructions for the children/had Spot neutered/moved into our house as a surprise." (All these examples are true. And please don't send me your tales of woe, guaranteed to curl my hair. My hair's already frizzy.)

Go into the talk with an open mind and give your mother-in-law a chance to explain herself. You may be surprised at her reasons for doing what she did. If you're not, at least she's been given the chance to explain her side of the situation. Clearing the air often leaves everyone feeling more satisfied, even if major problems remain unsettled. This paves the way for later resolutions and compromises.

The Other Woman in Your Marriage

Here's Ashley's story:

> It was the eve of the wedding. The rehearsal had gone off without a hitch, and the dinner was about to start. But first, Charles' mother grabbed him by the arm and pulled him off to the side. "Charles, you're my son, the light of my life, my reason for being. I've given the best years of my life for you; my youth, my health, my money. But believe me, it was worth every sacrifice. Please remember that the woman you're marrying will never be able to take care of you as I did. She will never love you as I do. No woman could. Just remember your poor old mother."

Flash forward 15 years:

> "I feel like an outsider when I'm around my mother-in-law," says Ashley. "Even though my husband and I have been married 15 years, she still treats me as though I'm a threat, someone who wants to take her son away from her. I'm not usually a competitive person, but when I'm with my mother-in-law, I find myself comparing, keeping score, and being unsure of my status in the family."

Unfortunately, there's a built-in sense of rivalry in every daughter-in-law/mother-in-law relationship. A woman and her mother-in-law are in a triangular relationship with the same man. The daughter-in-law's gain is frequently the mother-in-law's loss. And when another woman has caused you a loss, no matter how intellectually understandable it is, it's hard to take. Try these ideas for solving this situation with your mother-in-law.

Family Matters
When dealing with your in-laws has you feeling like you've walked through the metal detector at the airport once too often, remind yourself that having a good relationship with your mother-in-law is part of having a strong family. And you want a strong family, so don't give up.

1. An effective strategy for dealing with competitive feelings is to realize that part of your mother-in-law's possessiveness is natural aspect of being a mother. Your mother-in-law may never stop feeling it's her job to be a caretaker to your husband. Asking her to give up control completely and let you be the only influential woman in your husband's life is asking the impossible.

2. Do you feel as though you're not measuring up to your (sainted) mother-in-law? If so, you're not

alone. Many wives feel this way. Don't. Stop comparing yourself to your mother-in-law. First off, you're not your mother-in-law. Second, you don't have to live your life according to her terms. The earlier you establish this as a framework for your marriage, the happier you will be.

Me and My Shadow

"I adore my mother-in-law," says Kim. "The problem is, she's retired and lives alone and has lots of free time on her hands. I've got two toddlers, a husband, and house to take care of, as well as a full-time job. A few minutes after I'm home from work, she'll stop over, wanting to sit and chat. But I need to get dinner going, the kids want attention, I haven't seen my husband all day. If I tell her I don't have time to talk, I feel so guilty."

To keep from being separated while sleeping, sea otters tie themselves together with kelp, often drifting miles out to sea during the night. Do you feel like you and your mother-in-law are tied together with kelp, joined at the hip—or shackled at the ankle? One of the trickiest mother-in-law situations occurs when she wants more companionship from you than you are willing or able to give. This is especially touchy when you genuinely enjoy your mother-in-law's company.

If your mother-in-law is making too many demands on your time, be honest with her about how you feel. Tell her what you'd like to see in the relationship, and try to establish the right level of involvement for both of you. I know what you're thinking. "How can be honest? She's very sensitive and I'll just hurt her feelings. She's such a nice lady and I really do enjoy her company. Besides, talking to her about issues like this is as tough as trying to communicate with the president of North Korea."

Are you leery of upsetting the apple cart by speaking your piece to your mother-in-law? Not to worry; do I have a worksheet for you! Completing the following worksheet can help you set feasible parameters if you're suffering from too much of a good thing.

Complete each question. Attach separate sheets of paper if you're long-winded or write big.

Don't Go There
This problem works both ways: A daughter-in-law may be crowding her mother-in-law by making too many demands on her time. This is especially true when the daughter-in-law has lost her own mother or prefers her mother-in-law to her own mother.

1. How often do my mother-in-law and I speak on the phone? (For example: once a day, twice a day, every fifteen seconds, etc.) _____

   _____

2. How often do I think we *should* speak on the phone? _____

   _____

   _____

3. How often do my mother-in-law and I get together? How much time do we spend together every week? _____

   _____

4. How often would I *like* to get together with my mother-in-law? _____

   _____

   _____

5. Does my mother-in-law stop over my house unannounced? _____

   _____

6. Do her surprise visits annoy me? Hubby? The kids? Rolf, the wonder pooch?

   _____

7. Do we have keys to each other's houses? _____

   _____

8. Does this bother me? If so, why? (For example: She catches me wrapped in Saran, waiting to give the meter reader a cheap thrill.) _____

   _____

   _____

9. What upsets me the most about my mother-in-law's unannounced visits? (Examples: She takes time away from the rest of the family, she upsets my schedule, she insists on watching reruns of *Family Ties*, etc.) _____

   _____

   _____

10. What's my husband's take on the matter? How does *he* feel about his mother's frequent calls and visits?_____

   _____

Okay, so we've established that Houston, we have a problem. Now, tell her that you definitely want to spend time together, but that you need to be able to plan when and how often.

Set clear boundaries you both can agree on. You'll do less damage if you frame your words positively. Here's a model you can use:

Family Matters
Your mother-in-law may be widowed or suffering from poor health and genuinely needs a lot of your time. Don't feel guilty if you can't fill all your mother-in-law's needs. Knowing your own limits is the key to giving sincerely. More on this in Chapters 22 and 24.

Yes: "We all enjoy being with you, but it's unsettling for us to have you just stop by without calling first."

No: "We don't like it when you come over uninvited." (Or: "You make me nuts when you drop by," or "Next time you drop over without calling first, at least bring a European kick boxer named Serge instead of a coffee cake.")

Mothers-in-law, arrange visits with your adult married children in the same way you would with your adult friends. Follow the rules in your son- or daughter-in-law's home without projecting your own. Your company will be more sought-after if you wait to be invited, suiting their wishes, even if you have an open-door policy. When everyone settles into a routine, your married children will be more likely to appreciate your goodwill and thoughtfulness.

Surrogate's Court(ship)

Here's a story that I heard from my recently engaged friend Susan:

> I lost my mother, with whom I was very close, to cancer eight years ago. I have been lucky enough to not only become engaged to a wonderful man, but one who has a great mom. I adore the woman; I'm very lucky. She's wonderful and I have great affection for her. The thing that I'm finding difficult, though, is how to include my future mother-in-law in the wedding plans. It's awkward. She's NOT my mom and although we get along very, very well our tastes are very different. She's more traditional than I am, and instead of voicing her opinion about things, she clams up and mopes when she's not happy about a decision we make. Plus, I feel a little guilty, like I'm trying to replace my own mom.

There is genuine affection between Susan and her future mother-in-law; but they're both too worried about stepping on each others' toes. If this type of predicament isn't dealt with early on, the awkwardness may not go away after the wedding. To avoid lots of polite, surface conversations in the future, there are a few questions you may want to ask yourself:

➤ **Do you feel like you're being a traitor?** Don't—your mother would be happy that you're happy. Your mother-in-law can't help that she's a great woman and you can't help liking her. There's nothing in the world wrong with that. (Didn't you read all those nightmare mother-in-law stories earlier in this chapter? You're *lucky* to have a great mother-in-law!)

➤ **Are you worried that your mother-in-law feels like she's second banana?** If you have a good, loving relationship with your mother-in-law, she won't feel she has to compete with your mother's ghost. Don't go overboard trying to make her feel better. It'll end up making both of you feel awkward.

➤ **Do you and your mother-in-law have different tastes?** Maybe you're very comfortable including your mother-in-law in the plans, but your tastes clash as badly as chocolate with sardines. Find other ways to include her. For instance, Susan's future mother-in-law is a seamstress. Although their tastes in dresses were different, she involved her mother-in-law in the dress selection process by having her oversee the all-important alterations.

➤ **Are you trying to guess what your mother "would have wanted" and ignoring all other suggestions, especially those of your future mother-in-law?** Your mother probably would have wanted you to do what makes you happiest. If your mother-in-law makes a suggestion that you like, take it. It's okay. There are ways of incorporating special things into the day that represent your mom, like wearing a piece of her jewelry or including her favorite flower in your bouquet. But don't base all your decisions on what you think she would have preferred. You'll end up alienating those who want to be included in your day (like your nice mother-in-law) and losing sight of why you're doing this in the first place (you love her son, silly).

Let It Go

Brad told me, "My mother-in-law is totally oblivious to her faults. When I try to tell her about something she did that upset us, she either acts like she doesn't know what I'm talking about or spends an hour defending her actions. She won't admit her mistakes But until she starts apologizing, I don't care to be around her."

So what happens if you've taken my advice but your mother-in-law is just not getting it? I mean, the woman is totally clueless. She's one step away from wearing an aluminum foil hat and barking at dogs. Then what?

Even if your mother-in-law can't see or refuses to acknowledge how she's hurt you, you can try to forgive her. Forgiveness is not a matter of you insisting your mother-in-law says she's sorry. Rather, it's a

Family Matters
Whereas forgiveness is granted, trust is earned, and that doesn't happen overnight.

matter of you letting go of the anger you have for her. Peace, like weight loss, isn't easy or painless. It will take time to reconcile with your mother-in-law. You have to rebuild trust.

It's All Relative

There's nothing new about mother-in-law conflicts. Even in ancient Rome, the writer Juvenal said, "Domestic concord is impossible as long as the mother-in-law lives."

But until you bury the past, you will not be able to move onto the future. Follow these three steps. (I wish I could say that forgiving is as easy as 1-2-3, but it's not.) Forgiving is harder than climbing Mount Everest, bungee jumping off Niagara Falls, or keeping up with a hyperactive three-year old. And let's not push the envelope. Go for forgiving, not forgetting.

Here are the three steps:

1. Set aside your anger.

2. Try to understand your mother-in-law's perspective. You may come to see that she wasn't being as malicious as you once thought. And even if she was, be the bigger person here.

3. Realize that you may not have done the same thing to her but you've probably hurt other people. Don't throw stones at glass houses.

The more you understand what motivates your mother-in-law when she does things to get on your nerves, the less likely you will be to overreact and turn every itty-bitty incident into a major catastrophe.

I Dream of Jeannie?

One day while cleaning his attic, a young man found a vase. He got rag to wipe it clean to see if it was worth saving. As he was wiping it, out popped a genie! The genie said, "For releasing me, you will get three wishes."

The man shouted, "I want a million dollars." The genie replied, "Here's the catch: whatever you ask for, your mother-in-law will get twice."

The young man said, "I can live with that." Again, he asks for a million dollars. The genie said, "Your mother-in-law will get two million dollars." The young man agreed and it was so.

"For my second wish I want a new mansion," the young man said. The genie replied, "Your mother-in-law will get a mansion twice as nice." The man agreed and the genie made it so.

After some time the genie asked the young man for his third and final wish. After some thought, the young man asked to be beaten half to death. The genie replied, "Done!"

All kidding aside, your relationship with your mother-in-law doesn't have to be this tricky. It might always be a little difficult, perhaps a bit touchy, but with some effort you can achieve détente.

The Least You Need to Know

➤ Realize that part of your mother-in-law's possessiveness is a natural aspect of being a mother.

➤ Stop comparing yourself to your mother-in-law.

➤ Analyze the cause of the strife with your mother-in-law. What does she do that drives you 'round the bend? (And don't forget *your* role in the conflict.)

➤ Communicate your concerns in a frank but nonjudgmental (or hurtful) way.

➤ If all else fails, forgive—even if you can't forget.

➤ There are lots of genuinely terrific mothers-in-law. I know, because I have one, my dear Yia Yia Marie. And you can't have her. Nah, Nah.

Chapter 9

Daddy-In-Law Dearest

In This Chapter

➤ Compare and contrast the abilities of mothers-in-law and fathers-in-law to make trouble

➤ See why some fathers have difficulty making the transition to father-*in-law*

➤ Learn why some sons-in-law find their relationship with their fathers-in-law problematic

➤ Develop strategies for solving common problems with fathers-in-law

➤ Discover the rewards of a close relationship with your father-in-law

According to my highly idiosyncratic and definitely unscientific poll, here are the top 10 biggest lies of all time...

  10. The check is in the mail.

   9. ...then take a left. You can't miss it.

   8. Drinking? Why, no, Officer.

   7. Don't worry, I can go another 20 miles when the gauge is on empty.

   6. I gave at the office.

   5. We'll release the upgrade by the end of the year.

4. I never watch television except for PBS.

3. Don't worry, he's never bitten anyone.

2. ...but we can still be good friends.

and the number one biggest lie of all time?

1. Fathers-in-law rarely cause problems with their married children. *Mothers-in law* have the market cornered on in-law strife.

Saadam Hussein, the mother of all fathers-in-law, had two of his sons-in-law shot for what he called "treason." And you thought *you* had problems with your father-in-law?

In this chapter, you'll explore some of the most common issues that couples encounter with their fathers-in-law. You'll see that some of the difficulties that arise from the relationship between fathers-in-law and their married children are eerily similar to the strife we encountered with mothers-in-law, but there are some new twists as well. You also know that I'd never leave you hanging, dear reader, so you'll get plenty of solutions, too.

It's All Relative

A German proverb for in-laws advises: "Remember the three *S*s: 'Schenken, schveigen, and schlungen.'" Freely translated, this means: "Give great gifts, keep your mouth shut and avoid giving advice, and swallow the insults and hurts you may receive." And you thought all we got from the Germans were great clocks, sausage, and beer.

Shoot to Kill

The August 25, 1997 issue of the Long Island newspaper *Newsday* reported the following incident:

> In the violent culmination of a night of marital arguing, a North Amityville man was arrested yesterday after he fired an automatic pistol at his wife's father, police said. No one was injured in the episode, which was sparked by problems in the couple's marriage. About three hours later, the alleged assailant was arrested at a friend's house in Copague. He was charged with first-degree reckless endangerment and two counts of criminal possession of a weapon. He was being held last night for an arraignment scheduled today.

Bertrand Russell once claimed that the place of the father in the modern suburban family is a very small one, particularly if he plays golf. A father-in-law, however, can exert considerable pressure in a marriage, as the shoot-'em-up example shows. Fortunately, the situation rarely reaches this level of tension. And if you're that close to bang-bang, you really need me. Better read fast.

A mother-in-law's difficulty in adjusting to her new status is well documented. Fathers-in-law, however, often experience just as much difficulty—if not more—in moving away from the central position as "Dad" or "Father of the Princess." In some respects, mothers-in-law have it easier because women are usually more willing to share their feelings. Society encourages it; talk shows thrive on it. Men, in contrast, still tend to play that John Wayne/Ernest Hemingway "nothing wrong with me, ma'am" routine. As a result, many men have a surprisingly hard time adjusting to their new status as father-*in-law*.

> **Family Matters**
> If possible, check your father-in-law's relationship with *his* father-in-law. If they got along well, you might be looking at smooth sailing, too, because the pattern for family harmony is already established.

Measuring Up

It's no picnic being a son-in-law, either. Paradoxically, it can be as difficult getting along with a superlative father (and father-in-law) as it is with a lousy one. Maybe even harder.

Have you ever asked yourself these questions when your father-in-law calls?

➤ Does he really want to talk to me or am I merely the conduit to his Flesh and Blood?

➤ Does he regard me a person in my own right?

➤ Does he think of me as a necessary evil, like rice cakes and the Nordic Track?

➤ Will he ever consider me as a son, or will I forever be a level removed; a son-*in-law*?

At least with a louse for a father-in-law, you don't feel intimidated. You know the man will never play Arnold Schwartzenegger to your Danny DeVito, nor even pretend. But with a really good man, you stand in fear. Can you measure up to his model? Let's take a turn at the Fear-o-Meter.

Check every item that describes your feelings toward your father-in-law.

I regard my father-in-law as...

_____ **1.** a rival for my wife's affections

_____ **2.** my wife's first love

_____ **3.** an incomparable model for the role of husband, father, man

> **Don't Go There**
> Husbands raised by single mothers may have an especially difficult time forging a satisfactory relationship with their father-in-law because they often don't have a clear idea what to expect from a "father figure."

_____ **4.** someone who saw right through me, penetrating my bluff that I was worthy of his precious daughter

_____ **5.** an impossible act to follow

Score Yourself

5 check marks	Your father-in-law really did a number on your head, didn't he?
4 check marks	You're almost ready for tabloid TV.
3 check marks	Everything's okay, baby. Mama's here now.
2 check marks	Help is just a few pages away.
0–1 check mark	Don't you ever sweat?
None checked	Who *is* your father-in-law? Mr. Rogers?

See my point? Being a son-in-law can be as frightening as being a father-in-law. But not to worry. You can do this, men. It's time to win one for the Gipper. Stay with me here. I'll save you. Promise.

Daddy's Little Princess

Tim and Heather were that fabled duo, the boy and girl next door. As children, they ran in and out of each other's houses at will; their parents bowled and played cards together. A recipe for paradise, you say. Think again. One day, Tim and Heather grew up and fell in love.

"All of a sudden, Heather's father George started acting like something out of the Dark Ages," Tim said. "This man had known me all his life and suddenly I'm defiling his precious daughter. When Heather and I finally got engaged, I was ready to put on full body armor so he couldn't run a sword through me. You'd think I was some marauder stealing his daughter. Heck, this man taught me how to catch a football!"

A year later, George called Tim and finally apologized. "I might have been overreacting a little," he told Tim. "After all, Heather is my princess, my baby girl," the older man admitted.

Generally, parents will do what they perceive is right for their child, but perception and reality can be as far apart as Wayne Newton and a Fig Newton. That's where the trouble starts.

Shifting Sands

After the wedding, the situation suddenly changes for everyone involved. Neither fathers nor fathers-in-law have the same privileges they had before the Big Day. And being a father-in-law involves a whole new set of rules.

Old Geezers, are you worried that your children will never again make an appearance at your Thanksgiving spread because they'll be going to their in-laws? That the closets are now all yours? That the oil stain is gone from the driveway? That with the reduction in the food bill you can finally afford the Miata? It's not all negative, you know!

Rest assured that the kids may be married, but they're not gone. Far from it. But I'd be lying if I didn't tell you that things *will* be different now.

For most of us, this change in status is a frightening thing. Suddenly, you're not the most important man in your son's or daughter's life. You're not the one he or she will call when trouble arises. "You want to know you're important, to know you're respected, to know that what you do is appreciated and means something," one father-in-law told me. Fathers-in-law are especially susceptible to these feelings because they are traditionally the providers in the family. Even if they don't earn the bulk of the bucks, they are still often the titular head of the tribe. This was George's problem.

> **Don't Go There**
> When a couple ties the nuptial knot, they are apt to worry that their bonds to their own folks will be severed as they become part of a new family. This can cause a great deal of anxiety.

Space, the Final Frontier

Because Americans stress the importance of independence and "standing on your own two feet," newlyweds often feel duty-bound to sever the parental umbilical cord with a sharp *yank*. Their parents, in contrast, are ambivalent about this sudden independence. "We don't want to lose the kids," they tell me, "yet we don't want to prevent them from growing up and forming their own family."

All couples *must* pull away from their parents initially to have the time and privacy they need to get to know each other. But after the immediate pulling away, the couple can interact with their in-laws in a more mature fashion. Rest assured that the tie we have with our parents is like a bungee cord. We can pull and pull, but they will always come back. That's assuming that the in-laws (that's *you*, dear reader) are mature, of course.

The Other Man in Your Marriage

Here's Vinny's story:

> For 20 years, my marriage and family were fairly normal. Like everyone else, we had our ups and downs, but we did okay. Then my mother-in-law became ill. We moved

back to my wife's home town to be near my in-laws so we could help out. Two years ago, my mother-in-law died. And I have now lost my wife, Lisa—to her father! She has become daddy's little girl all over again.

My father-in-law is an energetic, intelligent man who retired from his job shortly after my mother-in-law became ill. Even when we lived 500 miles away, he tried to run our lives. Now that we live nearby, he completely runs everything. On the plus side, he has time to supervise our home repairs, take the kids on trips, and run errands for us. But there's a lot on the negative side.

The man is a control freak. He tells us what utility company to use, what brand of paint is best, how to invest our money. He buys the attention of our children with things that we can't afford and prefer that they don't have. He criticizes the way we raise our children, how much I earn, and just about everything else. Even though my wife manages a division of a major corporation, she has never been able to stand up to her father. Her mother always acted as the buffer. She was able to tone down my father-in-law's most flagrant power plays, but now she's gone.

Don't Go There

Under what I call the "Parental Law of Inertia," most parents continue to treat their married children as though they were still toddlers. Fathers-in-law are especially prone to this problem, so be forewarned. Long after you are married, they are still likely to slip you a $20 bill or check the air pressure in your tires.

What does a husband do when the "other man" in his marriage is his father-in-law?

When you and your spouse form your nuclear family, you are setting its boundaries. You decide who gets past Checkpoint Charlie—and who gets detained at the border. Setting limits protects you as a couple from intrusions from the outside world, especially from those nearest and dearest.

But what happens when you're 20 years into the marriage and the rules suddenly change? In this instance, Vinny's mother-in-law kept her husband in check. When she died, however, the balance shifted. Now Vinny's father-in-law is successfully driving a wedge between the couple by his need to control and his loneliness. What can you do if this is your situation? Try these ideas to reestablish the equilibrium in your family.

➤ **The old-switcheroo.** Put yourself in your father-in-law's position. What is motivating him to act this way? Vinny says that his father-in-law is a "control freak." No doubt this is true, but it's also quite possible that Vinny's father-in-law genuinely believes that he is being helpful, especially where the grandchildren are concerned. Perhaps, too, he is lonely with his wife gone. He's probably at loose ends as well, not having envisioned spending his retirement alone.

➤ **Make a choice.** It's hard to have it both ways. You can't accept your father-in-law's largess and then deny him access to his grandchildren without really good cause. Similarly, don't expect him to become your personal Bob Vila and then freeze him out of easy and pleasurable decisions, like choosing the paint colors.

➤ **Conference, communicate, converse.** I know: Been there, done that. It's not easy for most of us to upset the apple cart and say what needs to be said. Notice, however, that nowhere in his complaint did Vinny say that he tried to explain his feelings to his father-in-law. At the very least, Vinny owes his father-in-law of 20 years the courtesy of truthfulness.

➤ **Get a neutral party.** Cat got your tongue? Why not try an intermediary? Find a respected person, such as a trained counselor or a religious leader, to mediate as you and your father-in-law hash out the issue.

➤ **Matchmaker, matchmaker.** Start looking for another woman—for your father-in-law! With all that energy, he needs an outlet other than his daughter, son-in-law, and grandchildren. Hey, he should live and be well. Always consult your spouse about your matchmaking plans. Fixing up your father-in-law with a new tootsie can be a little sticky, considering how your beloved felt about his mother (assuming, of course, that the last wife *was* his mother).

> **Don't Go There**
> If you decide to ask your spiritual leader to help you solve a problem with your father-in-law, make sure that you're all singing from the same hymnal. Pick a religious leader whose views everyone respects.

> **Family Matters**
> To improve your relationship with your father-in-law, take time to validate each other and show interest. This can be done in simple ways such as having brunch together every Sunday or meeting for a walk once a month. There's no magic formula, only effort, caring, and kindness.

Hell on Wheels

Vinny's father-in-law was disrupting Vinny's marriage, but he was also giving the family quite a bit of help. This is not always the case. Sometimes, fathers-in-law can be quite a bit more destructive. Think "tsunami" rather than "gentle wave."

Here's what a friend I'll call Max told me about his father-in-law and the problems his behavior caused in the family. How does his situation compare to yours?

I've married into a disastrously messed-up family. My father-in-law is incredibly domineering and rude to his sons and wife, utterly destroying their self-confidence. His daughter (my wife), on the other hand, is the princess and not to be criticized in any way. I couldn't begin to say why he acts like this, but it's painful to be around.

Don't Go There
In domestic disputes, police have been injured and even killed when the husband and wife turn on the officer who was trying to protect one or the other spouse or an in-law.

Family Matters
Marriage counseling might help this couple discuss their needs regarding this painful ordeal. An outside mediator might also be able to guide Max and his wife (and other couples who face the same father-in-law problems) to focus on strengthening their marriage and not trying to save a family that can only save itself.

His sons, in turn, demean and criticize their wives and joke about how fat and useless they are (as if it would be easy to remain thin and athletic when you're stuck in a house all day with no car and two kids in subdivisions 15 miles from the nearest store or sidewalk).

I would really like to help, but more importantly, I *really* don't want to get dragged into this. How can I keep this guy off my back, because he definitely seems to have a problem relating positively to other men?

The only issue Max can address in this "disastrously messed-up family" is his own relationship with his wife. I suggested that he stay out of the larger family fracas and focus on keeping his father-in-law off his back. The minute he tries to step in to help the sons and their mother stand up to this man, they will all turn on him because blood loyalty almost always wins out. Getting between his wife and her loyalty/hatred of her father might cause fireworks that Max can best do without.

Max is a prime target for the family to use as their savior, telling him all the war stories, but then not doing anything directly about it. If they ask, Max should encourage them to get their own help from professionals and change the conversation to something else or politely listen, disengage, and leave.

Unfortunately, in a situation like this one, it is hard not to get involved. These family dynamics create a whirlpool that suck in anyone who tries to help into the chaos. Instead of going down the drain with this group of boneheads, spouses should

➤ talk to each other about their needs and the family situation

➤ work to strengthen the bond in the primary family

➤ limit their involvement with the extended family

➤ especially avoid conversations about the father-in-law-from-hell

Best Buddies

Gary Stevens says his father-in-law, "Red" Caldon, was bossy and critical during the first seven years of Gary's marriage. But this year, he was looking forward to spending Father's Day with him.

"Father's Day is a day when we have the opportunity to show him we do care and that he's special," said Gary, who said that both he and his 80-year-old father-in-law have mellowed with age. The two former strangers now chat daily and watch golf together, Gary said, and have forged a friendship.

It's All Relative

The fastest-growing Father's Day cards in the Hallmark line this year are those designed for fathers-in-law, suggesting in sales figures that many sons-in-law and daughters-in-law are working to improve their relationship with their fathers-in-law.

Both sides of the in-law equation are responsible for developing a healthy relationship, but the father-in-law often sets the tone because of his age and experience.

Gary told me that he talks over life's big decisions with his father-in-law during their weekly poker games. Some say they never thought about befriending their father-in-law, but it just happened over time. When Marie Giambrovo's father died, her father-in-law Lou Citrano stepped up and became a second parent to her. The two opened an insurance agency together soon after and have been business partners ever since. "She's my daughter as much as my own blood daughter is," Lou said.

Family Matters

Sons- and daughters-in-law sometimes hold back their affection for their father-in-law out of fear they'll betray their own fathers. However, a father-in-law can often be a second opportunity for love by offering you guidance you could never get from your own father.

The Least You Need to Know

➤ Your mother-in-law doesn't have the market cornered on disrupting your marriage. Your father-in-law can be a real handful, too.

➤ Many fathers have a difficult time making the change to father-*in-law* and letting go of their adult children.

➤ It's no picnic being a son-in-law, either.

➤ Communicate, see your father-in-law's side, and strengthen your bonds with your spouse.

➤ If necessary, limit involvement with a disruptive father-in-law.

➤ Your father-in-law might become your best friend.

➤ There are lots of genuinely terrific fathers-in-law. I know, because I have one, my dear Ol' Nas. And you can't have him, either. Nah, Nah.

Chapter 10

Crazy Quilt

In This Chapter

➤ Learn how America's melting pot has gone multicultural

➤ See what this means for you and your in-laws

➤ Get culturally hip

➤ Polish your multicultural manners; you'll very likely need them to get along with your in-laws

A newcomer, intrigued by stories of Coney Island, got up the courage to ask a woman friend to go there with him. The next day he met a friend.

"So, how was it?" the friend asked.

"A disappointment, really," the newcomer replied. "The Tunnel of Love was so wet we both caught cold."

"Your boat leaked so much?" his friend replied.

The newcomer looked aghast. "There's a *boat*?"

Hey, you're no greenhorn. You know the score because you're a true-blue American. But what *is* an American? In this chapter, you'll learn how the face of America is changing. Today's true-blue Americans come in all colors, all flavors, and from all countries. The "melting pot" of the seventeenth century has become the "crazy quilt" of today.

America is the most democratic and unrestricted country that has ever existed. We have welcomed into our families people from scores of other nations, near and far, ancient and modern. While this has given our country a richness and strength unparalleled throughout the world (as well as some great music and excellent take-out), it has made for some tense in-law relationships.

This chapter looks at how America is changing. Then I'll explain how this affects your family, especially your relationship with your in-laws. On our journey, you'll learn some multicultural manners. That way, if you don't get along with your in-laws, it won't be because you're a cultural lout.

It's All Relative

Arguably, one of the most useful contributions from immigrants are curses. Yiddish is ideally suited to especially effective curses. I humbly offer you my favorites:

➤ May all your teeth fall out—but one should remain for a headache.

➤ May all your enemies move in with you.

➤ May your sex life be as good as your credit.

John/Jean/Juan Q. Public

Who's the "typical" American today?

According to the most recent census, there are an estimated 264.6 million people living in the United States. Nearly a third of all Americans chose to identify themselves as minorities. Here's how we describe ourselves:

➤ 33.5 million (13 percent) of us are black;

➤ 27.7 million (11 percent) of us are Hispanic;

➤ 2.3 million (1 percent) of us are Native American/Inuit;

➤ 9.5 million (4 percent) of us are Asians and Pacific Islanders.

[Source: *1997 World Almanac*]

All told, 23 million of us are foreign-born, the highest level since before World War II. Just how diverse are we? Here are some stats to set your head spinning:

➤ More than 100 languages are spoken in the school systems of New York City, Chicago, Los Angeles, and Fairfax County (Virginia).

➤ More than 30 million people speak English as a second language, which means that roughly 14 percent of the American population speaks about 140 different languages. (And you thought you have trouble communicating with *your* in-laws!)

➤ Employees in the Digital Equipment Corporation plant in Boston come from 44 countries and speak 19 languages; the plant's announcements are printed in English, Chinese, French, Spanish, Portuguese, Haitian Creole, and Vietnamese.

➤ More than 40 percent of Californians are black, Hispanic, or Asian.

➤ There are more than 2,000 Hmong from Laos living in Wisconsin alone.

The Census Bureau doesn't have a crystal ball, but their data does suggest that by the year 2050, our country will be even more diverse than it is now. Here's how the face of America is projected to change:

➤ The non-Hispanic white share of the population is projected to fall from the current 73 percent to 53 percent.

➤ At the same time, persons of Hispanic origin should increase from 11 percent to 24 percent of the population.

➤ Asians and Pacific Islanders should see their numbers more than double.

➤ There should be an increase in the number of black Americans as well.

It's All Relative

More than 25 percent of America's immigrants—6.7 million—were born in Mexico. Other common immigrant homelands include the Philippines (1.2 million Americans hail from there), China/Taiwan (816,000); Cuba (797,000), Canada (695,000), El Salvador (650,000), Great Britain (617,000), Germany (598,000), Poland (538,000), Jamaica (531,000), and the Dominican Republic (509,000). [Source: *1997 World Almanac*]

Lingua Franca

And even if all your in-laws *do* speak English, they may not speak the same English that you do. Many Americans born in Europe, Asia, India, Africa, and the Caribbean have

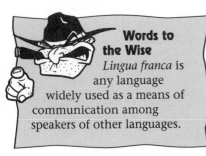

learned British English, not the U.S. variety. Like those classic TV twins Patty and Cathy, British and American English walk alike, but they don't exactly talk alike.

How good are you at understanding British English? Take a quick jaunt across the pond by matching each of the following British words with its American equivalent. Write the letter of the correct American word in the space by the British word.

British English	American English
_____ 1. bold	a. curb
_____ 2. lift	b. line up
_____ 3. lorry	c. telephone booth
_____ 4. nappies	d. rude
_____ 5. queue	e. road underpass
_____ 6. call box	f. potato chips
_____ 7. crisps	g. elevator
_____ 8. subway	h. diapers
_____ 9. kerb	i. french fries
_____ 10. chips	j. truck

Answers

1. d	6. c
2. g	7. f
3. j	8. e
4. h	9. a
5. b	10. i

Reality Check

How do these cultural realities affect *your* life? They suggest that at least some of your in-laws are likely to be from vastly different cultures than your own. As a result, in addition to dealing with the garden variety in-law battles over control, money, and grandchildren, you're going to have to cope with cultural matters as well.

While people from other backgrounds can vastly enrich our lives (where *would* I be without Chinese take-out?), it's inevitable that misunderstandings will occur over customs and culture. Read on to find out how you can minimize these potential hazards.

Bridgette Loves Abdul

How culturally clued-in are you? Take this quiz to see. Circle the correct answer for each scenario.

1. Abdul, a young man from Egypt, fell in love with Italian-American Gina. Adbul's first meeting with Gina's father Vito went very badly, however, when Adbul assumed Vito hated him. Why?

   a. Vito made him watch two episodes of *Hee Haw* and a *Partridge Family* rerun.

   b. Vito called him by the dog's name and then denied it.

   c. Vito superglued the toilet seat in the "down" position.

   d. Vito sat in the living room with his feet on the coffee table, his soles toward Adbul.

2. Irish-American Geraldine was horrified when her otherwise exceedingly polite Japanese-born in-laws started to talk about...

   a. Rush Limbaugh.

   b. Beavis and Butthead.

   c. William Shatner's hair piece.

   d. constipation.

3. Aphrodite, born in Greece, was scandalized when her new mother-in-law...

   a. showed her nude baby pictures of her husband.

   b. offered her *domestic* feta cheese rather than imported.

   c. handed her a copy of *The Complete Idiot's Guide to Dealing with In-Laws*.

   d. made a thumbs-up sign.

4. Grace Zhang, born in China, tried to dive under the table in embarrassment when her brother-in-law called for a waiter by

   a. knocking his fist on the table.

   b. clapping his hands.

   c. singing an aria from *Madame Butterfly*.

   d. waving his index finger.

5. Lisa's Iranian-born in-laws were furious when she
    a. made macaroni and cheese from a box rather than from scratch.
    b. put too much starch in her husband's boxer shorts.
    c. said that Pat Buchannan is a tad too liberal.
    d. hugged her husband in public.

Answers

Every answer is d. Here's why:

1. Arab culture sees the foot in general and the sole in particular as unclean. Showing the soles of the foot is an insult.
2. Although the Japanese have a reputation for reticence, they are comfortable discussing bodily functions such as constipation very openly. Thankfully, most Americans keep the progress of their bowels to themselves.
3. Greeks consider the "thumbs-up" (go ahead) sign a vulgar insult.
4. People from Asia and the Pacific Islands consider it uncouth to call a restaurant server by waving your index finger. It's on the level of calling a dog. (Choice c made her think he was tone deaf, but not rude.)
5. Among Iranians, even handshakes between men and women are seen as improper; never mind open hugs.

Score Yourself

0–1 correct	Madeline Albright's job is safe from any competition from you.
2–3 correct	Don't get out much, do you?
4 correct	You'll be okay if you keep your mouth shut and your ears open.
5 correct	Bet you do the *New York Times* crossword puzzle in ink, too.

It's All Relative

The top 10 American destinations for immigrants are New York City, Los Angeles, Chicago, Miami, Washington, DC, Orange County (CA), Boston, San Francisco, Houston, San Jose. New York City is far and away the most popular destination, with 15.5 percent of all immigrants settling there. Next comes Los Angeles, with 7.6 percent of the newcomers. [Source: *1997 World Almanac*]

The Greek Way

George Papas was 32 years old when he came to America from Sparta, Greece. Soon after, most of his family followed and settled nearby. George spoke English well enough to manage a prosperous diner. He employed most of his siblings as cooks, serving staff, and bookkeepers. His mother made the pastry for the diner; his father managed the rental properties that George owned. A hard-working man, George was proud of his status as a successful American businessman but was determined not to lose sight of his Greek roots. His wife Christine was an attractive 25-year-old American of Greek ancestry. "George thought he was marrying a real Greek," she told me. "Boy, was he fooled. All I know of my heritage is souvlaki and olive oil."

As a traditional Greek man, George refused to let Christine work in the diner—or anyplace else for that matter. "A wife's place is in the home," he said. "Her job is to keep the house and raise our child. That's how a Greek man takes care of his woman."

Sunday was George's one day off, and he wanted to spend it with his brothers and sisters at his parents' house. All day long, they ate Greek foods and swapped stories. Of course, everyone spoke Greek—everyone except Christine, that is. "I feel invisible," Christine told me. "Nobody cares if I'm there or not. Besides, they spend all week together. Can't I get one day alone with my husband?"

George's side? "My family and I don't understand Christine's problem," he said. "I make plenty of money so Christine can stay home and raise our children. I treat her as a good Greek husband treats his wife. She lives like a princess. What more could a wife want?"

In-law problems often have special complications when the husband and wife come from different ethnic backgrounds. Christine resented the time her husband spent with his family. George, in contrast, couldn't understand why his wife was dissatisfied. George's parents were equally baffled by Christine's behavior.

Family Matters
Culturegrams offers four-page overviews on each of 110 countries. Updated annually, they cost $40 a set. Write or call:

Brigham Young University
The David M. Kennedy Center for International Studies
P.O. Box 24538
Provo, Utah 84602-4538
1-800-528-6279

Don't Go There
This situation, as with the others in this chapter, does not apply to every Greek man. There will be exceptions to every rule because conduct differs with individuals. Furthermore, the acculturation process is not completely predictable. Many variables influence how quickly your in-laws will replace their traditional behavior with America's customs and values.

Stroll Through the Cultural Minefield

Here are some other areas to watch if your in-laws are from a culture different from yours:

1. **Groove to the beat: Body language**

   Let me hear your body talk? Please, keep it to a whisper when you're dealing with in-laws from another culture. Among Chinese people from Vietnam, for example, a man and a woman are discouraged from hugging or kissing if they are not married. Likewise, Orthodox Jews avoid contact with members of the opposite sex. Many Latinos, in contrast, expect body contact. The moral of the story? Always ask before you reach out and touch someone.

> **Words to the Wise**
>
> Among people from Hispanic backgrounds, it is good manners for friends to embrace and simultaneously pat each other on the back. This is called the *abrazo*.

> **Don't Go There**
>
> A doctor was upset when his patient, an Orthodox Jew, bled profusely and then died. The doctor was shocked, however, when the patient's in-laws demanded his blood-covered medical scrubs. When buried, Orthodox Jews must have everything containing their bodily fluids interred with the body. This includes bandages, fluids from tubes, and any and all amputated limbs.

2. **Flying from the nest: Childrearing practices**

   Your foreign-born in-laws might regard American attitudes toward a child's independence and responsibility as stingy and unloving. In Colombia, for example, relatives help each other with no questions asked and no strings attached. This is rarely the case in American today.

   A big difference between Europeans and Americans is the independence issue. Many acculturated Americans are out the door at 18, but it's not uncommon for people from the Old Side to live at home well into their twenties. In America, living at home is looked upon as, well, freakish. This is especially true for men—"What are you, a momma's boy?" In Europe, it's more common for the kids to remain in the nest until they're married.

   My friend Toni's future in-laws went nuts when Vito, their baby boy, their only son and the light of their lives, moved out. But when he moved in with Toni, they threatened coronaries on a daily basis. At first, every time Vito's parents called, they were astonished that Toni answered the phone. So what if it was *her* phone? Invariably, they asked what Toni was doing there. Of course, they eventually got used to the situation and even ended up going furniture shopping with the couple.

3. **Dress to excess: Clothing**

In general, Americans are not a modest bunch. People from other countries are apt to show much less flesh. Considering what most people look like uncovered, there's a lot to be said for more being more.

If you have any female in-laws from Thailand, for example, they'll likely cover as much of their body as possible. Islamic women are also very modest.

4. **Eat, drink, and be merry: Food**

Are your in-laws Jewish or Muslim? If so, nix on the pork and shellfish. Hindus don't eat beef. Seventh Day Adventists don't eat any meat.

Muslims, Hindus, Mormons, and some Protestant sects do not drink alcoholic beverages. To be on the safe side, just serve water (and maybe a Little Debbie or two). Or, you can run the menu by your spouse and in-laws before you serve it.

It's All Relative

In a number of eastern countries, it's perfectly acceptable to eat dog. In recognition of the American taboo against eating Fido or his canine companions, during the 1988 Olympics, Korean restaurants in Seoul removed dog entrees from their menus.

5. **Diamonds are a girl's best friend: Gifts**

Are your in-laws Chinese? If you like them, don't offer gifts of umbrellas, knives, scissors, or clocks. Umbrellas and sharp objects indicate that you wish a separation; clocks hint that life is running out. If you give your Chinese in-laws cash gifts, the amount must be in even numbers and the gift given with both hands. Pretty tricky, no? Check and double-check your in-laws' cultural beliefs before you whip out that AmEx for gift giving.

6. **Battle of the sexes: Male/female relationships**

A young woman was captured by a young man and taken to his home, where she was sexually molested. The victim called the police, who charged the man with kidnapping and rape. The young man was shocked: according to his culture, he is married to the girl and thus innocent of any wrongdoing.

Family Matters
Every culture has its traditions about the evil eye. In Yiddish, some people utter the magical phrase *kine-ahora* to ward off the evil eye.

117

Some marriage customs illegal in America are customary in other cultures. Among the Hmong, marriage can take place when a young man takes a girl (often as young as fourteen) to his home and consummates the marriage. In exchange, the groom's family pays a "bride price" to the girl's family. This practice is called *zij poj niam*, "marriage by capture."

The moral of the story? Hold out for a black-tie wedding and honeymoon cruise to the islands and be very careful to consider your in-laws' heritage as you plan weddings and other family celebrations.

7. **Yo! Adrienne: Forms of address**

   Most cultures are more formal than the United States. If your in-laws were born in another country, err on the side of formality when addressing them. For example, refer to them by their titles, not their first names, unless they tell you otherwise.

8. **On thin ice: Compliments**

   Be careful if you compliment your in-laws, because the statements that people interpret as compliments and the socially correct way to respond to compliments varies widely among cultures. For example, an American who is complimented would likely say "Thank you." A Japanese person, in contrast, would probably apologize by saying, "No, it wasn't very good."

When in Rome (or America Today)...

Hope, a native Californian, married Miguel, a newcomer from El Salvador. Hope's in-laws welcomed her warmly, and their relationship was smooth in part because Hope speaks Spanish fluently. Everything was going along beautifully until Hope planned a big meal for about 50 of her new in-laws. Anxious to please Miguel's family, Hope cooked many traditional El Salvadorian foods, including barbecued beef, rice, beans, and salads. Because the group was so large, she set out the food buffet style, on a long table. Hope proudly announced that the meal was ready, but to her astonishment, no one stepped forward to eat. Despite her good intentions, Hope blundered—many Salvadorans are formal about serving food.

As a new wife, Hope was expected to serve her in-laws personally. To Hope's in-laws, serving themselves from a buffet table was embarrassing and impersonal. Culture clash redux.

Each of us grows up in a culture that provides patterns of acceptable—and unacceptable—behavior and beliefs. Understanding the culture of your in-laws is crucial if you want to avoid blowing the lid off the relationship.

Don't Go There
Every culture has its traditions governing food and how it should be served. Many Asians and Saudi Arabians make eating noises to show their appreciation of the food; people from Arabic countries, parts of Africa, India, Sri Lanka, and the Philippines often eat with their fingers from a common platter. So it's not enough to check *what* you're serving; you also have to check *how* you're serving it.

Do You Have Anything to Declare?

When American actress Melanie Griffith and Spanish heartthrob Antonio Banderas recently tied the knot (obviously, Antonio got tired of waiting for *me*), they decided to split their time between Griffith's home in Los Angeles and Banderas' home in Spain. Because Banderas' family speaks no English and Griffith's speaks no Spanish, communication must be a challenge. "It's really great!" Melanie counters. "He must have 200 relatives in Spain—his mother has 16 siblings." *Great?* What is wrong with this woman? Maybe she has a point, however. Not speaking to your in-laws is one way to avoid misunderstandings....

But you're too cool for that dodge. None of that chicken "No speak the language" stuff for you. Instead, you're going to walk the walk and talk the talk. You may never serve matzoh balls a la fried rice with a side of salsa, but at least you're going to make the effort to learn your in-laws' cultural heritage and share your own with them. Use the following checklist to make the task a little easier.

Am I...

____ 1. aware of my in-laws' cultural values and beliefs?

____ 2. sensitive to cultural differences among my in-laws?

____ 3. aware that my preferred values and behaviors are influenced by my culture and not necessarily "right"?

____ 4. flexible and open to change?

____ 5. sensitive to nonverbal as well as verbal cues?

The Least You Need to Know

➤ America is changing. Be there or be square.

➤ Odds are good that your in-laws are going to have a radically different cultural background from your own.

➤ It's easy to make a big boo-boo. Check and double-check cultural practices.

➤ Smooth the way by asking your in-laws about their culture. Don't be shy about sharing your own heritage, too.

Vive la Difference!

Two men, sentenced to die in the electric chair on the same day, were led down to the room in which they would meet their maker. The priest had given the last rites, the formal speech had been given by the warden, and a final prayer had been said among the participants. The warden, turning to the first man, solemnly asked, "Son, do you have a last request?"

To which the man replied, "Yes sir, I do. I love dance music. Could you please play the Macarena for me one last time?"

"Certainly," replied the warden. He turned to the other man and asked, "Well, what about you, son? What is your final request?"

"Please," said the condemned man, "kill me first."

Each to his own taste, as the cannibal said to the missionary. The problem? Your in-laws might not have learned this lesson yet. As a result, they may have some difficulty dealing with difference. And this is one dance you shouldn't sit out, no matter what your taste.

Intolerance poses challenges under normal circumstances, but it can be even trickier when you—or someone you love—is the odd in-law out. No one wants to be the pork chop at the bar mitzvah. But as you've discovered so far in this book, with increasing diversity comes increasing potential for problems with your in-laws.

In Chapter 10, you learned that America is becoming more culturally diverse. Our diversity extends to gender, race, and religious differences as well as cultural variety. As a result, your in-laws may not share your appearance, spiritual beliefs, or heritage. In this chapter, I'll help you become aware of today's realities. Then I'll teach you a whole bunch of effective strategies for coping with intolerant in-laws.

Adam and Steve

A woman sent this letter to a newspaper advice columnist:

> Dear Advice Columnist:
>
> A couple of women moved in across the hall from me. One is a middle-aged gym teacher and the other is a social worker in her mid-twenties. These two women go everywhere together and I've never seen a man go into their apartment or come out. Do you think they could be Lebanese? Signed, "Curious"

Now, I have to tell you that this letter posed a bit of a problem for me: Does it belong in this chapter on same-sex relationships or does it belong in the next chapter on moronic in-laws? Ultimately, I decided to place it here because it makes the point that much of the fear and hatred that haunts same-sex relationships comes from ignorance.

> Dean Semler, cinematographer for *Dances With Wolves*, is one of those select Americans who got to meet Queen Elizabeth before her most recent state visit to the United States. During their brief meeting, he said, "I am a director of photography," to which she replied, "Oh, how terribly interesting. Actually, I have a former brother-in-law who is a photographer."
>
> Semler replied, "Oh, how terribly coincidental. I have a current brother-in-law who's a queen." The Queen moved on without saying another word.

According to the venerable Kinsey report, at least 10 percent of all Americans (that's 26.4 million) are gay. As a result, chances are good that one of your in-laws may be gay or bisexual. You may even be the one. What can you do in this situation? Here are some ideas:

1. **Combat ignorance.**

   Much prejudice comes from stupidity. Educate your in-laws about your in-laws' lifestyle—or your own.

2. **To thine own self be true, but respect other's beliefs.**

   The Birdcage, a movie starring Nathan Lane and Robin Williams as gay lovers, was funny, but also terribly sad. Lane felt that he had to disguise himself as a woman so that Williams's son would not be embarrassed in front of his new in-laws. Don't betray yourself, but temper the action to the situation.

3. **Face facts.**

   You can change some of the in-laws all of the time, you can change all of the in-laws some of the time, but you can't change all of the in-laws all the time. Some in-laws will never accept you; others will.

Gimme That Old Time Religion

"Look up the word 'WASP' in the dictionary and you'll find a picture of my in-laws," said Marla Berkowitz. "They're from the Midwest, the mayonnaise-and-white-bread Midwest. The women are blond, blue-eyed, and demure; the men are all named "Bud" or "Chip." And here I am, a Jewish girl from New York, with dark curly hair, brown eyes, and a big mouth. They don't know what to make of me. For a long time, they called me "The New York Girl" in a way that my folks wouldn't appreciate. Even when I try to look and act like Donna Reed, I feel like Barbra Streisand."

It's All Relative

According to one estimate, there may be twice as many Muslims as Episcopalians in America today. ("Marketing in the Islamic Context," Sixth Annual Eastern University Michigan University Conference on Languages and Communication for World Business and the Professions, 1987.)

The freedom to worship as we please is one of the foundations of American life. Nonetheless, everyone knows that the law of the land is different from the law of the family. Most of the time, fuss about intermarriage develops out of a sincere concern for the family's unity and well-being; other times, however, it is a result of fear and even prejudice. Whatever the reason for the friction among your in-laws when someone marries outside the fold, their reactions can usually be categorized under one of the following reasons:

➤ **Fear of losing your child.** No one's going anywhere so fast. Fear aside, these parents have usually done a great job of raising independent children who feel secure enough to separate from the family and grow as individuals. Marrying out of the faith doesn't mean losing your child.

➤ **Fear of the unknown.** These parents often worry that their child has joined cult. But there are cults and then there are cults: It's often a matter of perception. A friend of mine who is a devout Catholic views the Methodists as a cult.

➤ **Fear of embarrassment.** Many in-laws worry what their neighbors, friends, business associates, and other in-laws will think about their child and his or her spouse. We can say, "Who cares?" but people care about public appearances—very much indeed.

➤ **Fear or disobedience.** Some parents see intermarriage as deliberate disloyalty to their heritage. That this is rarely the case has no merit; if it's what someone believes, then the issue must be addressed.

No matter what motivates an in-law's fear after an intermarriage, family pressure rarely resolves the issue to anyone's satisfaction. Often, some aspects of a person's heritage can be incorporated into the relationship and a compromise can be reached. Read on to find out how.

Praise the Lord (and Pass the Mashed Potatoes)

While it may not be the primary cause of all family feuds, religion ranks in the top five reasons for family friction and the crumbling of relationships. What can you do if you find yourself half of an interfaith couple? How can you demonstrate that you're more than who you pray to? Here are some ways:

1. **United we stand, divided we fall.**

   First of all, it's essential that you and your spouse present a united front. You and your beloved must explain to your families, in private, that you chose your mate. Cat got your tongue? Try this line: "If you love and respect me, you'll need to respect my choice and my mate."

2. **Show interest in your in-laws' faith.**

   For example, if you're Catholic and your in-laws are Jewish, attend their Passover seder. (Watch the matzoh balls; a bad matzoh ball makes a good paperweight. They repeat like episodes of *I Dream of Jeannie*.)

3. **Invite them to learn more about your religion.**

   Difference is scary; knowledge lessens fear. When your in-laws see that you don't handle snakes or sacrifice raccoons, they are likely to feel less threatened by your religious beliefs (unless you *do* handle snakes and sacrifice raccoons. Thanks for not sharing).

Whatever you believe, recognize that none of your in-laws is under any obligation to worship as you do. They have to respect your beliefs, not follow them. So share and share alike, but don't insist that yours is the one true faith. No proselytizing, please. No tracts on pillows, no earnest sermons.

4. **Try to avoid confrontations.**

   Religious beliefs are a funny thing; you either have them or you don't. And if you do, nobody's going to sway what you deeply hold to be true. You won't get anywhere by antagonizing your in-laws. Here are my big three no-no topics: Abortion, birth control, sexual practices.

Don't Go There
Never degrade yourself or your beliefs—no matter how different they may be from what your in-laws believe.

5. **Compromise.**

   One couple I know were married in a Unitarian church, because, being Jewish and Episcopalian, they sought to find some middle ground of civilization where family members on both sides were less likely to kill themselves or each other. They selected that particular Unitarian church because on the day they checked out the church they were dedicating a pew to a cat. This leads to the final suggestion...

6. **Try a little humor.**

   As you've probably figured out by now, I think a little humor goes a long way to defuse tough and touchy situations. But keep the humor light and playful; never snide or sarcastic. And never make one of your in-laws the butt of a joke—no matter how much they deserve it.

The Eternal Jewish Truths

A woman sent this query into an advice columnist:

> Our son writes that he is taking Judo. Why would a boy who was raised in a good Christian home turn against his own?

Good question, silly woman. But on the odd chance that her son is converting to Judaism rather than taking up the marital arts, I hereby present some eternal Jewish truths to get you started. (You can also use the following knowledge if one of your in-laws is Jewish or if you need to educate your in-laws about your beliefs. No martial arts required.)

➤ The optimist sees the bagel, the pessimist sees the hole.

➤ If you can't say something nice, say it in Yiddish.

➤ WASPs leave and never say good-bye. Jews say good-bye and never leave.

➤ Israel is the land of milk and honey; Florida is the land of milk of magnesia.

➤ The High Holidays have absolutely nothing to do with marijuana.

➤ If your name was Lipschitz, you'd change it, too.

➤ Prune Danish is definitely an acquired taste.

➤ Laugh now, but one day you'll be driving a big Cadillac and eating dinner at four in the afternoon.

➤ Prozac is like chicken soup: It doesn't cure anything, but it makes you feel better.

➤ If you're going to whisper at the movies, make sure it's loud enough for everyone else to hear.

It's All Relative

The United States now has 1,100 mosques and Islamic centers, 1,500 Buddhist centers, and 800 Hindu centers. [Source: "Harvard Tracking Religious Diversity," *The Columbus Dispatch*, November 13, 1993.]

Sloppy Seconds

Diane married Glenn after a brief courtship that began about two years after his divorce from his previous wife, Lisa. "Out of curiosity, I asked Glenn how his mother, Rita, had felt about Lisa," said Diane. "He said Lisa had been like a daughter to Rita. The alarms went off. I knew I might have some trouble winning Rita over to my side—and boy, I was right."

Diane remembers her first Thanksgiving with her new in-laws. "Lisa called just as we were sitting down to dinner. It seems that she was very upset about not being with Glenn's folks at Thanksgiving; she even started crying on the phone. Rita spent over an hour comforting her. It was an awful situation. I was completely left out as Rita focused on her real favorite, her former daughter-in-law."

Ever been in this situation? Afraid you might be? Because half of all marriages end in divorce and a significant number of the participants choose to remarry and remarry and remarry, it's not unlikely that you could end up in Lisa and Glenn's situation—or in Rita's shoes. The first spouse automatically becomes a cross between Henry Kissinger, the Dali Lama, and Mother Teresa. And the second spouse? Cold, three-day-old tuna casserole, anyone?

The *subject* is second marriages (specifically coming on after a boffo first act), but the *issue* is boundaries. Rita should not have talked to her former daughter-in-law while her current daughter-in-law was there. But because she did, Diane should have cleared the air by speaking to Rita later about her feelings. Here's a model opening that Diane (and you) can use: "I understand that Glenn's divorce from Lisa has been hard to accept, and that you still feel close to Lisa. However, perhaps you didn't realize that it hurts me to have you talk to her while I'm here."

Here are some additional guidelines to help you build a good relationship with your in-laws when you're not their child's first spouse.

➤ Don't force yourself on your mother- or father-in-law. But don't be a cold fish either!

➤ Recognize that your in-law's special bond with your spouse's ex isn't a statement about you.

➤ Rome wasn't built in a day, and your relationship won't be, either. Give your relationship time to develop.

➤ If your in-law's compare you to the ex, try to accept that the ex must have had some good qualities—at least one, maybe two.

➤ Highlight your individuality.

➤ Develop your own connection with your in-laws.

Family Matters
When a remarriage occurs, the whole family goes through a transition period. Sensitivity and thoughtfulness to the new spouse are essential to make the passage go smoothly.

Don't Go There
Under no circumstances should Diane get her husband to speak to his mother on her behalf. She should settle the issue directly, without involving intermediaries. Diane can explain her feelings to her husband, but she must settle the problem with her mother-in-law herself.

Age Before Beauty

Tricia was a real beauty, a stunning redhead. On a quick glance, she looked no more than 25. Her figure was outrageous; her grooming impeccable. Only her hands and a few tell-tale wrinkles on her neck revealed that she was closing in on 40. But Ted, himself 25, loved Tricia's wit, generosity, and great looks. The 15-year age difference didn't matter to either of them—but it mattered a whole lot to Ted's parents. They were furious that Ted had selected Tricia. "She's too old to have children," they wailed. "When you're in your prime, she'll be an old lady," they moaned. "You could have anyone you wanted; why would you marry someone old enough to be your mother?" they screamed.

News flash: Life's not fair. (I know; "Tell me something that I *don't* know.") If a woman is more than five years older than her husband, a number of issues can sour the in-law relationship. The envelope, please:

1. It's not uncommon for mothers-in-law to feel threatened when their daughters-in-law are older than their sons, because the role of the mother is more obviously replaced.

2. In these situations, the competitiveness that accompanies most mother-in-law/daughter-in-law relationships is usually intensified. A lot.

3. A mother may feel uncomfortable to realize that her son is having sexual feelings for a woman closer to her own age. This is apt to intensify if she no longer feels attractive.

4. A mother-in-law might also worry that her little boy has been seduced by a cheap floozy. (Notice that no one ever worries about an *expensive* floozy?)

5. Commonly in these situations, a mother- and father-in-law worry that they'll never have grandchildren, because their daughter-in-law is over the hill.

It's All Relative

Are you feeling old? If not, consider that the people who are starting college this fall across the nation were born in 1980 and...

➤ the Iranian hostage crisis occurred before they were conceived.

➤ they have no meaningful recollection of the Reagan era.

➤ Atari predates them, as do vinyl albums and cassette audiotapes; they may have heard of an 8-track, but probably never actually seen (or heard) one.

➤ having not lived through the Disco Scare, they can romanticize the 1970s.

There's usually not such a flap when an older man marries a younger woman.

However, it's not always as simple as it seems, as my in my friend Virginia's case:

> I've got two May/December romances in my family. My 42-year-old sister and her 30-year-old boyfriend—and me (34-years-old) and my 60-year-old husband. My sister gets relatively no bunk about the relationship. A little, maybe; but she's fully accepted by his family, and we like him, too (well, usually).

> My father, however, has maintained a strong, 14-year burning flame of hatred for the "old man that dared to look at his little girl." We became a couple when I was 20, which didn't make my family roll out the red carpet any faster either. My father has never accepted it. It's a nightmare.

What can you do to pour oil on troubled waters?

➤ Take charge. Don't wait for the in-laws to come to you.

➤ Discuss the issue of the parents with your spouse first. Sometimes, there are lots of age issues to work out between the couple, too.

➤ Get your significant other involved. You can't fight this battle alone. And present a unified front. It won't work if your beloved sits there and says, "Yeah, well my folks have a point. You *are* old!"

➤ Have your husband or wife tell your in-laws that they don't have to love you, but they must respect you.

➤ Hopefully, as your in-laws see your relationship last, they will move from respect to like and maybe even to love.

➤ Bottom line: Demand respect. You deserve it.

Statistically, marriages are most likely to succeed when the partners share common interests—but there are no carved-in-granite rules about ideal age differences between spouses. However, if you and your spouse are comfortable with each other's ages, then it will at least give you some solid ground with which to deal with any naysaying in-laws.

> **Don't Go There**
> Warning lights should flash when the bride is very young, (as in under legal age) and the groom is pushy. But before you pull the plug on the nuptials, consider the consequences. Do you run the risk of losing your child if they marry anyway? Will you be unable to help your child later if the marriage sours?

The In-Laws Who Came to Dinner

Matt and Jessica met at the law office where Jessica was a secretary. At first, Jessica's parents were thrilled to hear that she was dating a very high-powered attorney. When they discovered that Matt was black, their opinion shifted 180 degrees. The situation got so unpleasant that Jessica's parents refused to attend the wedding. They did not speak to the couple for two years, until the birth of their first grandchild. It took them many more years to become something approaching friendly. "I give a lot of credit to Matt for being patient," Jessica says.

> **Don't Go There**
> A friend of mine whose child is dating someone of a different race assured me that her problems with her child's intended are not about black versus white. "Oh, this is harder than race," she said. "This is family."

Although interracial marriage has become more common today, many people still find it very difficult to adapt to an interracial couple. I often think that interracial marriages are like scenes from *West Side*

Story. In addition to slinging knives, the in-laws may as well break into a chorus of: "A boy like that he kill your brother. Forget that boy and find another—one of your own kind, stick to your own kind!"

My husband once claimed that we have a mixed marriage because he's a man and I'm a woman. My husband is a smart man. In effect, every marriage *is* mixed because we bring our own unique heritage and background to the table. But interracial marriages still push special buttons in many parts of America. In one respect, that's because people who think their families are liberal are often in for a very rude awakening. Be sure to watch your back here: The problems can come from your sisters-in-law and brothers-in-law as well as your parents-in-law.

I've Looked at Love from Both Sides Now

Robert Benchley, the American humorist and critic, took a course in international law while he was a student at Harvard University. On the final exam, Benchley was asked to discuss the arbitration of an international fishing dispute between the United States and Great Britain. He was supposed to pay special attention to hatcheries, protocol, and dragnet and trawl procedures. Benchley, who was not prepared for the exam, began his essay by announcing that he knew absolutely nothing about the point of view of the United States with respect to any international fishing controversy; he also confessed that he did not know where Great Britain stood on the issue. "Therefore," Benchley asserted in the introduction to his essay, "I shall discuss the question from the point of view of the fish."

Like Benchley, people who get along with their in-laws when there are serious problems with same-sex relationships, religious differences, second marriages, age differences, and interracial marriages have learned to see the same issue from different points of view. This ability enables them to cope with the problem more effectively. Give it a shot yourself!

The Least You Need to Know

➤ Same-sex relationships, religious differences, second marriages, age differences, and interracial marriages are potential minefields. Be prepared.

➤ Acknowledge your in-laws' concerns but present a united front and demand respect.

➤ Combat ignorance with information.

➤ To thine own self be true, but respect other's beliefs.

➤ Stress your individuality and try to develop your own relationship with your in-laws.

➤ Try the 3 C's: Compassion, caring, and compromise.

Chapter 12

Evolution's Missing Link

In This Chapter

➤ Not all your in-laws will be rocket scientists. This might be a problem with your in-laws who *do* have a brain

➤ Varying educational levels can also cause rifts among in-laws

➤ Differences in social class can pull apart even the closest in-laws

➤ Discover strategies to deal with these differences

Chuck Nevitt, North Carolina State basketball player, explained to Coach Jim Valvano why he appeared nervous at practice: "My sister's expecting a baby, and I don't know if I'm going to be an uncle or an aunt."

In the previous chapter, you explored some of the factors that can strain relationships among in-laws: Same-sex partners, religious differences, second marriages, older women marrying younger men, and racial prejudice. Here, you'll delve into three other sources of friction within families: Differences in educational levels, social class, and (dare I say it?) intelligence.

I'll first show you how these forces affected one family. Then you can take a simple test to see how likely you are to encounter these problems with your in-laws. Next, we'll explore how these differences can make it difficult to get along with your in-laws. Along the way, you'll read some first-person accounts of in-law problems caused by differences in class and intelligence. Because the odds are good that you're going to face these situations, I'll teach you practical tactics for dealing with these in-law dilemmas. (You know me by now. I'd *never* leave you twisting in any wind generated by irate in-laws!)

Almost as Smart as Neanderthals

There are many forces that cause conflicts among in-laws. Some, like religion and race, are obvious and often spoken of openly—or at least whispered about at weddings, funerals, and pig roasts. Others factors, such as socio-economic status, education, and intelligence, are often swept under the rug. After all, who wants to admit that her in-laws are trailer trash? Would *you* confess that your brother-in-law is one taco short of a combination plate? Who wants to concede that her mother-in-law enjoys watching paint dry?

Here's what my brilliant and well-educated friend Liz, an Asian-American, said about her relationship with her dim and less well-educated in-laws:

Don't Go There

Don't judge intelligence on IQ points. A person can score in the stratosphere on an IQ test and still be a potato-head when it comes to dealing with life. Level of education isn't a reliable benchmark, either. It's not always an indication of how bright your bulb is. Instead, consider practical as well "testable" intelligence when you condemn your in-laws.

My relationships with my in-laws have been less than ideal, possibly because my in-laws and I came from such different backgrounds—they are, for the most part, as blue-collar as one can possibly imagine, while I'm from a very well-educated, professional family.

One of my cousins-in-law earned my undying affection when I overheard him telling Jap jokes behind my back and he then borrowed money from us. While my mother-in-law and I got along okay for the most part, she really would have preferred a daughter-in-law from the same approximate gene pool (Irish-Catholic-Polish New York, the makeup of Mike's previous girlfriend, who also went to college with him). She would also have preferred that Mike marry a woman who did not pursue a career. Someone who made clever bird feeders from plastic milk containers would have suited her just fine.

The hardest time I ever had keeping my mouth shut came during election time in the 1980s—1984, I think it was—when my mother-in-law, aunt-in-law and grandmother-in-law were all sitting around trashing Geraldine Ferraro because she had the temerity to 1) get an education and 2) go for a job that a man should have. And that's what they said in front of me, who should have stayed home and had babies (unspoken but understood).

It's All Relative

The median American income is $38,782. About eight percent of all American families earned more than $100,000 a year, while 12 percent were below the official government poverty level ($15,141 for a family of four). [Source: *1997 World Almanac*]

Surprisingly, differences in background—socio-economic, educational, or cultural—pull families apart more often than you'd think. Read on to find out how these forces tear families apart and what you can do to prevent *your* extended family from becoming a casualty in this war.

Dumber and Dumbest

Each of the following stories appeared in a recent newspaper. Even *I* couldn't make this stuff up.

➤ The Portsmouth, Rhode Island police, charged a young man with a string of vending machine robberies in January when he 1) fled from police inexplicably when they spotted him loitering around a vending machine and 2) later tried to post his $400 bail in coins.

➤ A 20-year old woman was arrested in Lake City, Florida, for robbery of a Howard Johnson's motel. She was armed with only an electric chain saw, which was not plugged in.

➤ The *Ann Arbor News* crime column reported that a man walked into Burger King in Ypsilanti, Michigan, at 7:50 A.M., flashed a gun and demanded cash. The clerk turned him down because he said he couldn't open the cash register without a food order. When the man ordered onion rings, the clerk said they just weren't available for breakfast. The man, frustrated, walked away.

➤ A 34-year-old man in Alamo, Michigan, was killed in March as he was trying to repair what police described as a "farm-type truck." The victim got a friend to drive the truck on a highway while he hung underneath so that he could ascertain the source of a troubling noise. The victim's clothes caught on something, however, and the driver found him "wrapped in the drive shaft."

Family Matters

My in-laws are generous in all things, including humorous anecdotes from their past. We often recount these family legends at holiday dinners. As a result, these stories have become a source of unity in our family. If your in-laws can laugh at themselves, their stories can become a way to bring together your family, too.

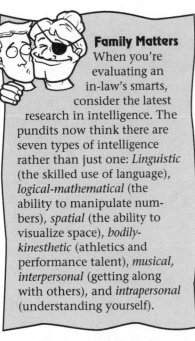

Family Matters
When you're evaluating an in-law's smarts, consider the latest research in intelligence. The pundits now think there are seven types of intelligence rather than just one: *Linguistic* (the skilled use of language), *logical-mathematical* (the ability to manipulate numbers), *spatial* (the ability to visualize space), *bodily-kinesthetic* (athletics and performance talent), *musical, interpersonal* (getting along with others), and *intrapersonal* (understanding yourself).

➤ A 19-year-old Bowling Green, Ohio, student had his head bloodied when he was struck by a Conrail train. He told police he was trying to see how close to the moving train he could place his head without getting hit.

➤ Ken Charles Barger, 47, accidentally shot himself to death in December in Newton, N.C., when, awakening to the sound of a ringing telephone beside his bed, he reached for the phone but grabbed instead a Smith & Wesson. 38 Special, which discharged when he drew it to his ear.

➤ MacArthur Wheeler, 46, was convicted of bank robbery after his face was caught in a surveillance camera; he and his partners had rubbed lemon juice on their faces in the belief that it would blur their image and make masks unnecessary.

All these people are someone's in-laws. They could be yours.

A One-Way Ticket to Palookaville

"I didn't think my in-laws were bothered by my master's degree," Wilma told me, "but ever since I got that piece of paper, they seem to be carping on my cooking, housekeeping, and cleaning all the time. My husband Trevor and I used to share the chores pretty equally, but when I went back to college, he started doing the lion's share. He's just kept doing it, but suddenly my in-laws are on my case all the time. They leave *him* alone, but everything is my fault! They think I'm taking away his manhood or something. What's sort of funny about this is that Trevor is perfectly happy about our arrangement and very proud of my accomplishments. His parents are the ones who are threatened by my education."

Family values differ regarding education. High-achieving parents are likely to sneer at an in-law who lacks the right initials after his or her name. Many a posh parent has bellowed: "My child marry a (pick one) (a) stevedore, (b) dog catcher, K-mart greeter rather than a (pick one) (a) doctor, (b) lawyer, Indian chief! We'll see about that!"

Blue-collar parents, in contrast, may feel threatened by a college-educated child-in-law. Someone with a sheepskin may make the rest of the clan feel inferior. Remember that ground-breaking sitcom *All in the Family*? Do you recall what blue-collar Archie called his college-educated son-in-law Mike? "Meathead," wasn't it? "Meathead" isn't what I'd call a term of endearment.

Communication can be very dicey in these situations. For example, what type of conversation can you expect to have with your prospective in-laws if they're rednecks? Here are the top ten things you'll absolutely never hear a redneck say, in reverse order:

10. Honey, did you mail that donation to Greenpeace?

9. Has anybody seen the sideburn trimmer?

8. Lee, do you think my hair is too big?

7. Wrasslin's fake.

6. Cappuccino tastes better than espresso.

5. I thought Graceland was tacky.

4. Those shorts ought to be a little longer, Darla.

3. Honey, these bonsai trees need watering.

2. I've got it all on a floppy disk.

And the number one thing you'll never hear a redneck say is...

1. Elvis who?

Here are the three most common fears that the less-educated in-laws have when their child marries someone with more education:

➤ They will be outclassed by their new son- or daughter-in-law's education. They'll look foolish in comparison.

➤ Fathers-in-law may feel especially threatened by the perceived lack of status.

➤ The in-laws may worry that the better-educated partner will "steal" their child and alienate him or her from the family.

> **Don't Go There**
> It's not only parents-in-law who feel threatened when a new daughter- or son-in-law has more education. Siblings-in-law may also measure themselves against the educational accomplishments of the new addition to the family—and decide that they come up short.

Stupid Is as Stupid Does

How can you tell if you and your in-laws are going to have problems in this area? Try my simple test. Check the statements that are so stupid your in-laws might have said them (or wish they had).

_____ 1. Here's what a basketball coach at Texas A&M told a player who received four Fs and one D: "Son, looks to me like you're spending too much time on one subject."

____ 2. An advice columnist received this letter: "I am a 23-year-old liberated woman who has been on the Pill for two years. It's getting expensive and I think my boyfriend should share half the cost, but I don't know him well enough to discuss money with him. What should I do?"

____ 3. Lou Duva, veteran boxing trainer, had the following comment on the Spartan training regimen of heavyweight Andrew Golota: "He's a guy who gets up at six o'clock in the morning regardless of what time it is."

____ 4. Another plea for advice: "I suspected that my husband had been fooling around, and when I confronted him with the evidence he denied everything and said it would never happen again."

____ 5. "They X-rayed my head and found nothing."—Jerome "Dizzy" Dean

____ 6. A comment overheard on a bus: "I have a man I never could trust. Why, he cheats so much I'm not even sure this baby I'm carrying is his."

____ 7. Frank Layden, Utah Jazz president, remarked to a former player: "I told him, 'Son, what is it with you. Is it ignorance or apathy?' He said, 'Coach, I don't know and I don't care.'"

____ 8. When asked how to pronounce his name, Brent Motycka replied, "Brent."

____ 9. Still another request for advice: "Will you please rush me the name of a reliable illegitimate doctor?"

____10. Torrin Polk, University of Houston receiver, on his coach, John Jenkins: "He treats us like men. He lets us wear earrings."

Score Yourself

10 check marks	The wheel's spinning, but the hamster's dead.
8–9 check marks	Your in-laws have an intellect rivaled only by garden tools.
6–7 check marks	They're as smart as bait.
4–5 check marks	Your in-laws couldn't pour water out of a boot with instructions on the heel.
2–3 check marks	There's still too much yardage between the goal posts.
1 check mark	Not bad. They're only one Fruit Loop shy of a full bowl.
No check marks	You've got my in-laws; give them back!

If You're Not Part of the Solution, You're Part of the Problem

Here's what Dan said about his in-laws:

> My in-laws are nice people, but we communicate on a different wavelength. If I didn't like them, it would be simpler. I think they genuinely care about me, but the relationship is enormously frustrating because we have so little in common. As a result, they're not sensitive to what's important to me as an individual.

Parents who are unwilling to accept a child-in-law as he or she is are often viewed as critical and intrusive. As a result, the child-in-law does not feel respected and dissatisfaction results. Constant criticism is draining and annoying. It can also chip away at your self-esteem, no matter what your accomplishments.

What can you do to level the playing field when it comes to unequal educational levels? Here are some ideas:

➤ **First, recognize the problem.** The elephant's in the room and no one can hide it (i.e., there's a big problem and you can't make it go away by pretending it isn't there).

➤ **This is one time when silence *is* golden.** Don't openly acknowledge the issue, because this can be like rubbing salt in a wound. ("I know I have more education than you and that probably makes you feel inferior" is not going to win you any allies among your in-laws.)

➤ **There are some things you should flaunt, but your education isn't one of them.** Put a Band-Aid over the Harvard logo tattooed across your chest; ditch the Yale sweatshirt. Resist the urge to show off your book learning. You don't have to *always* win at Trivial Pursuit.

➤ **Find common bonds with your in-laws.** Play a round of golf, bowl a few frames, try some poker. You don't have to spend the afternoon watching reruns of *Lost in Space* with your in-laws, but neither do you have to lecture them for two-hours about the best way to solve a quadratic equation.

➤ **If your in-laws express an interest in furthering their education, help them sign up for courses at a local high school, community college, university, or trade school.** This is a big "If," however. Never force any in-law to get an education. The decision must be theirs, not yours. But if you do lend a hand, do it as a peer. *Never* be patronizing.

It's All Relative

Some of the smartest and most well-educated people I know are the most modest. Because they know so much, they realize how much they still need to know.

Movin' Uptown

We like to believe that America is a classless society. We also like to believe that celery has negative calories, the outfit in the back of the closet will come back into style, and wrinkles are a sign of good character. Anyone who has felt out-classed by an in-law will be quick to agree that social standing matters. A lot.

What happens if someone (say, *you*) brings a mate into the family who doesn't quite measure up to the family's social standing? If your spouse makes less money than is expected, odds are the family will light a fire under his or her bottom. If your spouse lacks what your family considers the proper amount of ambition, I'll bet my Flash Gordon secret decoder ring that the family will make him or her a pet project. The family will take it upon themselves to correct the spouse's wayward thinking. Here's what a friend of mine told me about her family's reaction to her husband:

> I fell in love with Marv because he is sensitive, sweet, and laid-back—just the opposite of my obtuse, sarcastic, hard-driving father. Unfortunately, the traits that make my father such a pain also make him a great success in business. Marv is just too nice to push and shove his way to the top of the heap. As a result, he's still a security guard at a local department store. He doesn't earn enough money to meet the bills, but he's perfectly happy there. He has no desire to get ahead. I thought I was really happy with him, but my parents' constant criticisms have almost convinced me that I'm wasting my life with a loser.

Differences in socioeconomic status can drive a big wedge between in-laws. This can be the case whether your in-laws are poor and less-educated or rich and well-educated. Any sharp disparity in income and education between you and them can be tricky to overcome. The problems usually start from the very beginning, when the couples meet.

> **Family Matters**
> Education and socioeconomic factors are very closely linked. A person's income rises quite nicely with his or her education, so stay in school until the scholarship runs out. (Men: you also earn more money for every inch of height you have, up to about 6'5". See? Size *does* matter.)

> **Family Matters**
> Everything in life is a matter of perception. Where one person sees crisis, another sees opportunity. Optimists and pessimists will always view identical situations in different ways. Why not walk on the sunny side of the street and see these differences as a chance for greater personal growth?

Make My Doris Day

In the men's room at work, the Boss had placed a sign directly above the sink. It had a single word on it—"Think!"

The next day, when the employee went to the men's room, he looked at the sign, and right below, immediately above the soap dispenser, someone had carefully lettered another sign, which read—"Thoap!"

So far, we've looked at the problem from one side: You're reasonably accomplished and educated and one or more of your in-laws is a cement-head. But what if you're Average Joe or Joannie and one or more of your in-laws is a brain surgeon or rocket scientist or something equally intimidating? (My husband's late uncle, Jim Nestor, *was* a rocket scientist. He worked for NASA on the Mercury, Gemini, and Apollo programs. Fortunately, he was also a modest man who wore his brilliance well. He was so smart that he dealt with his in-laws by leaving town when they came to visit—but that's another story.)

So, what if *you* only have a high-school education or a two-year degree from a local community college and you marry into a family of Ivy League attorneys and fancy-schmancy doctors? You may feel very, very intimidated about your achievements. This is especially true if your in-laws are narrow-minded: Anyone who didn't row crew for Yale is relegated to the Pale.

It's All Relative

While 18 percent of Americans aged 25 and older lacked a high school diploma in 1995, 23 percent had a bachelor's degree or higher. The proportions differed greatly by age, however. For example, 88 percent of 35 to 44-year-olds had a high school diploma and 27 percent had a bachelor's degree or more. But among those Americans age 75 or older, only 57 percent had a high school diploma and only 11 percent had a bachelor's degree or more. [Source: *1997 World Almanac*]

Or, what if one of your in-laws is making money so fast that the Mercedes are stacking up like cordwood outside the 10-car garage? How would you feel if your in-laws' biggest problem is whether to vacation to Barbados or St. Lucia (traveling there in their private jet, of course)? Relations might be a little strained if they have a house the size of San Simeon and you're living in a vinyl-sided modest cape cod.

Don't Go There
If the socio-economic disparity between one in-law and the rest of the family is too great, it can be nearly impossible to find a common ground.

In this case, the shoe is on the other foot. You feel inadequate, outclassed, maybe even cheated. You're probably afraid that you won't be unable to reciprocate socially. Who wants to have franks and beans when they can have caviar and brie?

What can you do if you feel outclassed by your in-laws?

1. Celebrate your own accomplishments. You don't have to stand on the roof and crow, but you should enjoy your victories—and stop counting your in-laws' money.

2. Be aware that things may not be as peachy on the inside as they appear on the outside. Your in-laws may seem to be living the life of Riley, but appearances can be deceiving.

3. Realize that money can buy some impressive houses, cars, and jewels, but it can't buy what really matters: Health and happiness. I know, I know…it is a cliché, but with good cause—it's *true*.

4. Invite them over anyway. If your in-law's clan are the poster family for *Lifestyles of the Rich and Famous*, don't make assumptions on their snootiness. The rich-and-mighty might enjoy slumming with nifty in-laws like you. Be yourself and have fun. Throw some chicken on the grill, put up the volleyball net, and party hearty.

5. Find a common ground. No, you can't match them vacation for vacation, but you probably can enjoy seeing a movie together, grabbing a burger, or spending a day at the lake or beach.

The Least You Need to Know

➤ Differences in intelligence, educational level, and social class can cause friction among in-laws.

➤ People fear they will be outclassed by their new son- or daughter-in-law's education.

➤ In-laws may also worry that the better-educated partner will "steal" their child.

➤ Well-educated in-laws often want to re-make less-educated or socially polished in-laws. Beware: You could become someone's pet "project."

➤ Rather than flaunting your brains or education, develop common bonds with your in-laws.

➤ Invite your in-laws to parties and family gatherings. Leave the decision to attend up to them.

Part 3
In-Law and Order

A man in a Ford Granada pulled up next to a Rolls. He yelled at the guy in the Rolls, "Hey, you got a telephone in there?"

The guy in the Rolls said, "Yes, of course I do."

"I got one too—see?"

"Uh-huh, yes, that's very nice."

Then the man in the Granada said, "You got a fax machine?"

"Why, actually, yes, I do."

"I do too! See? It's right here!"

"Uh-huh."

The light was just about to turn green and the guy in the Granada said, "So, do you have a double-bed in back there?"

And the guy in the Rolls said, "No! Do you?"

"Yep, got my double-bed right in back here. See?"

The light turned and the man in the Granada zoomed off. Well, the guy in the Rolls immediately ordered a double-bed for the back of his car. When the job was done, he drove all over town until he found the Granada. The Granada's windows were all fogged up and he felt a little awkward, but he tapped on the foggy window anyway.

The man in the Granada finally opened the window and peeked out. The guy in the Rolls said, "I got a double-bed installed in my Rolls."

"You got me out of the shower to tell me that?" the man in the Granada replied.

The two main conflicts among in-laws are money and power. If your in-laws are like everyone else's, the arguments in your family range from the distribution of material goods to wrangles over turf issues. In this section, you'll learn how to use conflict to bring your family closer together.

Chapter 13

Getting to Know You, Getting to Know All About You

In This Chapter

➤ Learn what happens when a new in-law joins the family circle

➤ Explore the four stages of adjustment: Greeting, Meeting, Seating, Completing

➤ Deal with in-law power struggles by recognizing the stages in the relationship

➤ Understand that the process of adjusting is not linear

Three guys were about to be shot in a prison camp. The first one thought, "If I could just find a distraction, maybe I could escape."

Just as the squad leader said, "Ready, aim…" the guy shouted, "Tornado!" The members of the firing squad looked around and the prisoner ran away.

The second prisoner decided to try the same thing. The squad leader said, "Ready, aim…" and the second guy yelled, "Flood!" The members of the firing squad looked around and the prisoner ran away.

The third guy thought, "Hey, we're on to something here." But when the leader yelled, "Ready, aim…," the third guy yelled, "Fire!"

In this chapter, you'll learn how to avoid being in the line of fire when it comes to setting up your household. We'll start off by exploring how people react to outsiders (that's *you,* petunia) joining their family. Next, I'll explain the stages you go through when you become part of your in-laws' family: Greeting, Meeting, Seating, Completing. Along the way, I'll equip you with strategies for dealing with power struggles among your in-laws.

Invasion of the Body Snatchers

"When I met Jeff's parents, I thought I'd died and gone to heaven," Audra said. "My family was selfish and unpredictable—and very hostile toward Jeff. It was such a relief that Jeff's folks seemed so stable and welcoming. As a result of their guidance, the wedding was wonderful. Things started to fall apart soon after, however. They became critical, judgmental, and downright nasty. It was almost spooky, like my pleasant in-laws had been invaded by evil aliens from outer space."

Don't Go There

Nearly all of us put our best foot forward in the beginning of any relationship because we want people to think we're swell. In-laws are especially prone to using those "company manners" to impress newcomers to the fold. Sooner or later, the facade will crack, the honeymoon will be over, and you'll have to deal with the real person behind the mask.

Whether your in-laws are the Waltons or the Bundys, becoming part of a new family follows a predictable series of stages. First off, the family will have to adjust itself to accommodate the newcomer. This isn't easy, folks. As a matter of fact, it can be downright difficult.

When a new in-law enters the family circle, the focus shifts. In large part, this is because we have to make room for a new series of behaviors. No matter how "normal" you think your way of doing things is, it's bound to look weird to the newcomer. My family is a case in point.

Having Your Cake and Eating It, Too

We had an odd after-dinner ritual when I was living with my parents and siblings. Every night after dinner, my mother or father would announce, "You know, dessert would be nice." At that point, one of us would scamper to the freezer and take out a rock-solid Sara Lee cake. (Sometimes we had Pepperidge Farm cakes, and let me tell you, they freeze just as solid.) Then one of us would hack off a few chunks with a cleaver and we all happily munched on frozen cake. We did this every night. For some strange reason that no one has ever been able to figure out, we never planned ahead and took out a cake to defrost. It never even occurred to me that cake was ever served defrosted.

When I was about 19 years old, I brought my future husband, Bob, home to have dinner with my family. Sure enough, out came the frozen cake. As we cheerfully gnawed through the ice crystals, my husband-to-be patiently waited for his cake to defrost. Never a family to stand on manners, we finished sucking on our impenetrable cake, cleared the table around him, and mopped the floor. Bob was still patiently waiting for his cake to get soft enough to pierce with a fork, much less consume. My mother said, "What *is* wrong with him? Doesn't he like cake?" My sisters kindly offered to eat his piece of cake for him.

Bob revealed to me later that most people ate their cake defrosted. What a concept!

> **Don't Go There**
> Trouble can arise when the new-comer points out the family's peculiar behaviors. This makes it far more difficult for the new in-law to be integrated into the family.

Odd Ducks

No matter how conventional you think your family is, the new in-law will find something peculiar about your clan. I guarantee it. How can you lessen the shock—and your honey's sudden terror that he or she might have hooked up with a nut job?

Rather than hitting the panic button and shunning the new in-law, welcome the person and his or her customs. As a result of my marriage, my family made the radical move to defrosted cake. It was a revelation to us all.

Because people tend to marry people who are similar to them in appearance, background, and habits, odds are that the new in-law isn't going to have terribly radical new ideas. This can make it easier for the families to merge. Nevertheless, if the new in-laws have a very different cultural, religious, or social heritage, it's not going to be as easy to meld the two families.

How can you prevent disaster? Aside from defrosting the cake, you can try these ideas:

> **Family Matters**
> In-laws can't start to relax with each other until they achieve mutual acceptance. Like anything worth having, this process takes time. If you can make it to this stage, however, you're well on your way to a sturdy friendship.

➤ Watch and wait. Take it all in and think about it.

➤ Withhold judgments. Don't be so quick to speak your mind—and caution your family to zip their lips as well.

➤ Welcome the new customs as a way to bring fresh blood into the family.

➤ Try not to alienate the new in-laws. What's so terrible about doing things a little differently at first to make guests feel comfortable?

Stage Fright

You can't walk before you crawl. (Okay, so maybe *you* did, but could you speak Serbo-Croatian by the time you were four? Dance the tango at six? Get a varsity letter in the luge? Well, neither could I, but I'm sure someone who's reading this book could.) In the same way, you have to pass through four stages on your way to developing a satisfying relationship with your in-laws. The four stages are:

Stage	Definition
1. Greeting	Saying "Howdy" to the new in-laws
2. Meeting	Figuring out how things are done
3. Seating	Becoming part of the family
4. Completing	Feeling that you really belong to the family

Even though each stage brings its own special challenges, there's no reason for stage fright. After all, you have plenty of time to settle in. Rome wasn't built in a day, and neither is your relationship with your in-laws. Let's take a look at each stage more closely.

Greeting: Putting on a Happy Face

Stage #1: Introductions. This stage begins with the First Encounter, when your honey takes you to meet his or her folks. Depending on the number of siblings involved, this stage can stretch on longer than a tax audit. Here are occasions where you're likely to undergo the greeting ritual:

➤ Dating

➤ Informal family functions

➤ Formal family functions

➤ Business functions involving family members

How can you make this stage go more smoothly? Start by recognizing that there *will* be differences in viewpoints and culture between you and your in-laws. Unless these differences are abusive, keep an open mind. And remember: Because you love your honey, there are bound to be some aspects of your in-laws that you can respect and admire as well. After all, they did raise your beloved, so how bad could they be?

Family Matters

Most in-laws want the process to work as much as you do, because they do want their precious baby to be happy. At the beginning, assume the best of your in-laws; you're more likely to be pleasantly surprised.

Don't Go There

Under normal circumstances, the Greeting stage takes place before marriage. In some rare situations, however, you may not meet your future in-laws until after the wedding. In these instances, the Greeting and Meeting stages can get compressed, putting extra strain on everyone.

Second, recognize that first impressions can be misleading, especially when so much is at stake. What you perceive as phoniness might just be nervousness; ditto for what you take to be standoffishness.

Family Matters

If something they do upsets you, address it as soon as possible. They'll be more likely to stay calm and listen.

You can make the Greeting stage easier by doing things together that you all find mutually enjoyable, such as eating out, playing sports, or dancing. Get to know your in-laws as people, and give them a chance to get to know you.

Meeting: Letting It All Hang Out

Stage #2: Getting the lay of the land. Here, you scope out the situation to see how things are done. By now, the honeymoon has ended and reality is rearing its ugly head. There's probably a lot of scratching, odd noises, and grousing going on as you try to figure out how the game is played.

It usually takes about a year for in-laws to reach the Meeting stage when they set aside their "company manners" and reveal their real natures. Warning: This is when you'll start seeing your father-in-law in his T-shirt or your mother-in-law in her well-worn house dress at Sunday dinner. This could be what's in store for your hunk or beauty queen in 25 years.

Family Matters

Give the sucker an even break, in-laws. Make the rules as clear as you can. State them outright, as in "Everyone loads his own plates in the dishwasher" or "No one sits in the cat's chair—but the cat."

How can you tell if you've reached this stage with your in-laws? Try administering the following test to your husband, wife, fathers-in-law, mothers-in-law, brothers-in-law, and sisters-in-law.

Ask them to circle the best answers to each question.

1. Men, as you grow older, what lost quality of your youthful life do you miss the most?

    a. Innocence

    b. Idealism

    c. Cherry bombs

2. Women, as you grow older, what lost quality of your youthful life do you miss the most?

    a. Innocence

    b. Idealism

    c. Perky breasts

3. Men, complete this sentence: A funeral is a good time to…

    a. …remember the deceased and console his loved ones.

    b. …reflect upon the fleeting transience of earthly life.

    c. …tell the joke about the guy who has Alzheimer's disease and cancer.

4. Women, complete this sentence: A funeral is a good time to…

    a. …remember the deceased and console his loved ones.

    b. …reflect upon the fleeting transience of earthly life.

    c. …determine how much the rock on the third wife's finger set back the deceased.

5. Men, in your opinion, the ideal pet is:

    a. A cat

    b. A dog

    c. A dog that eats cats

6. Women, a sentence you'll never hear from your honey is…

    a. You mean chips and pizza isn't a balanced meal?

    b. A washer? So that's what the machine in the basement is.

    c. You're right; I *do* need some new T-shirts.

7. Women what, in your opinion, is the most reasonable explanation for the fact that Moses led the Israelites all over the place for 40 years before they finally got to the Promised Land?

    a. He was being tested.

    b. He wanted them to really appreciate the Promised Land when they finally got there.

    c. He refused to ask for directions.

8. Men, what is the human race's single greatest achievement?

    a. Democracy

    b. Religion

    c. The remote control

Score Them Yourself

Mostly A's and B's	They're still at the Greeting stage. You're safe for a while.
Mostly C's	You're definitely at Stage #2. Soon, you'll be drinking OJ from the carton and eating peanut butter straight from the jar.

The Meeting stage can be very tense as you learn the rules that govern your in-laws' lives. Jimmy's experience was fairly typical:

> I was staying at my in-laws' house for the weekend shortly after Beth and I got married. I took a shower in the morning and decided to shower again after tennis. My mother-in-law was furious. "We have a cesspool problem in this area," she hissed between clenched teeth. "No one takes two showers. How inconsiderate you are." I was shocked because she had always been so nice to me. Who gets so bent out of shape over a shower or two?

It's not the shower, bunky. It's the tension of redefining roles and welcoming a newcomer into the family dynamic. No matter how careful you are, you're bound to step on someone's toes. Relax; that's natural at this stage of forming a relationship with your in-laws.

Your in-laws are not under any obligation to make the process easier for you, though. Some in-laws are just not ready to accept newcomers to the family. By not making it easy for the newcomer, some parents try to maintain their roles as they existed before the marriage. But you can't go home again, as novelist Tom Wolfe said. Holding on too tightly can damage the relationship on all ends.

Sometimes, the new in-law (probably *you*) becomes the focus of existing tension within the family. This helps the family relieve its own fears—by dumping them all on you.

If you encounter this problem, try a little communication. No armchair psychology, please. Instead, simply state your feelings and wait for the person's response. Even if your attempt doesn't work, take heart: Matters usually get easier as the relationship continues. People often run out of energy. Besides, time has a way of putting matters into perspective.

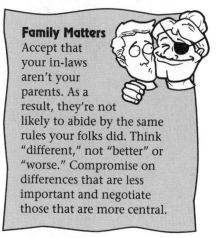

Family Matters
Accept that your in-laws aren't your parents. As a result, they're not likely to abide by the same rules your folks did. Think "different," not "better" or "worse." Compromise on differences that are less important and negotiate those that are more central.

Seating: Hello, I Came to Say I'm Going to Stay

Stage #3: Getting chummy. Within a few years, everyone has begun to settle into their new roles as in-laws. During this time, you can expect to be...

➤ Resetting boundaries

➤ Redefining rules

➤ Understanding ranking order

Family Matters
During this stage, in-laws often forgive each other for real as well as perceived slights. Being invited to a key family function—a christening, bris, or naming ceremony, for example—often signals that forgiveness is afoot. Do your share: Forgive (even if you can't forget).

Don't Go There
Never assume that your mother-in-law or your father-in-law is the boss. It can just as easily be a sister- or brother-in-law who holds the reigns of power. And don't discount the influence of a sister-in-law. She can cause just as much turmoil as a mother-in-law—sometimes even more.

Family Matters
With the possible exception of traffic, very little in the world proceeds in a linear fashion. The process of melding families is no exception. While I've given rough guidelines for the amount of time that each step could take, be aware that this formula is written in sand, not carved in granite.

Here's where you begin to close the gap between appearance and reality. You may think that your blowhard father-in-law runs the show, but a closer examination reveals that your meek mother-in-law is the brains of the outfit.

It's crucial that you figure out the power structure. My friend Kenny had this problem when he married Kerry. Here's what he told me:

> "Kerry's mother is a formidable woman, both in size and impact. Since she makes so much fuss, I just figured that she controlled the show. As I became more familiar with Kerry's family, though, I came to see the power behind the throne: Kerry's sister Leslie. No one would make a move without checking with Leslie. If a party was called for 2:00, Leslie would come sailing in at 4:00—and everyone would wait for her. If we all wanted to go for Italian food and Leslie preferred Chinese, it was Chinese. Everyone in the family gave in to Leslie. Amazing, no one seemed aware of what was going on."

Once you figure out which in-law is calling the shots, you can work with that person rather than against him or her. This will save you years of needless aggravation. Later on, you can challenge the power structure if you wish. But this way, you'll know who you're fighting against.

Completing: Grow Old Along with Me, The Best Is Yet to Be

Stage #4: In the groove. By this stage of the relationship, everyone understands and obeys the ground rules. The in-laws with brains have stopped tiptoeing around each other; the rest of the family may still be in the dark. There's a strong enough foundation in place that everyone is relatively comfortable with each other. In short, the stage is set for mature growth.

Nonetheless, don't be so quick to throw the life preserver overboard. Even the strongest family can be rattled by change, especially issues such as chronic illness, abuse, death, and divorce. I cover these issues in depth in Part 5, "Circumstance-in-Law." You can lower your shields, but never stop working toward family comprehension and cohesion.

Feud for Growth

Listen up, now, class. It's time for review. Read the following situation and select the correct answer. (No, you can't leave early if you finish before the bell rings.)

> Cynthia Bartlett didn't want to take her husband Stan's last name when they got married last year. Not only did she like her name, "Bartlett," but she had also established an impressive reputation as a graphic artist under that name. Thus began her repeated trips to the Motor Vehicle Department.

> "First, I took Stan's name because I felt pressure from my in-laws to do so. That was the first trip to Motor Vehicle. But after we were married for a year, I decided to hyphenate our two names, so back to Motor Vehicle for me. A few years later, I went the full monty and changed back to 'Bartlett.' My mother-in-law was angry, but she's mellowed about it. I've reached the stage where I feel comfortable using the name I want."

Where is this family in the adjustment process?

1. Greeting
2. Meeting
3. Seating
4. Completing

The answer is choice 4. Cynthia and her in-laws have reached an understanding. Peace has been declared; the treaties have been signed. No one's sweating the issues that years ago would have erupted like Mount St. Helens.

Not long ago, a woman didn't have any option about keeping her birth name. When I was married more than 20 years ago, I never even considered not taking my husband's last name, "Rozakis." (The decision was greatly influenced by the fact that my birth name had occasioned many jokes, none of them funny. I was thrilled to be dumping that name and taking one that did not lend itself to faux humor.)

It's All Relative

Okay, so I'll tell you already. My maiden name was "Neu." Are you happy now? Are you going to say, "What's new?" or "Anything new with you?" Don't.

Today, in contrast, many women wouldn't consider changing their birth names. But this issue is a minefield for in-laws who cling like the high-priced plastic wrap to traditional ways. A friend told me that even after she told her mother-in-law-to-be that she did not want to take her fiancé's name, her mother-in-law gave her a set of monogrammed towels—with only her husband's last initial on them.

And look at what happened to Hillary Rodham Clinton, aka Hillary Clinton and Hillary Rodham. She's flip-flopped on the name issue more often than Madonna has changed her hair color.

Initially, Cynthia's mother-in-law most likely decided that Cynthia was rejecting her new family and not being loyal to her son. Because Cynthia's mother-in-law never had the option of keeping her name, she was very likely threatened by her daughter-in-law's independence. She probably envied it, too.

But with the passage of years, she has likely come to see that a woman's decision to keep her own name isn't about rejection; rather, it's about staying connected to your own identity. Or, she's just decided that the battle isn't worth it. Whatever Cynthia calls herself, she's been a good wife and daughter-in-law, so the name isn't worth the battle. That's what happens when families reach the Completing stage in their relationship.

The Least You Need to Know

➤ You follow four stages of adjustment when you join two families: Greeting, Meeting, Seating, Completing.

➤ During the Greeting stage, the family forms those first impressions of each other.

➤ During the Meeting stage, you learn the family rules and the lay of the land.

➤ During the Seating stage, you become part of the family.

➤ During the Completing stage, you realize that you've arrived: You *are* part of the family.

➤ Identifying the family's stage in the process can help you deal with power struggles and other battles.

Home for the Holidays—But Whose Home?

Becky was on her deathbed, with her husband Jake at her side. He held her cold hand and tears silently streamed down his face. Her pale lips moved. "Jake," she said.

"Hush," he quickly interrupted. "Don't talk."

But she insisted. "Jake," she said in her tired voice. "I have to talk. I must confess."

"There is nothing to confess," said the weeping Jake. "It's all right. Everything's all right."

"No, no. I must die in peace. I must confess, Jake, that I have been unfaithful to you." Jake stroked her hand.

"Now Becky, don't be concerned. I know all about it," he sobbed. "Why else would I poison you?"

There's a lot of reasons why we want to poison our relatives, and holiday madness ranks right up there. Why do holidays make otherwise sane people want to do in their relatives —faithfulness aside? That's what this chapter is all about. So put away the arsenic, grab a cold one, and sit back. The party has just begun.

Tightly Wrapped

Some people approach holidays calmly. Maybe that's because their in-laws live in Guam, Sri Lanka, or Fiji. Perhaps they've discovered better living through chemistry, so everything looks a little fuzzy around the edges. Most likely they deal with the holidays by diving under the bed and staying there until the last relative has departed.

Words to the Wise
Holiday *n.* 1. A day fixed by law or custom on which ordinary business is suspended in commemoration of some event or person. 2. A time when families get together to celebrate key events, rekindle relationships, refuel feelings of familial love, and settle a few old scores.

For the majority of us, however, our in-laws live around the corner, we've run out of happy pills, and we're too scared to get under the bed. After all, who knows what's living *there*? That leaves us to deal with our in-laws and holidays.

Mention the words "holidays" and "in-laws" in the same sentence and even the stalwart flinch. Making dinner reservations doesn't help; it's not the cooking that's bumming you out. Even the witness protection program is useless. You can run but you can't hide.

How do *you* feel about spending the holidays with your in-laws? Take the following quiz to see. Check every answer that applies to you.

When the holidays approach, I get so nervous that I...

_____ 1. sleep with my eyes open.

_____ 2. channel surf faster without a remote.

_____ 3. forget to unwrap candy bars before eating them.

_____ 4. don't need a hammer to pound in nails.

_____ 5. help my dog chase its tail.

_____ 6. short out motion detectors.

_____ 7. only stand still during earthquakes.

_____ 8. walk 20 miles on my treadmill before I realize that it's not plugged in.

_____ 9. grind coffee beans in my mouth.

_____10. can ski uphill.

_____11. can take a picture of myself from 10 feet away without using the timer.

_____12. can jump-start my car without cables.

_____13. can test batteries in my ears.

_____14. can type 60 words per minute with my feet.

_____15. double as the Energizer bunny.

Score Yourself

10–15 check marks	You're so wired, you pick up AM radio.
5–9 check marks	Bet people could use your hands to blend their margaritas.
1–4 check marks	You only twitch when the doorbell rings.
0 check marks	We'll spend the holidays at *your* house this year.

There's no denying that the holidays are one of the top causes of tensions among in-laws. In some families, the holidays can be as strained as a cease-fire along the Israel-Palestine border, a truce in Bosnia, or a teenager in love. Why? What makes supposedly joyous times so very miserable? Read on to see.

It's All Relative

In their book on rituals, Evan Imber-Black and Janine Roberts distinguish between *outside calendar days,* holidays that are widely observed (such as Thanksgiving, the Fourth of July, Christmas, and Passover), and *inside calendar days,* personal and special family celebrations (such as anniversaries and birthdays). Both types of celebrations present equal opportunity for family conflict.

It's Party Time!

As you learned in Chapter 10, America is becoming increasingly multicultural. A generation ago, most families spent Thanksgiving gathered around a large dead bird, watched a little football, and threw some plates at each other. December called for Christmas; spring was Easter. Not any more, cupcake. The world has shifted and so have holidays. My family is a case is point.

I'm German-Jewish and my husband is Catholic-Irish-German-Greek. On my mother-in-law's side, this means the headline holidays are Christmas and Easter. On my father-in-law's side, we get Greek Christmas (Epiphany) and Greek Easter. As a result, the winter holiday season seems longer than an afternoon spent waiting to renew your driver's license.

If we give equal time to both sets of in-laws, we'd kick off with the neutral Thanksgiving, shift into a week of Hanukkah, crash into Christmas madness, do a New Year's debauch, and mop up with Greek Christmas. After a deep breath, we spin right into Passover, Easter, and Greek Easter. That's a lot of time spent cooking, arguing with relatives, shopping, arguing with relatives, cleaning, and arguing with relatives. The tension builds as we're pulled and tugged in many directions.

It's All Relative

Iranian-Americans may celebrate Noruz, while Native Americans have the traditional powwows and the Green Corn Dance. Hispanic Catholics often hold fiestas during the year to honor saints.

The Party Never Ends

So many holidays, so little time. How many of the following holidays have become a part of your family traditions because of marriage?

➤ Many Chinese-Americans celebrate their new year in January or February (the date varies), the beginning of the lunar new year.

➤ Mexican-Americans mark May 5 on their calendars Cinco de Mayo. The holiday commemorates the Mexicans' 1867 victory over the French.

➤ Are your in-laws Muslim? If so, Ramadan, celebrated on the ninth month of the lunar year, is an important holiday. It's marked by atonement and fasting from sunup to sundown.

➤ Japanese-Americans may honor their elderly relatives and friends on September 15, Respect for the Aged Day.

➤ Observant Jews mark the rededication of the temple in Jerusalem with the holiday of Hanukkah. The holiday lasts for eight days in December.

➤ Anyone in your new family from England? Boxing Day, celebrated on December 16, is the tradition of presenting small boxed gifts to service workers.

And that's just a nibble. What about the Carnival blow-out celebrated by Catholics who have come to America from Brazil, France, Haiti, Italy, the Caribbean? Let us not forget the Christian holidays of Christmas and Easter and the Jewish holy days of Passover, Sukkoth, and Rosh Hashanah.

Vietnamese-Americans may celebrate Tet, their new year, between January 21 and February 19. People make a fresh start for the new year by cleaning and painting their homes. They pay back any money they owe and try to avoid arguments.

It's All Relative

The first visitor of the new year is important to a Vietnamese-American family. A child or other relative is sent outside just before midnight and invited to reenter a few minutes later. This is to make sure the first visitor of the new year is one who brings the family good luck in the coming year.

Danger, Will Robinson

Tensions can arise over the specifics of each holiday. Here's what Todd told me about his dilemma with this issue:

> "I'm Catholic and my wife is Chinese, born in Taiwan. When we got married, I worried that I'd make a fool out of myself at my in-laws' holiday celebrations. Would I say the wrong things? Make the wrong gestures? How could I ever understand everything that I had to learn to honor my wife's heritage?"

And then there's the pressure that comes from trying to do too much in too little time. Help is on the way! Try these suggestions for taking some of the weight off your shoulders.

1. **Decide which holidays to celebrate.**

   Perhaps you can celebrate them all; perhaps you can't. Make your choices—but don't close the door. Be ready to shift gears if circumstances change.

2. **Learn, learn, learn.**

   Don't be afraid to ask. Until recently, I didn't know the difference between Virginia ham and fresh ham. As a result, when I saw a fresh ham at an in-law's holiday celebration, I had no idea what it was. The solution? I asked, "What is this meat-like substance? An albino pig?" You only feel like a dope for a second, but then you'll never have to ask again.

3. **Make sure you correctly observe all customs.**

   People born into the faith or culture have the leeway to be sloppy. You don't. Adhere to the letter of the law, at least in the beginning. Later, you can have some sausage on your matzo, too.

Border Disputes

What really causes the stress at holiday times? Are you terrified that Aunt Esther will once again chug-a-lug the cooking sherry and dance with the turkey? Do you panic at the thought of frying yourself on the tangled Christmas lights? Are you fearful that people will get ptomaine from your cooking?

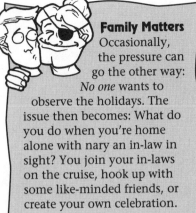

Family Matters
Occasionally, the pressure can go the other way: *No one* wants to observe the holidays. The issue then becomes: What do you do when you're home alone with nary an in-law in sight? You join your in-laws on the cruise, hook up with some like-minded friends, or create your own celebration.

Family Matters
The media and other outside forces put tremendous pressures on families to celebrate holidays the "right" way. All this hype generates high expectations, which are bound to be shattered one way or the other. Why not turn off the TV, pull the curtains, and do things your own way?

Don't Go There
Watch for unequal ritual styles. Do you spend two days at your in-laws' house celebrating Christmas, but only an hour and a half with your side during Passover? There's bound to be resentment if one side feels slighted.

What's the number one cause of turmoil at turkey time? Only the most snooty relatives lose sleep about Aunt Esther doing the Macarena with the bird. People shrug off a brief electrocution; no one frets about a little food poisoning among kinfolk. No, what really pushes the panic button is deciding which in-laws to spend the holidays with.

In large part, our turmoil comes from the pressure we get from our in-laws to spend the holidays with them. Married children often feel torn about which family to visit. That's because they're usually thrust into a position of keeping everyone happy. "I feel like I have to keep a 'scorecard' to see whose turn is next," a friend told me about her in-law holiday conflicts. "Heaven forbid I show any favoritism." Here's what Risa told me about her first holiday tug-of-war:

"What do you mean you're going to your in-laws' house for Christmas?" my mother whined the first year we were married.

"We're Jewish, ma," I said, "we don't celebrate Christmas. We don't have a big Christmas dinner."

"We always had dinner on Christmas," she said.

"We had dinner every night," I replied, "but that doesn't mean we celebrate Christmas."

My mother actually started to celebrate Christmas that year so she could undercut my in-laws. She was furious when we didn't show up to her "Christmas dinner."

While it's natural for the in-laws to want their kin present for special occasions, their demands can put unreasonable strains on you. Here's what one woman told me about holidays and her in-laws:

Everyone assumed that we would just divide the holidays among them. No one ever thought—least of all us—that we would develop our own family traditions. It never crossed our minds to spend the holidays with friends or on a vacation, either.

Magical Misery Tour

Often, both sets of parents demand equal time with you. And if they don't, you may put the pressure on yourself to play the game their way. Guilt is a very powerful motivator. After all, how can you favor your husband's parents over your own? Is it fair that your wife's sister hosts the family Christmas Eve party every year? What about your brother's tree-trimming party that same night? Some people attempt to solve this dilemma by trying to be all things to all people. Here's what Georgiana said about how she and her husband Joel celebrated the holidays in the beginning of their relationship:

> When Joel and I were first married, it was decided that we would spend Thanksgiving with Joel's parents and siblings, *and* my mother and her husband, *and* my father and his new family. We drove to his parents for an early dinner, dashing out the door before dessert to make it to my mother's apartment in time for late afternoon dinner. Then it was off for coffee and dessert at my father's house. About three years into the marriage, I calculated that we had actually spent more time on the road during Thanksgiving than we had spent at anyone's house. All anyone every said to us was "Leaving so soon?" and "Why are you always rushing out in the middle of a meal?" We tried so hard to make everyone happy that we made no one happy— least of all ourselves."

Don't Go There
Don't exclude your in-laws from your holiday celebrations because they treat your spouse or another member of the family badly during a holiday. Don't get sucked into the fray; let everyone fight their own battles.

Tug of War

What else pushes our buttons and makes holidays hellish? A number of hot spots are just built into holiday traditions, like the bike with 10,000 pieces that must be assembled on Christmas Eve. Here's how to recognize these buttons before they get pushed:

➤ **Great expectations.**

Every holiday brings its set of expectations. Your Halloween celebration may involve carving a pumpkin and drinking cider; your Kwanzaa observance may center around lighting candles and exchanging gifts. Even if the "kids" are 45 years old and long done with pumpkins and gifts, you may find it hard to shake those ideals.

➤ **Your side/my side.**

No matter how miserable your parents may make you during the holidays, most of us are drawn toward our own side during key events, like lemmings to the cliff. Fortunately, your parents aren't members of the Borg collective, so resistance *isn't* futile.

➤ **Party pooper.**

Every party has a pooper and that's why we invited you, party pooper. Every family has a relative who just sucks the fun right out of the day. Even though you know you should invite him or her, you just can't steel yourself to another afternoon of moans, tears, or dire predictions.

➤ **You call this a holiday?**

Celebrations vary from family to family. What one set of in-laws considers great fun, another set of in-laws considers a real snooze. An afternoon spent cooking, serving, and cleaning up while the men watch football? Hey, that's *my* idea of a swell time. See my point?

We Can Work It Out

Parents often don't realize the problems their married children experience as they try to balance loyalties to their own parents as well as to their in-laws and spouse. If the older generation didn't experience the same stress, they may not be able to understand how difficult this problem can be to their children, especially to young couples just setting their own boundaries in the relationship.

Family Matters
Make extra copies of the worksheet so you can target the problems that arise with specific holidays. You can also complete the checklist again when your family situation changes. This will happen if you have children, if your in-laws move closer to you or further away, or if you remarry and end up with still *more* holidays to celebrate.

And if they do realize it, they may not care. "We raised you and we deserve the pleasure of your company at least a few times a year," your parents may bellow. "You spent last New Year's with your sister-in-law. What about us?" your brother-in-law may complain.

Holiday pressure is especially tough on two-career families. Because both partners are working, there is little time for laundry, shopping, cleaning, and nurturing the relationship, much less seeing the in-laws. Women particularly may feel pressured to play the traditional roles at holidays to compensate for jealousy over their career success.

What can you do to deal with the conflicts in-laws can cause on holidays? Here are some suggestions:

Start by making a worksheet to solidify your thinking. This can help you decide where to go on those special days—or whether you would like to celebrate the holiday in your own home. Why not try this worksheet on for size?

1. Name of holiday: _____

2. Which childhood traditions linked to this holiday do you want to preserve? Why?

   _____

   _____

3. Which childhood traditions linked to this holiday do you want to ditch? Why?

   _____

   _____

4. Which traditions linked to this holiday from your spouse's childhood does he or she want to preserve? Why?

   _____

   _____

5. Which traditions linked to this holiday from your spouse's childhood does he or she want to ditch? Why? _____

   _____

6. How do *you* want to celebrate this holiday? _____

   _____

   _____

7. How does your *spouse* want to celebrate this holiday?

   _____

   _____

8. How do your *in-laws* want to celebrate this holiday?

   _____

   _____

9. What makes this holiday such a touchy issue in the family?

   _____

   _____

10. What other factors do you have to consider when you celebrate this holiday? (such as religious or cultural differences) _____

    _____

Got your checklist? Now you're armed and ready for the next step: Learning my ways to resolve holiday conflicts. Try the following ideas on for size. I guarantee that several will suit you perfectly! (How can I be so sure? I tried them all in the field myself...)

1. **Be loyal to your mate.**

   Your first allegiance is to your spouse. No matter how heavy a guilt trip your relatives lay on your shoulders at holiday time, recognize that you and your spouse are a couple. By promising to love, honor, and work through the toilet seat issue, you have created your own family. Now that you're a team, work as one.

   This doesn't mean that you should throw out your family and in-laws as you would your old Partridge Family albums. Instead, make your in-laws a part of your new family, the one you have formed with your beloved.

   > **Don't Go There**
   > Under no circumstances let your in-laws pit one of you against the other. Think of yourselves as the Great Wall of China: Present a solid, united front against outside assault.

2. **Make a decision.**

   There are times when you can sit on the fence—but making a decision about which in-laws to spend the holidays with isn't one of them. With your spouse, discuss all areas of potential conflict and then create a game plan. Figure out where you're going for the holiday, when, and why. Plan what you're going to say when the other side pitches a fit. Use the worksheet you filled out earlier to crystallize your thinking.

3. **Recognize that you can't be all things to all in-laws.**

   As you learned in previous chapters, whatever decision you make is going to upset someone. That's life. There are so many valid issues that you can chew yourself up over, so why make this one of them? Save the angst for other issues. Make your holiday decision, announce it to the relatives, and move on. I know this is a lot easier said than done (especially for someone like me who can hold a grudge until it reaches legal age), so work with me here.

   > **Family Matters**
   > Not sure whether you should indeed throw out those Partridge Family albums? Why not consult my *Complete Idiot's Guide to Buying and Selling Collectibles*? It covers albums, china, silver, crystal, paper money, stamps, coins, books, comic books, paper collectibles, games and toys, bottles, watches, quilts, radios, tools, furniture, photographs, drawings, prints and lithographs, rugs, jewelry, silver, and so much more. There's even a chapter on future collectibles!

4. **Tell people immediately of your plans.**

   Remember how angry you were when some of your wedding guests canceled at the last minute? "I'll never be such a stinker," you said. So don't be. No Scarlett O'Hara "tomorrow is another day" pronouncements on *this* issue.

If you can't or don't want to accept an in-law's holiday invitation, don't dodge the issue. Instead, bite the bullet and tell them as soon as possible. In addition to getting rid of an onerous duty, early notice also allows your in-laws to make alternate plans, if they so desire.

5. Respect your in-law's decisions.

If one or more of your in-laws doesn't want to come to your holiday celebration, don't be a sore loser. Don't whine, nag, or moan. And don't pressure your in-laws to change their plans. Respect their decisions and you have a better chance of having them respect yours.

6. Be sensitive.

There's no denying that the holidays can be very tense under normal circumstances, but they can be especially trying if the year has been difficult. If someone has become ill or, God forbid, passed on, you may want to vary the celebration to overcome the trauma. This might be a good year to set the party in a different place or even take a family vacation instead.

7. Look for workable solutions.

Life isn't always black-and-white; there's a lot of room for gray between the lines. For example, say you want to spend New Year's Eve home but your in-laws want to have a party instead. Instead of giving a flat refusal, see what compromise you can work out. Maybe your in-laws could come to your home for dinner and then you could ring in the New Year at their party. This won't always work, but it's worth a shot.

8. Involve your in-laws in your traditions.

I'd be messing with your head if I said that it's easy to get everyone to play together nicely. Most people never learn to share their toys. For instance, some in-laws want to be included in every party and get angry if they're excluded; others just have very different styles of entertaining. Nonetheless, set aside some time for a ritual or two. It doesn't have to be something major like chopping and trimming a

> **Don't Go There**
> Always check out all invitations with your spouse before you say yes or no. Try, "Thanks for the invitation. I'll talk it over with my beloved and get back to you." Never take it on yourself to make a decision about your whereabouts on a holiday—even if your spouse doesn't celebrate it. If you want to surprise your spouse, men, unload the dishwasher, wrap yourself in Saran, or drop a few diamonds in her Diet Coke. Ladies, ditto on the dishwasher and Saran, but a Porsche usually goes over better than a diamond.

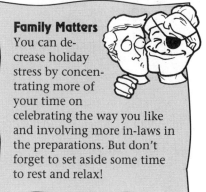

> **Family Matters**
> You can decrease holiday stress by concentrating more of your time on celebrating the way you like and involving more in-laws in the preparations. But don't forget to set aside some time to rest and relax!

200' blue spruce Christmas tree. Your rituals may be small and charming, like an hour of caroling or a evening of hot chocolate and cookies.

Aside From That, Mrs. Lincoln, How Did You Like the Play?

Where to go for the holidays isn't the only source of tension; how to act once you get there can also send your blood pressure to the stratosphere. Fortunately, we can usually muzzle ourselves, but it's harder to put some duct tape over your mother-in-law's mouth. A mother-in-law can put up a pretty fierce battle with that duct tape, let me tell you.

Keeping screwball in-laws in line during holiday dinners is a real dilemma in many families. We don't usually mind when an in-law or two swings from the chandelier or chews on the dog's tail, but things get a little dicey when they attack *you*—your cooking, childrearing, housekeeping, or repair skills. No one likes to have their self-esteem assaulted, especially on a national holiday. Here's what my friend Lois told me about her in-laws and holidays:

> Thanksgiving is here again, and I always have the family over for dinner. The problem is that my mother-in-law can never find anything right about anything. My house is never clean or neat enough; the centerpiece is never big or small enough; the cooking is always too slow, so dinner is never on time. She's like a mini-Martha Stewart, the K-Mart queen expert on everything. By the end of the day, I am frustrated, irritated, and just plain mad. I feel like a failure.

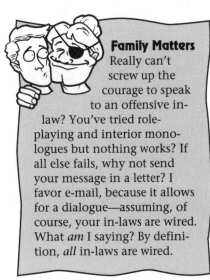

Family Matters
Really can't screw up the courage to speak to an offensive in-law? You've tried role-playing and interior monologues but nothing works? If all else fails, why not send your message in a letter? I favor e-mail, because it allows for a dialogue—assuming, of course, your in-laws are wired. What *am* I saying? By definition, *all* in-laws are wired.

How can Lois tell her mother-in-law to mind her own business and let her give a Thanksgiving dinner the way she wants—and still maintain the family relationship?

Master of Your Domain

Tell your mother-in-law (and by extension, any obnoxious in-law) how you feel, even though it can be painful and upsetting to voice our feelings. I'm not suggesting that you learn to love pain (that's a whole different issue), but when it comes to solving holiday conflicts, you have to make your feelings known. The situation isn't going to vanish like your socks in the dryer, your waistline, or the candy bar you hid from your kids.

In this case, Lois's mother-in-law is being a tyrant in Lois's home, her domain, where she does things the way she and her immediate family like them. Don't blame or judge when you express your feelings. Instead, explain how your in-law's actions make you feel. Here's a model: "Endora, I appreciate your caring that everything is just right for Thanksgiving, but your constant criticism makes me feel like a child. Please let me do Thanksgiving my way."

Share Your Toys

Another thing you might do to help overbearing in-laws feel part of the holiday is to invite them to take part in the preparations. Why not assign your mother-in-law the task of making and bringing the centerpiece or name cards, for example. In-laws who have trouble giving up control are often more comfortable when they can play a role in the festivities. Something like a centerpiece is nice because flowers rarely offend, unlike homemade liverwurst carved into the shape of a yule log, or 50-pound matzo balls.

Family Matters
The holidays are here again. What can you do with the in-laws no one can stand? Here are some ideas. Have dinner later, so these people aren't hanging around all day. Rather than inviting everybody over at say, 1:00, invite them over at 7:00—and serve at 7:15. If you have any in-laws who drink, eat dinner right away, before they get a chance to tank up and pound the table.

The Least You Need to Know

➤ Lessen the tension in multicultural families by learning all you can about your in-law's holiday celebrations.

➤ When planning how to spend your holidays, be loyal to your mate. Work as a team.

➤ Under no circumstances should you let your in-laws pit one of you against the other.

➤ Recognize that you can't be all things to all in-laws.

➤ Tell people immediately of your plans.

➤ Respect your in-law's decisions.

➤ Be sensitive to everyone's needs and look for workable solutions.

Chapter 15

Power Plays

> **In This Chapter**
>
> ➤ Explore family power struggles
>
> ➤ Discover the strategies your in-laws use to get power
>
> ➤ Survey key turf issues
>
> ➤ Learn how to adjust the balance of power—in your favor
>
> ➤ Make a game plan

There was an Orioles fan with really lousy seats at Camden Yards for the playoffs. Looking through his binoculars, he spotted an empty seat right behind the Orioles' dugout. "What a waste," he thought to himself, and decided to sneak into the empty seat.

When he arrived at the seat, he asked the man sitting next to it, "Is this seat taken?"

The man replied, "This was my wife's seat. She passed away. She was a big Orioles fan."

The other man answered, "I am so sorry to hear of your loss. May I ask why you didn't give the ticket to a friend or a relative?"

The man replied, "They're all at the funeral."

Family Matters

I think men who have a pierced ear are better prepared for marriage. They've experienced pain and bought jewelry.—Rita Rudner

Words to the Wise

Power is the ability to act; the capability of doing or accomplishing something. It's strength, might, and force. It's the ability to achieve your ends. Hmmm... sounds pretty good to me.

So, we all have our priorities. For some, it's watching the playoffs; for others, it's being the one to call the shots in the family. Setting priorities is a key issue when you deal with your in-laws. In this chapter, we'll explore different types of power struggles that can arise in any family and what you can do to resolve these crucial issues...with a minimum of bloodshed.

Power to the People

Most in-law relationships are power struggles. That's because power is well, *powerful*. Why, power can...

➤ make things happen

➤ get you what you want

➤ help you forge new bonds

➤ enable you to break old bonds

➤ change the way things are done

➤ make you feel like you're the head weenie at the roast

Regarding power, someone I respect a great deal once said to me that the smaller the cheese, the harder the mice fight over it. This advice struck me as words to live by because it suggests that you can't anticipate the size of the resulting fracas by the size of the original issue. Families will fight with the same vigor over small issues as they will over gargantuan ones.

Sometimes the issue even gets lost in the struggle for dominance: Witness some of the famous feuds that pepper the American consciousness or the less-famous but equally powerful feuds that have become legends in your family. Is it really true that your Aunt Paula won't talk to her sister-in-law Toby because Toby voted for Nixon? Could it be that your father-in-law won't talk to your brother because someone lost a garden tool a decade ago. Naw, couldn't be...but it probably is.

Might Makes Right

In-laws, like all other people, use several different tactics to get power. If they're smart, they go with the ones that work best, but for some people, any power play will do in a pinch. Here are some of the most common techniques people use to assert power over other people. Which ones describe how your in-laws get their way?

1. **Passive-submissive.**

   People like this often follow their in-laws' lead. They're usually relieved not to have to make decisions, because they aren't comfortable being in charge. These people are often very dependent, which means if they're not already on your side, you're not going to be able to sway them unless you thwack them on the side of the head with a two-by-four. This rarely engenders family harmony, however.

   These in-laws often find the most powerful family member and cling to them tighter than the high-priced plastic wrap that grips a bowl of left-over noodles.

2. **Passive-aggressive.**

   These clever folks use indirect manipulation to get what they want. Like a puppet master, they pull the strings behind the stage. These power players often seem to go along with family decisions but inwardly resent that they are doing so. As a result, they often subtly resist and even sabotage the plans that have been made.

   How can you identify a passive-aggressive family member? It's your sister-in-law who doesn't want to attend a party and so shows up an hour late. It's your father-in-law who goes to an event he'd rather skip and then embarrasses his wife in front of everyone.

Family Matters
These power play patterns are not mutually exclusive. Even in a particular situation, a person can use more than one method to get their own way. Watch for shifts in behavior; it's often a sign that there's been a change in tactic to adapt to changing situations.

Family Matters
Passive-aggressive players are often fearful of seeming to be pushy. They may also be afraid of rejection or disappointment.

3. **Passive-suffering.**

   These wily sorts control others by giving in. They govern by their seeming passivity. By turning over the reigns of power to others, they retain the ability to use recriminations. Here's the mantra: "See, I left you in charge and you screwed it up—again." A deep sigh also works well.

4. **Assertive-compromising.**

   Bingo! These healthy individuals can assert their needs but also compromise after hearing the other sides of the issue. They know how to balance power so everyone usually emerges feeling satisfied. They are comfortable exhibiting power, but also comfortable relinquishing it. Family members know where assertive-compromising in-laws stand on issues, and they're reassured that their needs are being taken into account.

Don't Go There
Beware of assertive-controlling in-laws. Since they are terrified of feeling powerless, they usually take no prisoners in their climb to the top.

5. **Assertive-controlling.**

We're into rigid and unyielding here. These people assert their own needs but usually insist on getting their own way. "Winning" means forcing others into submission. While they usually get their own way, they're unlikely to win "Most Popular Relative," or even get invited back to the party if anyone could help it. In extreme cases, it's not getting what they want that matters; it's just that they *won*.

Act Up

Where do you fit in this hit parade? Check the description that most closely applies to you.

____ A. Make a family decision? I'd sooner glue my nostrils together with crazy glue, chew ground glass, or spend an afternoon at an Ozzy Osbourne concert.

____ B. Of course you'll go to cousin Harvey's all-you-can eat eel feast, but somebody will pay...and big time.

____ C. Question: How many Jewish mothers does it take to screw in a light bulb?

Answer: None. "It's okay; I'll sit in the dark."

____ D. You know how to create a win-win situation. In your spare time, you negotiate for the UN.

____ E. It's my way or no way.

Score Yourself

If you answered A...you're passive-submissive

If you answered B...you're passive-aggressive

If you answered C...you're passive-suffering

If you answered D...you're assertive-compromising

If you answered E...you're assertive-controlling

Now, let's explore some of the most common in-law power struggles up close and personal.

In My Day, Things Were Different

I humbly offer you my philosophy of housekeeping, for it has served me well: "You make the beds, you do the dishes, and six months later you have to start all over again." Unfortunately, some homemakers from the previous generation may not always share my priorities—although I have done my very best to spread them far and wide.

Has your mother-in-law cast a cold eye on *your* housekeeping skills? Are you waiting for that white-gloved finger to snake over your dusty credenza? Many a contemporary wife has felt her mother-in-law's displeasure at the state of her home, especially if she works and has the temerity to share the housekeeping chores with her husband and children. There's a big-league power play going on here, petunia.

In part, this is because many older women were expected to do all the housekeeping without any help, even if they worked. As a result, older women may resent their daughter-in-law's freedom to sneer at dust bunnies, scoff at the vacuum, and speed-dial the pizza man. Some mothers-in-law have even been known to take matters in their own hands and clean or rearrange the furniture in their daughter-in-law's home!

Here's what Janine, a 35-year-old professor of speech at a large California university, told me about her first sustained encounter with her mother-in-law, Stella. The older woman lived across the country and rarely traveled. Janine and Dave had been married for more than a year when Stella came for a month-long visit.

> **Don't Go There**
> Mothers-in-law who worked throughout their marriage may feel equally threatened by a daughter-in-law who has chosen to be a homemaker. In the struggle for power, the mother-in-law may fear that her daughter-in-law will be a better nurturer than she was; the daughter-in-law, in contrast, may feel inferior and out-classed by her outwardly successful and independent mother-in-law.

"Mama had been with us in our tiny condo for just two days when she took me to task for not preparing Dave's breakfast. She was furious that I didn't lay out Dave's clothes the night before, fix him a bag lunch, and run the vacuum over the rugs before going off to work. She couldn't believe that I used paper napkins rather than the table linen she had sent me; she was speechless when I ordered take-out every night rather than cooking. What shocked her most of all, however, was my habit of coming home when I wanted to, rather than rushing home before my husband did so I could greet him. How could I not wait on my husband? How could I expect him to get his own food, do his own laundry, and clean the house?"

Stella firmly believed that her "child" was being neglected and emotionally shortchanged by his wife. Janine, in contrast, couldn't understand how her mother-in-law expected her to work and wait on her husband. Unlike Elvis, the generation gap is alive and well. It's one of our nasty little secrets, like fried pork rinds and raw cookie dough.

It's All Relative

Regarding laundry: Most women do laundry every couple of days. A man, in contrast, will usually wear every article of clothing he owns, including his bell bottoms that were hip in the seventies, before he will do his laundry. When he is finally out of clothes, he will wear a dirty T-shirt inside out, rent a U-Haul, and take his mountain of clothes to the laundromat. Men always expect to meet beautiful women at the laundromat, but this is a myth perpetuated by reruns of old episodes of *Love, American Style*.

Food Fight

Food is a surefire power issue, since the kitchen has been a traditional power base for women. The kitchen is a bulwark in this battle because it is here that the mother-in-law must give up her power base and the daughter-in-law must assert hers. Some mothers-in-law bow out of kitchen duty gracefully, probably because they've had enough of cooking years ago. Others, in contrast, are determined to use food as a way to prove love and capability. Ditto for daughters-in-law.

Don't believe me? How many of these tasty tidbits have you heard (or used?)

➤ "A way to a man's heart is through his stomach."

➤ "If you're a good boy, you get a cookie."

➤ "Show me how much you love Mommy by taking another spoonful."

➤ "I made it special for you. If you loved me, you'd eat it."

Carol had this experience when she first invited her mother-in-law over for lunch. Here's what she said:

> "I prepared a salad with a light pesto dressing, since I don't serve much meat. My mother-in-law looked in the bowl and grimaced. 'What do you call this?' she sneered. 'No wonder my Ralph is such a scarecrow if this is what you serve. This is nothing but rabbit food. He needs something to stick to his ribs, like some of my good sausage and potatoes. After all, he works a full day, you know.'"

Adding fuel to the fire, many daughters-in-law are starting out with a great deal more information about food than their mothers-in-law ever had. After all, how many non-Italian women prepared pesto or ratatouille 30 years ago? A generation ago, sushi was restricted to Japanese families; it was rare to find tortillas outside a Latino home. Today, these foods are commonplace, as are the ingredients and tools necessary to prepare them. Your mother-in-law may be a whiz with Jell-O, little marshmallows, and mayonnaise, but that's as outré as beehive hairdos, fire-and-ice lipstick, and cat's-eye glasses.

Tony experienced a variation on this power struggle with his in-laws. A nineties guy, Tony does all the cooking while Angela is the primary breadwinner. Angela's parents just can't get with the program. Here's Tony's problem:

> "My in-laws always have a comment on what we do and how we do it. I do the cooking in my family, so I got the kitchen criticism. Among the complaints: I don't arrange my spices correctly, I stack cans of tuna next to my soups, and I have more pasta than cream of chicken soup. They've criticized my use of broccoli ('It makes gas'), skim milk ('What's wrong with a little fat?') and tofu ('It tastes like erasers.') I've gotten a laundry list of my culinary shortcomings during our marriage. 'I can't please them!' I hollered at my wife last night. 'There's just no way. Nothing I do will get them to shut up.'"

It's All Relative

Regarding groceries: Most women make a list of things they need and then go to the store and buy them. Most men wait until the only items left in their fridge are half a lime and a beer, then they go grocery shopping. They buy everything that looks good. By the time they reach the checkout counter, their cart is packed tighter than the Clampett's jalopy on *Beverly Hillbillies*. Of course, this will not stop them from going to the 10-items-or-less lane.

Tiffs Over Turf

Tensions over food, as with similar issues, are often a cover for deeper power plays within the family. Regardless of the specific reasons, however, your sense of dignity and personal worth are attacked when your in-laws make you feel helpless.

A mother-in-law in particular may give too much advice because she fears that she's no longer needed. Mothers-in-law who have invested much of their time to child rearing are especially prone to these fears. Let's be fair here: No one warned women over 40 that being "Mom" wouldn't be enough for a lifetime. What happens when people invest a good part of their lives in a contract that society has rewritten?

Power struggles and conflicts are often very upsetting, but not all conflict is necessarily bad. Conflict directed properly can help in-laws bring up problems and work

Don't Go There

It's tempting to blame your spouse for your problems with the in-laws. Actually, it's tempting to blame your spouse for *everything,* from the Cuban missile crisis to your bad hair day. Fight the urge. Be a mensch, even if your beloved *is* being a knucklehead when it comes to in-law power struggles. You'll respect yourself in the morning.

through key issues to healthy resolutions. In some instances, bringing issues to the surface can help you and your in-laws lead happier lives by resolving long-standing power struggles.

However, I'm not a strong believer in letting it all hang out. There are some things that should stay in the closet, the cupboard, or wherever you keep them. For example, I don't suggest you bring up your past lives—or past loves. Being too honest is like eating too much candy: It's fun at the time but leaves you feeling vaguely nauseated in the morning.

When You Wish Upon a Star

Okay, now that we've been fair to both sides, it's time to roll up our sleeves and get to work. How can you straighten out the power plays in your family? Start by figuring out what *you* want within your family structure. It's a waste of time to realign the power structure unless you get want you want. And you can't get what you want unless you figure out what it is that you really want in the first place.

This isn't as easy as it sounds (not that it sounded all that easy). To lighten your task, I've prepared a little chart. All you have to do is pick the five most important items listed. Then arrange them from most to least important. The ones on the "most important" side are the ones you've decided are worth the effort to attain.

cleaning	money	recreation
cooking	status	travel
personal time	sex	hobbies and sports
education	respect	fame
power	appearance/grooming	other _____
family time	seeing in-laws	

Top Five Picks

1. _____
2. _____
3. _____
4. _____
5. _____

Most important   Important   Least Important

_____

_____

Power Lines

Next, figure out who has the power in your extended family. When you are trying to change the status quo, you have to understand your personal family culture. This can prevent you from making crucial tactical errors. Here are some clues to help you on your sleuthing.

➤ **Never assume that volume = force.** The most quiet member of the family may be the most powerful. My father made a lot of noise, but my mother called the shots.

➤ **See how the power is distributed.** For example, where do most family members go for the holidays? Why?

➤ **Look at the economic side.** Often, the golden rule of in-laws applies. You know that one: He who has the gold rules.

➤ **Consider gender.** Traditionally, women are the keepers of the family flame. They're the ones who set up the dinner dates, arrange the holidays, remember birthdays, shop for gifts, and take care of medical situations. While this is indeed changing in light of an increasing number of two-income families, the change hasn't been as swift as many think—or would like. As a result, more women than you'd realize are the power behind the throne.

Family Matters

In some rare instances, no one is in power. There's no one family member strong or savvy enough to run the show. If you suspect this is the case among your in-laws, study the situation closely. Perhaps the power just shifts with the situation, one member handling money issues, another taking over health-care problems.

Game Plan

Once you figured what you want and who's in charge, you can set about changing the power structure. The process will take time, so be patient. After all, it took years to set up the status quo, so unless you pull a coup d'etat, you're not going to change the family overnight.

➤ Step #1   Be assertive-compromising

➤ Step #2   State your needs, but be willing to see everyone else's sides as well.

➤ Step #3   Try to work out fair situation. Don't be a tyrant and ride roughshod over everyone else's feelings.

Family Matters

Take your time and calculate your moves carefully. Sometimes you can talk to your in-laws directly and resolve the situation, but other times your approach has to be more subtle.

Last Licks

Here are a few final suggestions to make it easier for you to solve power plays with your in-laws.

1. **Remember that revenge is indeed sweet, but it is a dish best served cold.**

   Don't be so quick to strike back. Let things simmer down before you extract what you consider justice. Everyone doesn't *always* have to get their just desserts.

2. **Look at your own behavior.**

   Sweetpea, no one is innocent in this situation. Consider what *you* may be doing to throw off the balance of power in the family.

3. **Choose your battles carefully.**

   You may win the battle but lose the war. Weigh each issue so you can decide if it's worth the effort to duke it out.

4. **Show respect.**

   Even if your in-laws *are* a pain in the you-know-where, they are your in-laws and they (usually) are older. Americans in general don't have a whole lot of respect for age (why else would I be thinking about that face lift already?) but age *does* deserve some deference. Even if you don't feel it, try to show your in-laws the respect they have earned by their greater experience.

5. **Don't forget irony.**

   If you stop sneaking spoonfuls of the super premium ice cream and lay off the bacon, odds are you'll make it to the stage where you'll be the mother- or father-in-law in the family photo. Let me tell you, Mouseketeers, it's a frightening moment when you first look in a mirror or store window and see your mother's or father's reflection staring back at you...but it's you, not them. If biology is indeed destiny, odds are you'll be mouthing those parental phrases you swore you'd never say. You know the ones: "Wait until your father gets home" and "I'll give you something to cry about." Ouch. So as you're judging your mother- and father-in-law now (as well as your older sisters- and brothers-in-law,) remember that it won't be too long before you're walking in their Reeboks.

6. **Maintain a good sense of humor.**

   Some things just aren't funny, but it's amazing how often you can find a germ of humor in even the grimmest situation. I'm not suggesting that you burst into gales of laughter when someone falls on his face in public, but you can make an effort to see the humor in most in-law power struggles.

Don't Go There
People are written off or discounted when mean behavior is expected or tolerated. As a result, old complaints and power struggles keep repeating like a foot-long chili dog.

7. **Never force anyone to make a choice. Almost.**

   "It's them or me" could leave you twisting in the wind. The only exception to this is an abusive in-law situation, where your emotional or physical health is in danger. I cover this in detail in Chapter 23.

8. **Don't bash your in-laws to make your own parents look good.**

   This isn't a zero-sum game. You *can* have your cake and eat it, too.

The Least You Need to Know

➤ Analyze the power tactics your in-laws use.

➤ Figure out who has the power in your extended family.

➤ If you've been wronged, resist the urge to get revenge.

➤ Choose your battles carefully.

➤ Show respect and maintain your sense of humor.

➤ Don't back your in-laws into a corner or bash them to make your own parents look good.

Gilt Trip

It's been called moolah, cash, bread, dough, lettuce, clams, bills, balloons, folding money, fins, ten-spots, yuppie food coupons, C-notes, travelin' money, bucks, and greenbacks. But no matter what we call it, we know what we mean—money. The word money comes from the Latin moneta, from moneo, "to warn." Let this chapter serve as a warning to you: Nothing causes in-law problems like money issues.

We like to think that love makes the world go round—but in many families, it's money, not blood, that's thicker than water. In this chapter, we'll see why money issues are among the most divisive that can occur within families. I'll show you how income disparities, gifts, and loans can cause marital problems and therefore have a tremendous impact on in-law relationships.

We're in the Money

Money, like sushi, summer vacations, and superstars, evokes strong responses in people. But unlike raw fish, endless days with the kids, and Madonna, money isn't a love/hate relationship; our reactions to money are much more subtle than that. That's because money is such a complicated issue with most people. It's not just how much you have and how much you want: Where you got it and how you spent it also enter into the equation.

Family Matters
Money is good for bribing yourself through the inconveniences of life.

Before you can figure out how to deal with in-laws and money issues, you have to figure out where *you* stand on the subject of money. Complete the following inventory to see where you stand. Check the responses that best reflect your feelings about money.

_____ 1. My problem lies in reconciling my gross habits with my net income.

_____ 2. Ebenezer Scrooge, my hero.

_____ 3. Enjoy money while you have it. Shrouds don't have pockets.

_____ 4. A fool and his money are soon parted.

_____ 5. Whoever said that money can't buy happiness doesn't know where to shop.

_____ 6. I still have the first buck I made.

_____ 7. Money can't buy friends, but it can get you a better class of enemy.

_____ 8. Thrift, thrift, thrift!

_____ 9. Save a little money each month and at the end of the year you'll be surprised at how little you have.

_____ 10. A penny saved is a penny earned.

_____ 11. I don't know much about being a millionaire, but I bet I'd be great at it.

_____ 12. Saving is next to godliness.

_____ 13. Better to be nouveau than never to have been riche at all.

_____ 14. Every morning I get up and look through the Forbes list of the richest people in America. If I'm not there, I go to work.

_____ 15. Any person who has $10,000 left when they die is a failure.

_____ 16. I can squeeze George so tight that he winces.

Score Yourself

All odd numbers   Your children won't be burdened with the problems of inherited wealth.

All even numbers   Remind me never to ask *you* for a loan, Scrooge McDuck.

> **Family Matters**
> Never get too deeply in debt to someone who cried at the end of *Scarface*.

Dollars and Sense

We like to believe that we can trust our family members to "do the right thing" where money's concerned. We also like to believe that we can drop that five pounds whenever we want, that we really weren't going *that* fast, officer, and that one day our ship will come in. Hold the phone: You mean I really *can't* fit into my high school cheerleader outfit?

> **Don't Go There**
> Second marriages are likely to carry especially heavy debt obligations, such as alimony and child support. These are often a source of contention among in-laws.

You're supposed to trust your family because they're on your side. In most cases, they usually *are* rooting for you. When it comes to money, however, the issue changes faster than a toddler's mood or Linda Evangelista's hairstyle. Greed can dissolve even the strongest bonds among in-laws.

Feuds over money arise when…

➤ one in-law feels the others have not contributed their "fair share."

➤ parents favor one in-law over the other when it comes to the allocation of funds.

➤ one member acts independently with family funds.

➤ some family members have more money than the others.

➤ people's expectations about money are thwarted.

Money Talks

Part of the American Dream is to have wealth—however we define "wealth." For some people, it's simply to have more money than their parents did. For others, however, it's the accumulation of a vast storehouse of pretty things—furniture, jewelry, art, cars, and so on. Family strife arises over who has money, how they got it, and how they use it.

Here's what Tracey told me:

"I'm one of six children from a blue-collar Irish Catholic family. My dad was a tool-and-die maker; my mother was a housewife. When I was a kid, we never had very much, but neither did anyone else in the family. My sisters married men like my father, hard-working custodians, bus drivers, and repair men. My brothers have similar jobs. None of my sisters works. I married a surgeon who does very well. He comes from the same background as I do, so none of my in-laws has much money, either. However, I've discovered that my husband's hard-earned success drives the family apart.

Our lifestyles are so different. When I get a new nanny or housekeeper, my brother-in-law says, 'How's the new slave working out?' When I put my kids in summer camp, my in-laws said, 'What's the matter? Are you too lazy to take care of your own kids in the summer?' When we bought a vacation house by the lake so my husband could get a rest from the pressures of his job, the whole family automatically decided it was their vacation home as well. They were furious when I told them to wait to be invited."

Family Matters
In 75 percent of American households, women manage the money and pay the bills.

Because financial success is all-too-often a measuring stick of worth today, it can be a sticky family situation no matter what size your stick happens to be. Some in-laws flaunt the fact that they don't have a lot of money. Their self-deprecating remarks serve to remind everybody else in the family how tough they have it and how guilty everyone should feel because of it. Any of your in-laws sing *this* song?

"I have a sister-in-law I love but I can't stand being around her,'" Victor said. She never passes up a chance to tell us how poor she and her husband are—if not directly, then more subtly. For example, if we're going on a vacation, she'll sit there with a sad face and say, 'Gee, I guess we'll never get a chance to go on a vacation, so take a lot of pictures for me.' I want to rip out her hair. Whenever she's around, we all have to downplay anything new we've bought—even if it's just a new pair of pants!"

Money Isn't Everything

You can bridge the money pit more easily if you separate the in-law from the dollar sign and focus on the real issue. Here are some possible issues that could be causing the problem:

➤ One in-law makes more money than another and people are jealous.

➤ Your in-law is really an ass and always has been, money or no money.

➤ Long-standing sibling rivalry is the issue.

➤ One family member is trying to seize power, using money as the lever.

➤ An in-law is foisting blame on another, using money as the smoke screen.

➤ An in-law is a born troublemaker and money is simply the issue du jour.

➤ Money has become a power issue.

Once you have identified the real issue behind the greenbacks, you can begin to solve the problem. Vast disparities in income are usually out in the open, unless one in-law lives well below his or her means. In that case, money is only an issue when the in-law shuffles off this mortal coil and people want a share of the pie. A much more dangerous family situation arises when things look straightforward on the surface...and then erupt like a volcano.

Don't Go There

Dual-income families can cause strife among in-laws who are more comfortable with traditional gender roles. Younger as well as older people can feel these strains; surprisingly, female homemakers are often more threatened by working women than men.

It's All Relative

The world's first true paper money originated in China, but scholars argue over the specifics. Some claim that the first paper money was created as early as 650 AD, during the Tang Dynasty, but none of the notes survive. Others contend that paper money was not freely circulated until the ninth century AD, during the T'ang Dynasty, and they can buttress their claims with actual samples from the era. Tang or T'ang: Take your pick.

Exploding Money

The roller coaster we call a stock market has added a whole new twist to family battles over money. It seems that everyone is investing in the stock market. Even people who used to stuff their money under their mattress are now stuffing it into mutual funds, Ginnie Maes, T-bills, and municipal bonds. Only a dolt could avoid making a bundle on this hot market or so we think. Here's what Dennis told me about how the stock market drove his family further apart than the Hatfields and the McCoys.

"I invested my money through my brother-in-law Alan, as did the rest of the family. Even though Alan tended to be a blowhard, the family believed in him. After all, why use a stranger to handle your investments when you have a broker in the clan? Everything went smoothly until October 1987. On Alan's recommendation, I began some big trades on margin. I was making big bucks, too, but it was so nerve-wracking that my ulcer started to kick in. In September, I reached my limit because I had hefty tuition bills coming up. I asked Alan to cash me out. Alan agreed.

In early October, I again called Alan and told him to pull out everything I had invested. I was ready for a nice, safe CD. On Black Monday, October 19, the market crashed, but I was cool—I had gotten out in time. But then Alan called. He hadn't listened to me and all my money was still invested. Alan's actions plunged us into financial ruin. His decision to ignore my wishes split the family: Half felt Alan had tried his best; the other half felt he should be flayed alive."

Family Matters
Investments and loans are a key component in all businesses. In Chapter 17, I cover the issue of money and family businesses.

Want to see the myth that you can trust an in-law with your money go nova? Start with investments and loans. People often get enmeshed in investments and property transfers with the idea that they can trust their family members to always do the right thing with their money. Unfortunately, even the best intentions can go south faster than a snow bird in February.

Neither a Borrower nor a Lender Be

So what if he left his wife his *second-best* bed (you don't want to ask what happened to his *best* bed). So what if he tortures generations of school kids with his "thee's" and "thou's"? Old William Shakespeare was onto something important when he penned these words in *Hamlet*:

> Neither a borrower nor a lender be,
> For loan oft loses both itself and friend
> And borrowing dulls th' edge of husbandry.*
> (*thriftiness)

The key to happiness with family economic transactions lies in knowing the meaning of the word *loan*. To in-laws with principles, it means that the money is temporary, like The New Kids on the Block or Liz Taylor's latest hubby. In these cases, the money is usually lent with love—and repaid with interest. However, these clear-cut loan situations are about as common as government efficiency or fun diets that work.

More often, a family loan is seen as...

➤ an obligation, as in "you owe me this money because I'm your in-law."

➤ a gift with no strings attached.

➤ a private source of income with a hazy repayment schedule.

➤ a sour situation that recycles like reheated take-out food.

➤ an advance on an inheritance.

Any loan officer worth his Rotary pin would know not to lend money to someone who didn't understand the concept of "loan." But loan officers rarely have to deal with the guilt from wildly different incomes among family members and the responsibility we feel about taking care of our "own."

Some family members make a hobby out of borrowing money from their in-laws that they never intend to repay—unless someone in the family has them fitted for a pair of cement overshoes for a swim with the fishies.

> **Words to the Wise**
> **Loan** 1. the act of lending. 2. something lent or furnished on condition of being returned, especially a sum of money lent at interest.

Other family members, in contrast, find themselves looking for loans when their situation changes. That's what happened when Lucia split from her hubby Sam. After their divorce, the whole family got on the loan bandwagon. Here's her sister-in-law Dina's feeling about the matter:

> "When Sam dumped Lucia, we were thrilled that we'd all finally be done with the Shop-'til-You-Drop Queen. Sam was fair with the alimony, but it wasn't enough to support Lucia in the style in which she wanted to become accustomed. How to bridge the gap between desire and reality? She began to borrow from all us. No in-law was left unturned.

> First she put the touch on her sister-in-law and brother. Then came her brothers-in-law. A few cousins chipped in; finally, she even hit up her former in-laws. At this point, no one's speaking to her. I know we'll never see a penny of the money we've 'lent' her. It's time she grew up and got with the program. The family 'bank' is closed."

> **Don't Go There**
> Having to ask a family member for a loan can be as embarrassing as putting on that Speedo after a holiday pig-out. But it's trickier when a loan is dangled before you in time of need, perhaps even unsolicited. If you rise to the bait, be aware that the repayment schedule may be binding and have some clauses you never bargained for.

You can save a lot of pain by making a family loan a real business transaction by drawing up a legally binding agreement. Don't be shy about having a lawyer help with the papers and having the final document signed as well as notarized. You may also want to have an impartial third-party act as a buffer. Yes, loan contracts are cold and impersonal, but isn't that preferable to a fiery family feud? Why not forestall problems before they arise?

Pass the Bucks

What about outright cash gifts? You know what I mean by the word "gifts"...money given with no strings attached. And if you believe that gifts come without obligations, boy, do I have some swamp land in Florida for you. Where in-laws are involved, it's rare that there are no strings attached. That's just plain old human nature, as Jon's experience reveals:

Family Matters

In-laws raised during the Great Depression may have an especially hard time forking over cash to their kith and kin, because they often fear for their own financial future—no matter how much money they have. They've seen it all vanish once and realize that it can all vanish again.

"My mother-in-law invested $25,000 in each of her kids' names, earmarking the money for down payments on their homes. That's all well and good, but she expects to be repaid for it by owning us. If we tried to give her the money, she'd be insulted. Instead, she wants to hold her 'gift' over our heads. She likes to feel needed, but I feel used. I'm sorry that we had to use her money to buy our house."

So-called "primitive" societies have the complex gift-giving situation clearly spelled out. Among these groups, there are three parts to the transaction: Giving, receiving, and repaying. No doubt where *they* stand on the issue. Unfortunately, our gift-giving rituals are about as clear as mud.

People give gifts for many reasons, depending on the person and the occasion. We give gifts to...

➤ show that we care.

➤ impress.

➤ atone for a guilty conscience.

➤ bribe someone.

➤ discharge an obligation.

➤ make us feel good.

It's All Relative

In the Japanese culture, the obligation of repayment is spelled out in the concept of *giri*. When you receive a gift, you must repay it or do better. Daughters-in-law must treat their mothers-in-law very well in this regard in order to please their own husband and family.

Heidi's parents, for example, give presents naturally to show their love. Her in-laws, in contrast, use gifts as a way to buy affection. Here's what she told me:

> "Even thought their intentions are good, my in-laws still use money as a way to bridge the gap between people. It's always bothered me that their gifts have an invisible price tag. It's like they're saying, 'Look at us. We're so generous. You have to love us.'"

It's Better to Give Than to Receive?

Further, recipients have an equally mixed reaction to being on the receiving end of someone's largess. Some people feel grateful, while others consider the gift no less than what they're due. We may feel embarrassed by someone's generosity or resentful that they've forced us into reciprocating. Here's what Pete told me about gift-giving among his in-laws:

> "When my side of the family gives us presents, I feel that they want to show their love or help us out. But when my in-laws give us something—especially money—it shows that we're not ready to stand on our own two feet. It's quasi-charity, not a true gift. I know I can never match their gift, so I always feel embarrassed."

Pride and loyalty also get tossed into the mix. This puts great stress on in-law relationships. Not surprisingly, in-laws who dole out big bucks are often more popular in the family than in-laws who may not be as free with their money or have as much to disperse. It's difficult for even the most resolute person to turn down an all-expense-paid vacation, a new car, or a down payment for a house.

Whether it's better to give or to receive depends on who's giving and getting what. In either case, you can't go wrong with these basic guidelines:

1. Give items that you think your in-laws would like, might need, or would find useful.

2. Don't be afraid to ask someone what they want—but be prepared to ante up if the answer is something major like a set of his-and-hers garage door openers.

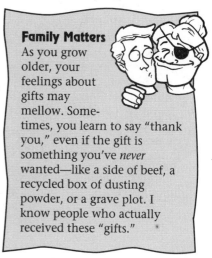

Family Matters

What happens if your kids won't write thank-you notes? You lock them in their rooms, but then they'd just play with their Pentium Pros, whiz-bang color printers, and $4 million video game systems. Instead, don't let them use the item until they have written the note. If that fails, you can always humiliate them in front of their friends.

Family Matters

As you grow older, your feelings about gifts may mellow. Sometimes, you learn to say "thank you," even if the gift is something you've *never* wanted—like a side of beef, a recycled box of dusting powder, or a grave plot. I know people who actually received these "gifts."

3. Don't give anything that presents a burden. Nix on adorable bunnies at Easter or the tickets to a Motley Crue concert in Sweden. My mother once gave me a bowl of goldfish. Although she said it was "for the children," I'm sure she was getting back at me for something I did in the seventies.

4. A gift doesn't always have to be something material. Some of the best gifts I've ever gotten were gifts of time—baby-sitting or a home-cooked dinner are hits here. (But I wouldn't turn down a large, gaudy diamond or an even larger, gaudier sports car.)

5. If you get a gift, be sure to say thanks. At the very least, it tells the generous in-law that you actually received the gift. At the most, it shows your appreciation.

In most cases, if you're contemplating whether to give an in-law a gift or a loan of money, you're better off with the gift. Unless you are willing to make the issue a legal matter by having a contract drawn up, giving a gift can save a lot of hard feelings. That way, no one expects the money to be repaid.

String of Steel

Do you know what "dating" is? Dating means doing a lot of fun things that you'll never do again if you get married. The fun stops with marriage because you're trying to save money for when you split up your property.

With the divorce rate at 50 percent, many in-laws are leery of giving cash gifts to their children and their spouses. Some even insist that the engaged couple sign a premarital agreement to keep money or valuable heirlooms in the family in case of a divorce.

Words to the Wise

A *prenuptial agreement* clearly documents what each couple is bringing to the marriage as well as the division of assets if the marriage dissolves. Although prenuptial agreements are legal documents, they are not entirely ironclad. A significant number of prenups have been overturned in court.

You've learned that financial disagreements are one of the biggest causes of marital mayhem and in-law antagonism. Some of these problems can be avoided if you and your honey are secure enough to draft and process a *prenuptial agreement*. Some people feel that prenups are a sign of impending doom, right up there with Olestra; others, in contrast, believe these legal documents show greater trust.

Because marriage is a legal as well as romantic relationship, the bottom line must be considered. I strongly recommend prenups when the distribution of wealth within a marriage is very unequal. This can occur when one partner brings a great deal of money or other valuables to the marriage or the other partner expects to inherit or earn a bundle.

The Least You Need to Know

➤ You can't always trust your in-laws to do the right thing where money is concerned.

➤ Greed can dissolve even the strongest bonds among in-laws.

➤ Identify the real issue behind money squabbles.

➤ Make loans to in-laws into formal business transactions by drawing up legally binding agreements.

➤ A gift doesn't always have to be something material. Time can be the best gift of all.

➤ Consider a prenuptial agreement if you are marrying someone with much more or much less money than you have.

Chapter 17

Taking Care of Business

In This Chapter

➤ Get the facts on family businesses

➤ Decide if you want to join the in-laws in the family firm

➤ Learn how struggles over money, power, and sibling rivalry can rip apart family businesses

➤ See that battles over succession are no picnic, either

A man found a strange, old bottle on a beach in Los Angeles. He popped the cork and a genie burst out. The genie shouted, "I am so grateful to get out of that bottle that I will grant you any one wish."

The man answered, "I have always wanted to go to Hawaii, but I've never been able to go because I won't fly. Boats are out, too, because the ocean makes me feel claustrophobic. So I wish for a road to be built from here to Hawaii."

The genie replied, "No, I don't think I can do that. Just think of all the work involved. Consider all the piling needed to hold up a highway and how deep they would have to go to reach the bottom of the ocean. Imagine all the pavement needed. No, that is just too much to ask."

The man said, "Okay, there's one other thing I have always wanted. I would like to be able to get along with my in-laws in our family business."

The genie considered for a few minutes and said, "So, do you want two lanes or four?"

From a pain-and-suffering point of view, in-laws can't be beat. Throw in a family business and you have a true recipe for disaster. But it doesn't have to be that way.

Most issues that relate to families also relate to family-owned businesses. Unfortunately, when problems in the workplace involve the family relationships of the key players, standard business advice has limited value. That's why in this chapter I'm going to give you advice specifically tailored to the issue of dealing with your in-laws and the family business.

Mind Your Own Business

Did you know that...

➤ about 90 percent of U.S. businesses are family-owned.

➤ family businesses account for 40 percent of the country's gross national product.

➤ family businesses create one-half of the jobs in the country.

➤ More than 150 firms in the legendary Fortune 500 are family-owned or family-controlled.

Words to the Wise
Family-owned businesses are defined as those in which family members have majority ownership, and at least two family members work in the company.

That's a lot of in-laws working together. Remember what you've learned so far about such heated in-law issues as rivalry, jealousy, power plays, money issues, role expectations, and unresolved conflict? In addition to making your Thanksgiving a real turkey, these factors can affect the success of your family business—and whether you go to work each day with a grin or a grimace.

Realizing this, I'll bet you're not shocked to learn that fewer than 39 percent of family-owned businesses make it to the second generation, and only 15 percent make it to the third. Hmmm…how much you want to bet this is because a family business can be more incendiary than Cruella De Vil on a bender?

It's All Relative

Sixth- or seventh-generation family businesses like Levi Strauss and the Rothschild banks are quite rare. The biggest family-managed business today, Italy's Fiat, is run by the third-generation of Agnellis, now in their sixties and seventies. Few people in the company expect it to be family managed 20 years hence.

Why is it so difficult for family businesses to endure? One reason is that old bugaboo, family conflict. The fault lines that you see between in-laws repeat in their family-run business. The business can survive a schism between generations one and two, but the pattern repeats and the business doesn't make it to generation three.

After all, at the end of a difficult work day, many people can go home and tell a sympathetic family member all about it. But what if the people you work with are your in-laws, and problems on the job are partly (or mainly) due to them? Here are some of the most common dilemmas that can arise when in-laws work together. Put a check mark next to each problem that you've experienced as a member of a family business:

____ **1.** You can't decide if you even want to become a member of the family firm—and the pressure feels like a 200-pound monkey on your back.

____ **2.** Your brother-in-law, Mr. Golden Boy, is a lazy slug. Since he can't make it to the office during any month than contains an "R," the company suffers.

____ **3.** You work harder than your sister-in-law—but she makes more money than you do because she's the boss's daughter and you're only the daughter-in- law.

____ **4.** Family members can't agree how the company should be run. As a result, no one's at the helm. Mayday!

____ **5.** You don't get promoted because dad always loved your brother-in-law more.

____ **6.** There are no rules for family members, so you feel like your job is as steady as Jell-O.

____ **7.** You can't let off steam about the boss because she's also your mother-in-law— and she makes a helluva apple pie.

____ **8.** Your father-in-law, the CEO, refuses to retire, even though the company's getting as stale as reruns of *Gilligan's Island*.

____ **9.** You're afraid that your father-in-law is going to leave the business to another in-law...and you'll be left out in the cold.

____**10.** Your in-laws have you by the cojones (pardon the expression).

It's All Relative

There are 42,000 family businesses in the United States alone, with revenues over $25 million. The cumulative effect of family business is equivalent to an economy larger than any in the world except the U.S. or Japan. As these numbers show, family businesses are big business indeed!

As you can see, being part of a family business can create quite a few problems. By the end of a typical day working with your in-laws, you're apt to feel like you've walked through a metal detector once too often. Not to worry; help is on the way! Read on.

To Join or Not to Join?

Mother: "Jen, we've given this lots of thought, and your Dad and I are really hoping that you'll join your brother, sister-in-law, and us in the family business after you graduate in May."

Dad: (jumping for joy) "This is one of my greatest dreams come true! And I'm sure you're as excited as I was when I joined my parents in the family business. So, what do you say, Jen?"

Jen: (stalling for time) "Well, I'm not surprised. I did work in the business during summers and school vacations just like my brother and his wife did, and now my college graduation is only a few months away. I, uh, guess it makes sense. It's sort of what I always expected, too. It's just that I've got, well, some concerns, and I guess I'd like to think about it some more…"

Family Matters
If you're thinking about joining the family business, first clarify any unstated expectations with other family members to avoid ambiguity and bizarro assumptions. This will help establish clear roles and responsibilities from the very beginning.

Why does Jen want to think further before she agrees to join the family business? Because she's smart, that's why. Jen realizes that becoming part of a family business can be a double-edged sword. Before *you* decide to join your in-laws in work as well as in play, you need time to assess your own skills, examine your career and personal goals, consider your relationships with your in-laws, and explore other options.

Be sure to lobby for a competitive salary, one that would be paid to a non-family employee performing a similar job. Obviously, your in-laws would be cheating you if they underpaid you, but overpaying can be even worse. If you're paid more than non-family members, you're getting into bondage—the golden handcuff variety. The inflated salary can easily tie you to a job you might neither like nor be suited for, but you can't afford to leave. Your big bucks can also raise the hackles among non-family members in the company.

The following questions can help you decide whether or not you're cut out for mixing business and family.

1. Are you strong enough to make decisions based on what's best for the business rather than what's best for the family? To keep the family business alive, you have to do what is best for the business.

2. Do you think the CEO—Dad, Mom, or another relative—has the necessary commitment to maintain long-term profitability?

3. Can you be in the family business and still be your own person?

4. Is there accountability in the business?

5. Is generating money in the family business the only reason the family stays together?

> **Family Matters**
> If you've decided to join your in-law's family business, you might want to spend a few years working elsewhere first. This gives you the chance to gain some experience in a more objective setting, earn some promotions, and report to different bosses. Then you'll bring greater knowledge, experience, and achievement into the family firm.

Blood Is Thicker Than Water

Eavesdrop on the conversation between Jeffrey and his father Sid to see what's going wrong in their business. I'll give you a hint: It concerns an in-law.

Jeffrey: "Okay, Dad, so he's your brother-in-law. But does that mean we have to put up with inferior work and an erratic schedule that we would never tolerate from anyone else in the business? Besides, he's way overpaid for what he's doing. You know we could hire two people, both more productive, for what he's making."

Sid: "Look, Jeffrey, Harry is my brother-in-law. There's really nothing more to discuss."

Jeffrey: "I'm trying to help this company and Harry is the biggest obstacle to progress. Dad, you won't confront him and it's driving me crazy. I'm working my tail off and don't earn anywhere near what he gets. He's becoming a drain on the business. So what do we do? Accept shoddy performance from him and carry him for life just because he's your brother-in-law?

> **Don't Go There**
> When a family business is undergoing stress because of in-law problems or outside issues, business relationships *and* personal ties among relatives are at stake. For example, if you have an argument in the office on the third Wednesday in November, you still have to sit down with your opponent the next day over Thanksgiving dinner.

Sid: "I know you take your job seriously and I can see how my brother-in-law can make it difficult, but I thought I raised you with some values and respect for family. What's the big deal? Harry was there for me when I needed him. That's what being a brother-in-law is all about. How can I get you to understand this?"

How can we help earnest Jeff, sweet Sid, and that toad Harry achieve harmony with each other, their in-laws, and the cosmos? We can start by laying down the rules. Yes, family is family, but business is also business. To make beautiful music together, we have to get them in tune. The best way is to get some guidelines in place.

It's All Relative

Be a CEO and lose weight! Here's how:

Exercise	Calories Used
Passing the Buck	25
Pouring Salt on the Wound	50
Swallowing Your Pride	50
Beating Around the Bush	75
Grasping at Straws	75
Bending Over Backward	75
Jumping to Conclusions	100
Beating Your Own Drum	100
Jogging Your Memory	125
Climbing the Walls	150
Adding Fuel to the Fire	150

Sanity Rules

Relatives working in a family business can prevent resentment, rancor, and ruin by setting down a series of rules—and then following them. Here are five key rules to ensure that your family business operates as smoothly as possible. (By the way; it may not be too late to set these rules into motion, even if the business is already long established.)

196

The Rules:

1. Have set rules for hiring all employees—especially in-laws.

2. Make sure everyone knows the rules. The rules are not intended to be family secrets, like Uncle Joe's Kathie Lee-and-Frank moment, your mother-in-law's tendency to nip at the cooking sherry, or your brother-in-law's thing about ladies' underwear.

3. Apply the rules as fairly as possible to every in-law. (Let's not kid ourselves; in-laws are usually going to be treated differently from the hoi polloi. And "differently" better mean "better" or you'll be hearing from Aunt Edna in the morning.)

4. There must be a way to adjust the rules to deal with changing business situations—like a decision to stop manufacturing slide rules, black-and-white TVs, or Edsels.

5. Everyone must be notified if the rules change. (See rule #2.)

Family Matters
The rules set forth for the family business depend on the family's philosophy, mission, size, industry, and resources available. Those guidelines must be consistent with the family's values.

What factors should you consider when you write the rules? Here are some of the most important ones:

➤ When and under what circumstances can in-laws enter the business?

➤ What experience and education are required?

➤ Will they fill a vacant position or can a position be created for them?

➤ Do they need to be a certain age to be employed in the business?

➤ Do they need to retire at a certain age?

Don't Go There
In-laws may act too tough on each other so as to not show favoritism or act too wussy because of the relationship, especially during trainee time. QED: Try not to have in-laws train in-laws.

➤ Is re-entry possible after a voluntary or involuntary exit? (Due to childrearing, attendance at graduate school, jail time, liposuction, argument with family members, etc.)

➤ Is part-time work permitted?

The Rules, Part II

The first five rules cover the basics: Hiring practices and fairness. Now, let's kick it up a notch by setting forth some guidelines for employment qualifications, staffing key positions, hiring non-family members, and communication. Here are five more rules that cover these issues.

6. In-laws working in the business must be at least as able and hard-working as any unrelated employee. This is a toughie, kids, nepotism being what it is, but starting with qualified people goes a long way to prevent problems down the line.

It's All Relative

DuPont, controlled and managed by family members from its founding in 1802 until professional management took over in the mid-seventies, grew into the world's largest chemical company. It prospered as a family business in part because it faced up to the in-law quality issue. All male duPonts were entitled to an entry-level job in the company, but their performance was carefully reviewed by senior family members. If this review concluded that the young family member was not likely to be top management material 10 years later, he was eased out.

7. Family-managed businesses, except perhaps for the smallest ones, increasingly need to staff key positions with non-family professionals. The demands for knowledge and expertise—whether in manufacturing, marketing, finance, research, or human resource management—can rarely be satisfied by family members alone.

Don't Go There

In a family-managed company, relatives are always "top management," whatever their official job or title. Remember, on Saturday evenings they're the ones schmoozing around the boss's dinner table.

8. No matter how many family members are in the company's management and how effective they are, one top job must be filled by a non-relative. Typically, this is either the financial executive or the head of research—the two positions in which technical qualifications are most important.

9. Be sure to make time away from the business. Everyone needs a break from the grind—especially in-laws who work, live, and socialize together.

10. Try for open communications. Tricky for kinfolk, but key for business success.

None of Your Business?

Succession is another troublesome issue for in-laws and their family business. That canny CEO Queen Elizabeth I solved the problem by deciding *not* to retire—but then again, she had the ultimate in job security. Difficulty deciding when to retire or not is a surprisingly common situation for the CEOs who rule by blood lines, whether they're royal or not.

It's All Relative

The Windsors' role in governing the British Empire is ceremonial, but they take it very seriously nonetheless. The ne plus ultra of in-laws as out-laws, they refer to their task as monarchs as carrying out "the family business." You think it's tough working for your in-laws? Try it if your boss is the queen!

I don't know what excuses today's Queen Elizabeth gives her son Charles, but I do know the Top 10 reasons that CEOs of family business often give for not turning the reigns of their companies over to their in-laws. And here they are, in reverse order:

10. "Too many people I've known have died soon after they retired (or acted like they were dead)."

9. "Without me, the business is nothing."

8. "Without the business, I'm nothing."

7. "I hate gardening, find cruises boring, and get sunburned if I play too much golf."

6. "I need someplace to go. My spouse married me for better or for worse—but not for lunch!"

5. "My in-laws want to change the way the business is run. If I'm not there, they will destroy what I've built!"

4. "I don't want to choose between my in-laws to name a successor."

3. "The business is my major source of income. My in-laws will run it to the ground."

2. "Nobody can run the business as well as I can."

1. "They may run it better than I did!"

And your ammunition for the response volley...

10. There's no correlation between mortality and retirement. (Though if you outstay your welcome in the business, there's no saying that an overly ambitious in-law won't cosh you a good one with a nine-iron.)

9. Hey, kid, can we rein in that ego? What are you—a legend in your own mind?

8. Retirement doesn't have to be an "all or nothing" proposition. There are many constructive ways you can maintain your identity and connection

Don't Go There
Members of a family businesses often take them-selves quite seriously. In part, that's because there's often constant job and family pressure. In family business, there's no let-up, no disengagement. Even though that's the nature of the beast, you *can* build in some pressure valves—and you *must*.

with the business. Why not spend time with your successors and trusted advisors investigating all the possibilities? (That should kill at least a year.)

Family Matters

As you learned in Chapter 16, money issues can be more delicate than a man's ego. To solve $$$ issues, it may be necessary to use experts to facilitate the dialogue in the beginning, or at points along the way.

Family Matters

While there's no link between early death and retirement, you can probably ensure a longer, healthier retirement if you develop interests outside the business. Women, consider golf, bridge, or visiting the Chippendales on a regular basis, for example.

7. So find other leisure activities that excite you. Do those things you've always wanted to do, but for which you never had the time.

6. True fact, boss. There is no denying that major life changes can stress any relationship. Get a new focus on your life, one that keeps you out of your spouse's face.

5. If the business doesn't change to keep up with new demands, it will suffer. Businesses thrive on fresh ideas and energy. Do you really mean to tell me that you didn't make any changes when *you* became the head honcho?

4. So let them duke it out after you're gone. Better yet, involve them in the decision now.

3. You ran a business and you don't know how to invest your money? Pleeze. This excuse is lame.

2. No one is indispensable; we can all be replaced. (Okay, maybe not Cindy Crawford and Brad Pitt, but even Rin Tin Tin lost his slot to a puppy.) Besides, you're probably not the only one running your business now. You may make major decisions, but chances are, you're not involved in all the details.

1. And what's wrong with that? Complete succession planning will help your business thrive under the next generation. This is one of the most important legacies you can create for your family.

Retiring Heroes

Not all CEOs of family businesses are as determined to die on the throne, however. Just when you thought it was safe to go back into the corporate in-law waters comes the cautionary tale of Legal Seafoods, a popular Boston-area chain of fish stores, restaurants, a processing center, and a frozen line. George Berkowitz started his business from nothing and built it into a major enterprise. But who would succeed him? Berkowitz had three sons, and the two oldest both wanted to run the family firm.

In some families, the brothers could have figured it out. But although Mark and Roger Berkowitz worked together in the firm for 17 years, their relationship had never been smooth. Even as kids they'd been rivals. Neither brother wanted to share power.

George Berkowitz chose his oldest son, Roger. Mark walked out, bitterly, severing ties with his father and brother—and separating his own children from their grandparents. Later, Mark Berkowitz opened a competing operation directly across the street from a Legal Seafoods.

George Berkowitz believes that spouses are important influences in such a situation, and that he made a serious mistake in not letting his sons' wives know exactly where they stood. "If you don't inform everybody of where you are, you don't know where you're going to be. In-laws should be informed that this is a family business and that's the way it's going to be. Maybe if the women or men who married into the business thought about how their actions will make the business blow up, maybe they would think differently about how to make decisions," he said. He cautions executives not to step in as an intermediary in family feuds that don't directly affect the business.

"It would have made it much easier if someone outside who had the ability to choose had made the choice. But the hurt would have been there. Mark would have felt that it was a biased opinion," George argues. And outsiders, he cautions, must recognize that the family is a unit beyond the business. "The dynamics are different. When we have a fight, it doesn't mean it's the end of the world. But we always come back. It's not dysfunctional—it's family business."

> **Family Matters**
> In many family businesses, the issue of succession—selection of the person or persons who will be in charge after the parent or founder is gone—exacerbates long-standing sibling tensions. Too often, this issue is never discussed, either because it seems impossible to resolve or, at a minimum, requires difficult and painful decision-making.

Aspiring Heroes

Just as family businesses need "rules of entry," so do they need "rules of exit." These are ideally planned before anyone is near retirement age so that discussions are not taken personally, but looked on as guidelines for the company. Here are some questions to consider:

> ➤ Is there to be a mandatory retirement age?
>
> ➤ What about a retirement compensation package?
>
> ➤ Should there be some consulting arrangement?
>
> ➤ What about plans for ownership transfer?
>
> ➤ Can this be done gradually over a period of a few years, rather than all at once?

> **Don't Go There**
> Heir issues can also become gender issues. Daughters, once relegated to hearth and home, now expect to receive a piece of the pie—not serve it.

Roots and Wings

One payday, when a young man came in to pick up his check, he was sent instead to meet with his father-in-law at the elder executive's country home. The father-in-law was wearing a reversible hat, the facing side sporting a button that said, "Boss." Wearing the hat, the father informed his son-in-law that he was fired—then reached up and turned the hat around to reveal another button that said, "Dad." He put his arm around his son-in-law and said, "I hear you just lost your job. Is there anything I can do to help?"

What's the best gift we can give our kids? It's roots and wings (though I probably wouldn't turn down a week in Montego Bay, a Mercedes, or a mink). This saying is a cliché for good reason: It's stood the test of time. Especially in a family business, it's vital to know when to hold on—and when to let go. We all have to grapple with the same issues as we get ready to leave the nest: Independence, maturity, work ethic, control over our finances, the right to make our own decisions (including our own mistakes). Sometimes giving our in-laws some freedom (those wings) lets them spread their wings and soar.

Mom Always Loved You Better

Len: "You know, Mom, Harriet is really unfair. She gives me the worst jobs possible. She says I'm sloppy and criticizes me in public. She makes me look bad in front of everyone else."

Mom: "I don't know what to tell you, Len. She's your sister-in-law. You've got to talk with her about it. I can't keep interfering in your behalf. This is how you used to act with your sisters and brothers where you were a child."

Len: "But she doesn't listen to me when I talk to her. She just mocks me and nothing seems to change. She treats me like I'm a child."

What's going on?

Whatever the issues between Len and Harriet, in Len's opinion, his sister-in-law is assigning him undesirable jobs, is overly critical, and embarrasses him in front of others. When confronted, Harriet seems to be unresponsive. Len sees himself as a helpless victim. His frustration and pain are significant and he sees his mother as his only refuge. Len places himself at Mom's mercy.

Meanwhile, Mom is trying to separate family and business and break childhood patterns by directing Len to communicate with his sister-in-law. But the past is too powerful for Len. He has counted on Mom to straighten things out before and is now disappointed at her unwillingness to do so.

Mom is in a squeeze. She recognizes that the caliber of Len's work is less than satisfactory, so standing up for Len can compromise the company's quality, yet if she doesn't support Len, she disappoints her son at a time when he seeks her support.

What to do? Try these ideas:

1. Len must realize that no matter how unjust he believes his sister-in-law is, mommy is no longer the court of last resort. He must confront his sister-in-law directly, or be prepared to tolerate the current situation.

2. Likewise, if Harriet has something to say about her brother-in-law, she should say it straight to him. To undermine her in-law to other employees is to destroy both her brother-in-law's credibility and his own standing as a manager.

3. Harriet must try to respect her brother-in-law's concerns and be willing to listen with an open mind.

4. In the absence of a more formal performance appraisal process, she can also make it clear to Len that certain standards of quality are expected and must be achieved for the sake of the business.

5. These in-laws should seriously assess the advisability of their current reporting relationship. Whenever possible, in-laws should not report to in-laws.

Family Matters
Mothers in a family business are typically charged with the role of "CEO"—chief emotional officer. This carries a special burden as well as an opportunity. Mothers are frequently counted on as the ones to achieve a sense of balance and fairness. They need to be on the lookout for childhood patterns of behavior and separate family and business issues.

The Least You Need to Know

➤ About 90 percent of U.S. businesses are family-owned. Most are affected by family conflicts along the line.

➤ Think long and hard before deciding to join the family business. If you do join, get a competitive salary.

➤ Once you're a member of the inner circle, have set rules for hiring all employees—especially in-laws—and apply them fairly across the board.

➤ Be sure to make time to get away from the business.

➤ Try for open communication.

➤ Have clear lines of succession.

➤ Give your children and in-laws roots to grow and wings to fly.

Part 4
And Baby Makes Power Play

Some questions are easy to answer. Here are the answers to life's most important questions. The only things missing are the questions...

1. *Trust me. I do this all the time.*

2. *No.*

3. *NO!*

4. *Unleaded.*

5. *If I had three pennies, I would have given them to you.*

6. *Forty-two, maybe fifty.*

7. *I was absent that day.*

8. *You'll break your mother's heart.*

9. *When hell freezes over.*

10. *Because the world would be a lot better off if things were done my way all the time.*

11. *I mailed it yesterday. It should be there by the end of the week.*

12. *No, honestly. I can't taste the freezer burn.*

Unfortunately, odds are that your in-laws aren't losing sleep about freezer burn, U.S. postage, or disinfectants. They are, however, probably obsessing about your sex life, reproductive plans, and child-rearing practices. In this section, I give you the answers and the questions so you'll be armed for these assaults.

Sexpectations

There once was a farmer who was raising three daughters on his own. He was very concerned about their well-being and always did his best to watch out for them.

As they entered their late teens, the girls began to date. One night, all three of his girls went out on dates for the first time. The farmer greeted each suitor at the door holding his shotgun, to make sure that the young men knew who was boss.

The doorbell rang and the first of the boys arrived. The farmer answered the door and the lad said,

"Hi, my name's Joe,
I'm here to see Flo.
We're going to the show.
Is she ready to go?"

The farmer looked him over and sent the kids on their way.

The next lad arrived and said,

"My name's Eddie.
I'm here to see Betty.
We're gonna get some spaghetti.
Do you know if she's ready?"

The farmer felt this one was okay too, so off the two kids went.

The final young man arrived and the farmer opened the door. The boy began,

"Hi, my name's Chuck..."

and the farmer shot him.

Some issues are loaded...and then some issues are *explosive*. The issue of s-e-x is as explosive as they come, especially when applied to family situations. In this chapter, you'll discover how people react to their children's maturity and growing sexuality. Then I'll teach you strategies for dealing with exhibitionists, those in-laws who show us more than we really care to see. You'll learn techniques for coping with vastly different attitudes toward sexuality among in-laws, too. Finally, I'll help you deal with the issue of cohabitation, so you can adjust to different standards of behavior.

The Naughty Bits

Don't Go There
In his book *100% American*, Daniel Evan Weiss notes that 47 percent of American men enjoy sex more than money. Amazing. I'll bet you're shocked.

Don't Go There
On average, people around the world first engage in intercourse at 17.6 years of age. Americans, in contrast, start earlier, at 16.2 years of age.

Sex. Just say the word and people sit up a little straighter and start paying attention. Sex sells everything from soap to snack foods, cars to cappuccino. Let us not forget the obvious links between alcohol, cigarettes, perfume, and sex—virtually every consumer good is sold through sex appeal. I'm sure that right now some overpaid suit on Madison Avenue is working on a way to sell cat food with sex. A sexy cat? Does Morris the Cat count?

Movies and TV shows are rife with sexual innuendoes. There's even a laugh track to make sure we don't miss the juicy parts. The rating system, designed to help adults screen their children's viewing habits, ironically makes it easier for kids to find the ribald shows—even if they don't get the jokes yet.

Increasingly, however, they *do* get the jokes—and at a younger and younger age. You'd think this would make it easier for parents to accept their children's sexuality, but paradoxically it can often have just the opposite effect. The nagging little issue that bothered us when the children were teens can become a screaming big issue when they mature. Frequently, the in-laws get swept up into the fracas. Sometimes, the in-laws can even be the cause of the turmoil. Read on to find out how.

Not With My Baby Girl You Don't!

Even though our society is permeated with sex, it can be very difficult for parents and in-laws to accept that their 30-year-old baby boy is "doing it" with his wife. It's no easier to contemplate their 30-year-old daughter having intimate relations with her hubby. Why do we find our adult children's sexuality so hard to accept? Primarily, our children's sexual actions…

Family Matters
In Kentucky, 50 percent of the people who get married for the first time are teenagers.

➤ underscore our own mortality. If the kids are sexually active, then we must be old. *Really* old.

➤ call our own values into question.

➤ cause us worry. Will they be happy? Have they made the right choices?

As a result, many of us have a tough time making the transition from parents to parents-in-law (not to mention grandparents, the subject of Chapter 20). My friend Marci had the following story to share about her experiences on this front:

> "I thought my parents and in-laws would be thrilled when Ken and I finally decided to have a child. We'd been married for three years when I became pregnant. When Ken and I announced our happy news, my in-laws seemed uneasy. An awkward silence settled over the room. It took several minutes before anyone congratulated us. Since Ken and I are both responsible, mature, and settled, I knew they weren't worried that we'd be bad parents. They just couldn't seem to believe that we would really be having a child. My mother-in-law kept saying, "'My baby is going to be a father? My baby is going to be a father?'"

You spend years telling those hulking, surly teenage boys to keep their filthy hands off your pristine daughter. You caution her about getting "in trouble," "knocked up," or "in the family way." Suddenly, your daughter marries one of those lumbering, sullen boys and you realize that he's really a shy, gentle young man. And now he's allowed to put his hands all over your daughter.

Don't Go There
The first known contraceptive was crocodile dung, used by Egyptians in 2000 B.C.

It works the other way, too. How many years did you spend furious at the bold hussies who called your innocent son at all hours of the day and night? They were shameless Jezebels. Suddenly, your son has plighted his troth and the strumpet is revealed as a sweetie pie. And now she's *supposed* to touch him all over his body. No wonder everyone's in an uproar.

Red Hot Mama

So far we've just been talking about the everyday Joe loves Jane stuff. What happens if one of your in-laws is a Yoo Hoo with a little extra Hoo? Hot mamas are great for getting laughs on *Married With Children* and at corporate holiday parties, but they're not quite as funny when they're *your* in-laws. Here's what Jeanette said about her sister-in-law Margot:

"My brother's wife Margot is like a cat in heat. She acts like a hooker on the prowl with any male members of the family—and my husband doesn't even seem to notice. She wears very short, tight clothes and high heels, even to family picnics. Even though she's been married for three years, nothing's changed. She puts her hands all over my husband and my other brother—even my father! When I pointed it out to my brother, he said, 'Oh, Margot's just affectionate, that's all. What's the big deal?' I'd think it was just me but my mother and other sister-in-law have the same reaction to Margot's brazen behavior. She presses herself up against the men, sits on their laps, and even pats them on their rear ends. It's way over the top. I really want to tell her off, but I don't want to alienate my brother. I love him, but I don't know how much more I can take of his wife's shameless behavior."

It's All Relative

The condom—made originally of linen—was invented in the early 1500s. Today's condoms are far more likely to be made of latex than fabric, but no matter what material it's made from, the condom has proven a useful little device.

What can you do if this situation is going on in your extended family? Here are some ideas:

Don't Go There
Under no circumstances gather all the sisters-in-law together as a mob with scarlet "A" and needle in hand. There may be strength in numbers, but ganging up on an in-law rarely accomplishes the desired aim of family harmony.

➤ Talk to your sister-in-law yourself. Explain that her actions make you feel uncomfortable, especially if children are present. Try not to be judgmental, but don't be afraid of making your case.

➤ Ask someone else in the family to intervene. Select someone she's more likely to respect, such as her mother or father.

➤ If all else fails, speak to her spouse.

➤ Don't be subtle. Because this woman is about as delicate as a smack upside the head, she's not likely to get it unless you paint in bold strokes.

Perhaps Catwoman thought she was acting appropriately; perhaps she just didn't give a hoot. Perhaps Jeanette was overreacting; perhaps she was right on the money.

What causes these differences in perception of sexual matters? In large part, they come from the way we were raised.

Blame It on the Bossa Nova

How did your parents explain the "birds and the bees" to you? Mine solved it the common way—by neatly and completely sidestepping the entire issue. I believe my mother said something along the lines of, "Be careful" some time during my teen years, but she could have been referring to my driving or cooking. Both required great diligence on my part.

Despite the sexual revolution of the 1960s (more on that in Chapter 20), our level of comfort in discussing sexual issues is most often based on our experiences as children. If your parents, relatives, and siblings were open about sexual matters, chances are you will be too. But if everyone in your family stayed buttoned up, odds are you're not about to babble to everyone about the great time you and your spouse had last night in bed with the whipped cream.

Not only do parents pass on factual information about the interaction of Tab A and Slot B, they also pass on their attitudes toward sex, their value system, and sexual beliefs. Here are some issues about sex that your family conveyed to you, either consciously or unconsciously:

➤ What is good and what is bad about sex?

➤ What is appropriate and what is inappropriate sexual behavior?

➤ What is acceptable and what is piggy?

➤ What is abnormal and downright weird?

It's All Relative

Here are some useful Latin sexual phrases for the nineties:

➤ "Erectionus finalum." (Anna Nicole Smith is here, Gramps.)

➤ "Log floggit cum palma folliculus." (If you don't stop it, you'll go blind.)

➤ "Motorolus interruptus." (Hold on, I'm going into a tunnel.)

➤ "Dumbassus! Hottie iste transvestitus!" (Fool! That gorgeous woman is a cross-dresser!)

Thanks for Not Sharing

There are often serious clashes when you marry into a family with a different attitude toward sex. There are other sexual issues that come up within families as well. What happens when your in-laws share more of their sex lives than you want to know, as Geoff's experience illustrates:

"My mother-in-law and father-in-law are very open about their sexual relation-ship—much too open for my taste. My wife and I (and any in-law within earshot) often get the play-by-play color commentary about their amorous adventures of the night before. Even though my in-laws are in their seventies, they have a very active sex life, judging by what they say, at least.

My father-in-law is so open about sex that he even spoke to all his grandchildren about it, even if their parents didn't agree. When each child turned seven or eight, he took it on himself to explain how babies were made. I come from a very conser-vative family, and we never, never talked openly about sex. Part of me admires how comfortable he is with the issue, but part of me is really upset, even shocked at his openness. All my in-laws have taken sides about swinging Gramps and Grandma. This is becoming a real hot issue in the family."

This might seem to be a sexual issue, but once again it's really a boundary issue. In this case, the dividing line is between privacy and secrecy. The words are not the same, any more than Michael Jackson and Diana Ross.

➤ *Privacy* is keeping things to yourself that you do not want to share with others. Privacy involves personal issues such as sex.

➤ *Secrecy*, in contrast, is hiding something. Secrets (if revealed) can often have a traumatic impact on your relationship with your spouse and in-laws. A secret can be destructive because it can interfere with a healthy family relationship.

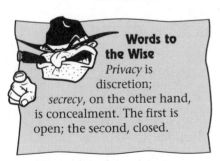

Words to the Wise
Privacy is discretion; *secrecy*, on the other hand, is concealment. The first is open; the second, closed.

Privacy is keeping your business to yourself. *Secrecy* is Watergate, Nannygate, and Marv Albertgate. You want privacy; you don't want secrecy.

In this instance, Geoff and his wife should explain to their in-laws that their views on the issue of sex differ from their in-laws' views. As a result, Geoff and his wife would prefer that their in-laws leave the sexual discussions with the kids to them. They would also prefer to skip the intimate details of their in-laws' romps in the hot tub.

Makin' Whoopie

Mandy was upset at the way her sister-in-law and brother act in public. Even though they are married, Mandy was offended to see them embrace in public. Here's what she said:

"My brother Nick and sister-in-law Tiffany have been married for three years. Nonetheless, they still act like two sappy teenagers: They hug and kiss in public and feel each other up. It is really obscene! I mean, they even rub against each other in public. I want to tell them to rent a room already. What are they trying to prove?"

Sometimes this is a cultural issue. The Japanese people, for example, do not approve of body contact. Touching members of the opposite sex is especially repugnant. As a result, kissing in public is considered extremely offensive.

Even at Japanese weddings, these rules are not relaxed. Actually, they become more strongly observed. There is no hugging, no kissing, no touching on the part of the bride and groom, and certainly not on the part of the wedding guests. Therefore, the Japanese have developed a complex system of bowing to express relationships.

But what if the difference over what's considered proper sexual behavior in public is not motivated by cultural issues? Mandy is on to something here when she says, "What are they trying to prove?" Sometimes our in-laws *are* trying to prove something with their blatant sexual behavior. What's the message? It doesn't take the Universal Translator on the Starship Enterprise to decode this one.

This couple, and others who act the same way, are often trying to show that they're desirable, attractive, and loved. Sometimes they really were wallflowers at the party; other times they just felt that way. Whatever scars their inner child suffered at the junior high holiday dance, they're going to show us now, by golly. They're hot to trot.

What can you do to cool their engines? Try talking to them about how uncomfortable their behavior makes you feel. To make the message sink in, though, be sure to reassure them that they really are all souped up. Yes, you do indeed find them attractive, and you can understand how their mates might find them hard to resist, but you'd feel a lot more comfortable if they would kick it down a notch in public, or at least in front of you.

> **Family Matters**
> Asians from countries other than Japan are equally disapproving when they see American men and women openly displaying affection in public. In their own countries, women are considered sexually licentious if they act this way.

More Than I Need to Know

And then we have in-laws who pursue libido-related hobbies. My friends Margaret's parents have been married for nearly 40 years. For most of that time, they worked together in the family business. Here's what Margaret's husband Juan told me about his in-laws:

"My father-in-law Pete is a very vital, active, and, well, sexy man. Although he's in his 60s, he looks at least 15 years younger—and often acts that way. Pete loves to

213

sail, but my mother-in-law gets seasick very easily. I think the picture on a box of fish sticks would set her off. As a result, she rarely wants to go sailing with her husband. We live on the Florida coast, and my father-in-law goes sailing nearly every weekend. He always brings one or more pretty young women with him on the boat to 'keep me company,' he says.

'Because your mother-in-law won't come along with me,' he told us, 'you can't expect me to be a monk.' Margaret and I don't expect him to be a monk, but we *do* expect him to be discrete about his extra-curricular activities. He actually invites us to go along. It's disgusting to see him carrying on like a teenager with the babe du jour! I'm very tempted to tell my mother-in-law what's going on during these pleasure cruises. After all, my father-in-law is the laughing stock of the whole family for carrying on like an old goat right under our noses. The whole family is up-in-arms about this."

Let's not fool ourselves here: Juan's mother-in-law knows exactly what's happening here. I'll bet my Captain Marvel decoder ring that Juan's mother-in-law has been savvy to her husband's fooling around for decades. She chooses to ignore the issue, and that's her right.

But how can the rest of the family cope with the situation? Here are some suggestions:

➤ Show some tolerance. It's tempting to pass judgment (Lord knows I love to do it), but until you've walked a mile in someone's Nikes, you don't know what's going on in their head. So stay cool. There's a long-term marriage involved here, and you don't want to be the one to force its collapse.

➤ Get some distance. Don't like the situation? Don't put yourself in the middle of it. If Pops is prancing around the catamaran in his Speedo with his a woman young enough to be his grandchild, don't go out on the boat with them. Instead, find a day to schedule a family day on the boat...without Bitsy and her perky twins.

Quasi-In-Law

For centuries, sex and marriage went together like Bogie and Bacall, Tracy and Hepburn, and cookies and milk. For some people, sex was the reason they got married. As George Bernard Shaw said, "Marriage is popular because it allows the maximum temptation with the maximum opportunity."

Not so today. In fact, many people choose to live together before they get married or just live together and dispense with that "married" part. This is fine with some in-laws, but not so fine with others. For many people, cohabitation is an uncomfortable issue. They may consider it embarrassing at best, immoral at worst.

It's not that difficult to ignore the issue when the couple is off on their own, but problems often arise when they come to stay with an in-law who does not approve of them sharing the same hair brush, much less the same bed. Here's what Monique said about her sister-in-law Tonya, who is living with her boyfriend Ed.

> "Ed is Tonya's third live-in boyfriend since college, so you'd think we'd have gotten used to the situation, but we haven't. I really would like Tonya to come and visit, since my kids love their aunt, but they're at very impressionable ages. How can I explain that their aunt is living with a man she's not married to? Should I acknowledge that they're living together and let them share a bedroom, or should I play the hypocrite and put them in separate bedrooms? I know where I stand, but you can't imagine all the trouble this is making in the family. Half my in-laws are on my side, and the other half aren't."

How can we solve this issue? First, remember that your home is your home and you have the right to set the standards that you want. That said, there is usually a way to compromise. Here's how:

➤ As always, start with some communication.

➤ Explain your feelings to the couple and listen to their side of the issue.

➤ Then make a decision based on all the information.

Very often in these cases, you're best off bending a little rather than being as inflexible as two-week old bagel.

Here's a different slant on the same issue, from my friend Gabriella:

> "When Dan and I moved in together, we knew we were very serious about each other. My family, although Italian and Irish Catholics, were fine. They knew I was nuts about the guy and he was definitely aces in their book. His parents freaked, though. 'How can you do this to us? You're

Family Matters

For centuries, sexual relations in marriage also served a practical function; people needed all the resulting offspring as a cheap source of labor.

Family Matters

According to some polls, 85 percent of all married people said "I will" before they said "I do." And more than 50 percent lived together before they married.

Don't Go There

Before you get on your high horse in front of all your in-laws, be sure you have identified the right issue: Is it sexual standards or a power struggle that's at the heart of the quandary? Be sure you're addressing—and solving—the right problem, not its evil twin.

embarrassing us! Move back home!' they screamed. For the whole first month we lived together his mother and I would have this funny little conversation when she'd call the apartment:

Me: Hello?

Mama: Gabriella?

Me: Yes. How are you, Mrs. Liotta?

Mama: What are you doing there?

Me: I live here, Mrs. Liotta, Remember?

Mama: (Gasp followed by silence.) Let me talk to my son!

If I didn't have a sense of humor, it would've been horrible. But we were entirely serious and very willing to respect their wishes (i.e., not sleeping together when we'd sleep over, and so on). However, out of sheer tradition, they couldn't accept the "arrangement" for a long, long time even though we always got along very, very well."

The moral of the story? A little respect goes a long way to establish good relations with your in-laws, especially when it comes to touchy issues like S-E-X.

The Least You Need to Know

➤ Few issues upset the family apple-cart as much as sex.

➤ Some people have a difficult time making the move from parents to parents-in-law because their children's growing sexuality underscores their own mortality.

➤ There can be serious clashes when you marry into a family with a different attitude toward sex. Sometimes it's best to speak up; other times you're better off keeping quiet.

➤ Be aware of different cultural attitudes toward sex.

➤ Have fun, but make sure the door is closed if your in-laws are over.

Kidding Around
with the In-Laws

A son bought a talking parrot as a gift for his mother's birthday. He spent $500 for the bird because it could speak six languages.

When he saw his mother the next day, the son asked, "How did you like the bird?" The mother answered, "It was delicious."

The son replied, "Ma! How could you eat that bird? Don't you know it could speak six languages?"

The mother replied, "If it could speak six languages, why didn't it say something?"

Unfortunately, many in-laws say too much, too often. Of course, all that advice, guidance, and counsel is dumped right on your head. Under the best of circumstances, unwanted advice from your in-laws can be annoying; when you're contemplating starting a family, however, it can be downright offensive.

In this chapter, you'll learn ways to deal with the helpful hints that well-meaning (and not so well-meaning) in-laws offer before that red-faced, screaming bundle of joy does or does not make its appearance.

What Do You Mean You're Not Pregnant Yet?

My husband and I were married for seven years before we had our first child. There was no mystery to the matter: I was earning first my master's degree and then my Ph.D., all the while teaching and writing. At the same time, my husband was establishing a successful career in publishing.

> ### It's All Relative
>
> An estimated 3,900,089 babies were born in the United States in 1995, a decline from the 4,952,767 births in 1994. The fertility rate (the number of live births per 1,000 women aged 15–44 years) for 1995 was 65.6— two percent lower than the rate for 1994 (66.7 percent). [Source: *The World Almanac and Book of Facts, 1997*]

Astonishingly, none of our in-laws pressured us to have children. I took their consideration for granted until I started listening to my friends who had also not yet gotten around to putting a dent in the Zero Population Growth movement. "The in-laws are on my case day and night about the baby issue," Jodi said. "Even if we wanted to have a baby, there's always some family member calling up to nag us about it. They don't let me off the phone long enough to even discuss it with my husband—much less *do* it." Terrel and Sami's story also is typical of the pressure that in-laws can apply on the reproduction front.

Pressure Points

Terrel and Sami had been married for a year when their in-laws began to drop some hints that it was time for a little action on the reproduction front. At first, the hints were gentle and joking; a few years later, however, the grandparents-to-be got more ferocious in their demands. Surprisingly, even the sisters- and brothers-in-law got in on the act: After all, wasn't it time for a new niece or nephew to make an appearance?

It's All Relative

➤ The lowest U.S. infant mortality rate ever (7.5 infant deaths per 1,000 live births) was recorded in 1995, the most recent year that statistics are available.

➤ Every eight seconds a baby is born in the United States.

➤ Every hour four babies die and one in five infant deaths is due to birth defects.

➤ Every year more than 5,500 babies are born weighing less than one pound.

➤ Every minute a baby is born to a teen mother.

➤ One in nine infants is born preterm (less than 37 weeks gestation).

➤ The U.S. infant mortality rate is higher than that of 24 other nations.

[Source: *The World Almanac and Book of Facts, 1997* and The March of Dimes web site.]

By the time two more years had passed, Sami's mother-in-law was openly moaning that her daughter-in-law was cold and unloving. Obviously, Sami didn't want to be bothered with kids—her career was far more important. Meanwhile, on the other front, Terrel's mother-in-law began to trumpet news of everyone else's pregnancies: Wasn't it wonderful that cousin Luci was pregnant? Such a joy that cousin Sarah was having her eighth (or was it ninth?) child. Ah, *there* was a dutiful daughter.

Then the men stepped up to the plate. Sami's father took Terrel aside for a father-in-law-to-son-in-law talk. "If the problem is money," the older man said, "you can relax. We'll help take care of expenses. We'll pay for the layette and a baby nurse for a week. We'll even set up a college fund for Junior."

A year later and still no baby. The Baby Issue (as Sami and Terrel began to call it) took on a life of its own. Sami's mother-in-law started giving lavish gifts to her sons and daughters who had children. She gave even more extravagant gifts to the grandchildren—but only token gifts to Sami and Terrel. "Why do Sami and Terrel need my gifts?" she asked. "They haven't seen fit to give me any joy."

Then, Terrel's father got in on the act. He gave the couple a week-long vacation in the Bahamas so things would "click." He even gave his son some hints about baby-making, in case Terrel wasn't sure (after seven years) how things worked in the mating game. Terrel and Sami had a great time at the straw market, the casino, and the beach. Bedtime was fun, too. But still no baby.

Ironically, Terrel and Sami hadn't given much thought to having a child until their in-laws began to apply all the pressure. They figured, as many couples do, that the issue would resolve itself in all good time. Mother Nature would take her course. But when the family started with their thumb screws and torture rack, the couple began to get really annoyed. What gave their in-laws the right to meddle in such personal business, they wondered.

Family Matters
On average, parents-in-law give the newly-weds a year before they start demanding kids. After that, all bets are off.

Not to worry: Rozakis to the rescue! What gives in-laws the right to meddle? This question is a no-brainer: *They're family*. In-laws don't "meddle"; they show "concern." Being family gives them the right to spin doctor their intrusion into "care."

A Pregnant Pause

Statistically, women are waiting longer to give birth to their first child. A generation or two ago, it was much more common for women to have all their children while they were still in their twenties. My husband's mother had all three of her children by the time she was 25, for example. I didn't have my first child until I was closing in on 30.

Why the wait today? In many cases, couples are postponing their families until they have established themselves in their careers. Further, the innovations in reproductive technologies allow many women to have children far later in life than their mothers could. Today, it's even possible in some cases for a woman to have a child even after she has completed menopause. To date, the oldest woman to have given birth with the aid of technology is 63 years old. A generation ago, a 63-year-old woman was far more likely to be playing canasta in Vero Beach than taking Lamaze classes—or even contemplating them.

In addition, many women today are marrying later than they did a generation or two ago. If you ask my late-marrying female friends, they'll tell you they postponed marriage because "all the good ones are taken." This may be true (after all, I *did* grab one of the good ones early on). Delayed marriage may also be due to career pressures and the greater variety of choices outside marriage that women are afforded today.

In addition, many women simply want to have some independence before they merge their lives with someone else's. Here's what Abby told me:

> "I distinctly remember having in the back of my mind since I was old enough to shave (a no-no until you were in your teens in my house) that I didn't want to even think about children until I was 30. Seemed like a good, round number and enough time to figure things out. Just so happens I'm right on schedule, but I can't imagine having been married at 21, 22, or even 25. I just wasn't ready (or mature enough, really). In fact, two close friends of mine that did marry at that age are now divorced. There's so much available to young women and so much more is "acceptable," I think many of us don't think twice about marriage until much later."

Whatever the causes, many women today are having children later than their mothers, mothers-in-law, and older sisters did. This can cause significant pressures within a family. Read on to see how.

Up Close and Personal

What makes otherwise sane in-laws butt into such a personal matter as a couple's choice whether or not to have children? In-laws' interference in your baby making (or lack thereof) isn't casual, Gentle Reader. In-laws often have very definite reasons for sticking their noses where they don't belong when it comes to the baby issue. Here are their Top 10 reasons for urging you to produce a child:

10. They want to see their bloodline continue.

9. They yearn to have the family name passed down through the generations.

8. They've built something they value, such as a family business, and they want to keep it in the family. Children can ensure the continuation of a business, in-laws often think.

> **Family Matters**
> Rule of thumb: The more dreadful the family name, the more anxious the in-laws are to saddle a kid with it. More on this in Chapter 20.

7. They believe that your decision not to have children (or to postpone having children) reflects badly on them. For example, your in-laws might fret that you don't want children because you had such a dreadful childhood. While this may indeed be the case, take your childhood trauma up with your therapist, not your in-laws. After all, that's why your shrink gets $95 an hour.

6. They see reproduction as a religious issue.

5. They feel threatened by difference. Married people have children; otherwise, why would they get married? By not having children, you are deviating from "normal" behavior, they reason.

4. They want to keep up with the neighbors, their colleagues, or the rest of the family. For some in-laws, kids are a status item, like cars, computers, or coffee.

3. A relative once told me to have kids for "payback." "I bought all those baby gifts," she said, "it's about time we got some of it back."

2. Grandchildren keep them busy. It gives them something to do when the bridge game has been canceled or the yacht race rained out.

> **Family Matters**
> It's not a bad idea to reassure your meddling in-laws that you *do* love them. No matter what motivates them to force you to pop out a tot or two, they most likely really believe that they are doing the Right Thing here.

And the number one reason why your in-laws pressure you to have children...

1. They genuinely enjoyed raising kids and they want the pleasure again. This is the most difficult reason to argue against. After all, what kind of ingrates would deny their family the pleasure of kids?

Okay, so now you know the reasons *why* your in-laws are on your case about creating a clone the old-fashioned way. What can you do about the meddling and pressure? Try these ideas:

➤ Assure your in-laws that you appreciate their concern. After all, they very likely *do* have your best interests at heart.

➤ Explain that your reproductive decisions are your own business, plain and simple. Stress to your in-laws that they don't have any input in this decision. Encourage them pick out your shower curtain or plastic pink flamingos, instead.

➤ Be tactful and stay cool.

➤ Stick to your guns. Don't provide any color commentary, play-by-play, or instant replays of your amorous adventures. Remember what you learned about *private* in the previous chapter?

➤ Keep your sense of humor. The first year she was married, my friend Shelley got baby gifts from her mother-in-law in lieu of Christmas gifts. Now, since Shelley wasn't pregnant and had no immediate plans to become so, she *could* have shoved the rattles and rompers down her mother-in-law's throat. Instead she just laughed about the too-obvious hint. (Then she returned all the gifts and bought the luscious cashmere sweater she wanted in the first place.)

> **Family Matters**
> Some researchers believe there's a biological clock ticking for grandparents, too. Just as women of childbearing age may feel a real biological urge to have a child, so a man or woman past childbearing age may feel the urge to have a grandchild. So don't come down too hard on the pushy parents-in-law; they may not be able to help their nagging you to reproduce.

Finally, the White Smoke

So the day finally comes when you announce that you have done your part to ensure the continuation of the family's bloodline. Alert the media—but don't let your guard down. The fun has just begun.

After your in-laws heave a collective sigh of relief (hey, this may be first time both sides have agreed on anything yet), you'll find that you've relinquished all control of your body. You're prepared for the doctor to have the monthly look-see, but that's just the beginning.

You might even be expecting total strangers to offer their completely unsolicited advice. A total stranger (thankfully, it wasn't a relative), actually said to me in a mall: "Don't look at ugly things or your baby will be ugly." Fat lot she knew. Nature makes all babies beautiful so they can be tolerated until they acquire some sense.

You expected the doctor to poke. You're not surprised that strangers prod. But in-laws? Surely they should have better sense than to invade your fast-expanding space. Ha! They're frequently the worst of all. Here are some areas where you can expect in-law advice, ad nauseum:

➤ Diet

➤ Rest (feet up vs. feet down)

➤ Sleep

➤ Medications

➤ Alcohol

➤ Prenatal testing

> **Don't Go There**
> With all this pressure, you may feel that freedom of choice has been taken from you. It hasn't been. Stick to your guns.

This is all well and good, but some in-laws get a little carried away with planning. I have a friend whose mother-in-law actually registered the baby for an exclusive nursery school…three months before the baby was even born! When my friend complained, her mother-in-law said, "There's a long waiting list, and you do want the very best for Pointdexter III, don't you?" Okay, so I made up the "Pointdexter" part. The rest is true; I swear.

Your in-laws may also bombard you with books; I got enough copies of Dr. Spock's *Baby and Child Care* to open up my own library. So what if I had 50 copies of the same book? It is a very good book, truth be told.

Anything You Can Do, I Can Do Better

Pregnancy can be a time for competition from your in-laws, too. Louise's mother-in-law demanded all the details of Louise's pregnancy: Nausea, leg cramps, back aches, cravings—the whole ball of wax. The problem? Anything Louise had, her mother-in-law had had ten times worse. "You call that water retention?" she said. "I retained 3,000 pounds of water with my Bobby. They had to give me a million water pills and keep me in bed for a year." "Swollen ankles? Those aren't swollen ankles. Mine were like tree trunks! I couldn't get my shoes on for months!"

You might also have competition over the actual delivery. Maggie's sister-in-law was delighted when Maggie delivered by Caesarean section. "I knew you didn't have the guts to go natural," she said. Some women have complained to me that their sisters-in-law

> **Don't Go There**
> Giving birth is like trying to push a piano through a transom.

even crowed over their decision to use painkillers in labor. Labor just wasn't labor if you didn't shatter glass with your bellowing.

And then it's all over and you bring home that little bundle of stinky joy. What do your in-laws say? "You're not stopping at one, are you?"

Baby Love

How can you deal with the meddling and competition from your in-laws? Here are my suggestions, culled from research studies, anecdotal records, and my personal experience as two-time mother. (See, I listened to my in-laws' parting comment and didn't stop at one.)

➤ **Recognize the problem.** Maybe your sister-in-law has been competing with you from Day 1. Do you really expect her to stop now? Your pregnancy has nothing to do with her attitude; she'll compete over any issue.

➤ **Weigh the advice your in-laws give you.** Some of it will be remarkably dopey, but among the dross you'll find nuggets of gold. For example, there is a lot to be said for getting rest during pregnancy and after delivery; I wish I had taken that advice! When my daughter was born, I was teaching Tuesdays and Thursdays at a major university. I taught on a Thursday, gave birth to my daughter on Friday, and was back in the class on Tuesday. What a hero! No, what an idiot. It took me a whole lot longer to heal and recover my strength than it would have had I rested.

➤ **Chill out. Recognize that your in-laws often mean well.** Don't take their meddling personally, even if it's meant that way.

➤ **Involve your in-laws in the process.** Having a baby is a blessed and joyous experience, excruciating pain notwithstanding. Besides, the sooner you involve them with the pregnancy, the more willing they'll be to baby-sit when you're so sick of diapers, bottles, and baby gas that you welcome the chance to watch linoleum curl or even— food shop.

Children of Choice

"My husband and I tried for years to have children," Lani told me, "but things just didn't click. Finally, we said enough to the infertility treatments and decided to adopt a child. We have been blessed with a beautiful baby girl from China whom we named Tina. You'd think everyone would be happy, wouldn't you? Just the opposite is the case. Some of my in-laws treat our daughter differently from the other cousins in the family. They act like she's not good enough. It was upsetting enough when Tina was a baby, but now that she's older, it's getting tragic—she's beginning to realize that she's not good enough to them. We've always been a close family, but this is driving a wedge between us."

It's All Relative

Of the 51,157 American children who were adopted in 1986 (the latest available published data on domestic adoptions by the NCFA), approximately one-half (24,589) were adoptions of healthy infants (under two years of age) of all races and ethnic backgrounds. The remainder were adoptions of older children or children with "special needs" (physical, mental, or emotional disabilities, being part of a sibling group, etc.).

Adoption can be a difficult issue for many in-laws to accept. As you learned previously in this chapter, some parents and parents-in-law want a grandchild to ensure the continuation of their bloodline. They want the baby to carry their genes and to look like them. As a result, a baby isn't just a sweet, smelly package. Rather, it's their ticket to immortality.

How can you deal with this issue? Start by explaining your feelings to the family. It's none of their business why you decided to adopt. Whether there's a fertility problem or not, adoption is the way you chose to build your family and that's it. Your in-laws have to accept your decision and respect it. They have to honor all your children, adopted or not, and treat them with equal respect. Demand this from your in-laws; you and your children deserve it.

It's All Relative

In addition to the domestic adoptions each year, American couples or individuals adopt several thousand foreign-born children. Begun first as a solution to emergency situations in foreign countries, these adoptions have now become an important adoption alternative.

Mix 'n' Match: Transracial Families

Parents who adopt transracially are often the subject of intense criticism from inside the family as well as outside it. By adopting transracial, you become a minority family, subject to criticism, odd remarks, and prejudice. In-laws of all races get in on the prejudice.

If you adopt a child who looks different from you, you might feel that you can handle the stares and loss of privacy that go with the territory. You may find, however, that the frequent questions and comments of strangers and relatives annoy and worry you. Of course, at the heart of your anger and anxiety is the fear that your adopted child will be hurt by thoughtless questions, or that their siblings will feel neglected.

Family Matters
Psychological studies have found that transracially adopted children appear to handle the identity issues all adopted children face better than most because, researchers theorize, they cannot pretend to be like everyone else. And children raised in such environments often are able to bridge the culture gap.

Here's what Patty told me about her first experience with insensitive in-laws:

"I remember taking Robyn, then four months old, to her first family party. She was immediately surrounded by cousins who wanted to look at her and touch her. Then one cousin asked, 'Why does she look like that?' referring to the fact that Robyn is black and I'm white. I was ready for this, so I launched into an explanation about Robyn's birth mother. What I wasn't ready for was my in-laws' reaction. Not a one of them stepped forward to explain the situation and help me out. Further, it was plain that not a one of them had explained Robyn's adoption to their children.

Finally, a small cousin came to my rescue. 'Because she was born that way,' the tot said. Thus, I learned my first lesson in handling insensitive remarks about our unusual family."

Doctor, Cure Thyself

To overcome prejudice from all quarters, parents who adopt transracially have to work a little harder. Start by working on your own attitudes.

A woman I met named Chris says her greatest surprise after she adopted two black children was facing her own racism. "I was raised as a white liberal and was not prejudiced in obvious ways," Chris said. "I never realized [my racism]. It was rather shocking and embarrassing."

Don't Go There
Although psychological studies generally have been positive about transracial adoptions, most professionals in the adoption field still oppose them. A California law, which took effect in January 1990, requires agencies to spend 90 days trying to match children ethnically before allowing transcultural placement.

An adoptive father named Julio had a similar experience. An Hispanic who grew up in a predominantly white neighborhood, he remembered feeling out of place as a child and being referred to negatively as an Indian. When he adopted his daughter, who was black, she looked to him even darker, like an Indian. He felt embarrassed and frightened. "When I was a child, I felt trapped by how I looked," he said. "There was nothing I could do about it. Looking at my daughter, I felt fear for myself and fear for her. But it disappeared when I could express my anger about how I was treated as a child and how my daughter is likely to be treated by some ignorant people." This positive attitude and acceptance will spill over to the entire family.

Remember, your in-laws often take their behavioral cues from you and the way you act toward your children.

If you're positive about the adoption, they are more likely to be, too. But if you have some issues to work about concerning adoption and race, these problems are likely to be picked up by the family and magnified.

Fortunately, even the most insensitive questions are nearly always well intentioned. Further, they actually provide a good way for you to express your pride in your adopted children (as well as in their siblings who were born to you).

In the nanosecond that you have to frame your response to bone-head questions from your in-laws, remember that your response should:

> **Family Matters**
> What can you say if an in-law asks, "What do you know about the real parents?" The answer? "Well, we're his real parents, actually, since we're bringing him up."

➤ Support your child's self-esteem

➤ Protect your child's privacy about his origins

➤ Clarify that adoption builds "real" families with your "own" children

Using these guidelines (and keeping your temper reined in), you can generally find a gracious answer that will affirm the child without sounding critical of your cement-head in-law asking the question. However, there *are* times when we may want or need to let a particular comment pass and help our child to understand it later.

Guess Who's Coming to Dinner?

A couple I know was entertaining one of the wife's important clients, and their Colombian-born son was present. The client remarked that she had friends who had adopted two Korean children and later had had two children "of their own." At the time, the adoptive parents decided it was best not to risk offending the woman by correcting her choice of words. The next day my friend asked her son if he had been bothered by the remark. They were then able to discuss the issue quietly and at length.

> **Family Matters**
> One of the best ways for a family to feel close is to talk. Talking about adoption and the different feelings that children might have about it can reaffirm their sense of belonging, even when insensitive or ignorant in-laws get into the mix.

The Least You Need to Know

➤ In-laws have many reasons for wanting you to pop out a tot or two.

➤ Your reproductive decisions are your own business, plain and simple.

➤ Nothing invites unsolicited advice like a pregnancy.

➤ Weigh the advice you get from your in-laws. Throw out the nonsense and follow the good stuff.

➤ Involve your in-laws in the pregnancy—it will make them more willing to baby-sit later on!

➤ Adoption brings a special set of problems. When in-laws offer rude comments, clarify that adoption builds "real" families with your "own" children.

➤ Keep your sense of humor. You'll need it.

Chapter 20

Baby Talk

In This Chapter

➤ Discover the world of grandparenting

➤ See how the arrival of a baby can throw all your in-laws off balance

➤ Play the name game, baby version

➤ Learn to deal with critical grandparents and overly generous ones

➤ Find out how working mothers can overcome guilt of not being Super Mom

There were two brothers, eight and ten years old, who were exceedingly mischievous. Whatever went wrong in the neighborhood, they surely had a hand in it. At their wit's end, the boys' parents asked their priest to talk with the hooligans. He agreed, and asked to see the younger boy alone first.

The priest sat the boy down across his huge, impressive desk. For about five minutes they sat and stared at each other. Finally, the priest pointed his forefinger at the boy and asked, "Where is God?"

The boy looked under the desk, in the corners of the room, all around, but said nothing.

Again, louder, the priest pointed at the boy and asked, "Where is God?"

Again the boy looked all around but said nothing. A third time, in an even louder and firmer voice, the priest leaned far across the desk, put his forefinger on the boy's nose, and boomed, "WHERE IS GOD?"

The boy panicked and ran all the way home. He dragged his older brother to their room where they usually plotted their mischief. "We are in BIG trouble," he cried.

The older boy asked, "What do you mean?"

"God is missing and they think we did it," the kid replied.

It's not easy raising kids, even with some outside help. That's one reason why in-laws feel so free to meddle in your parenting methods. Hey, why shouldn't you get the benefit of their superior experience? *Their* kids didn't turn out so badly, did they? (Don't answer that.) Actually, it doesn't matter. When it comes to childrearing, in-laws rarely take prisoners.

In this chapter, you'll first learn all about being a grandparent and how parenting and grandparenting has changed since you raised your children. Then I'll explain why baby names can be such a fiery issue among in-laws—and how to resolve this problem. Finally, I'll explore some of the most common problems that arise when a baby makes its appearance on the in-law scene. Let the fun begin!

Dazed and Confused

What's a grandparent? Now, we all know that grandparents are what your parents become when you have a child. But it's not quite that simple. There are certain rules that grandparents have to follow to be allowed in the union. For example, rule #154 of my Official Grandparents Rule Book reads: "When you are only six weeks old, a grandparent will buy you imitation lizard-skin cowboy boots that hang like weights from your adorable little feet." Here are five more grandparent rules, so you get the idea what's involved in this grandparent business:

1. A grandparent will believe you can read even when you have the book upside down.

2. Grandparents can always be counted on to buy anything you're selling, from seeds to cookies.

3. A grandparent is the only baby-sitter who doesn't charge money to keep you.

4. Grandparents will put a sweater on you when *they* are cold.

5. If a stranger so much as blinks an eye, a grandparent will whip out a display of pictures of you.

It's All Relative

Thanks to longer life spans, grandparents are more numerous than ever before in history. Currently, about 75 percent of all Americans are grandparents. In fact, we've even seen the inception of Grandparents Day.

In 1973, the state of West Virginia began a campaign to set aside a special day honoring grandparents. This campaign was spearheaded by Marian McQuade of Fayette County, West Virginia, who hoped to persuade grandchildren to tap the wisdom and heritage held by the elder generation. Senator Jennings Randolph (D-WV) introduced a resolution in the U.S. Senate and in 1978 Congress passed legislation. Then-President Jimmy Carter proclaimed that National Grandparents Day would be celebrated every year on the first Sunday after Labor Day.

Simple, yes? Not so fast, babycakes. Everything is different today. As a grandparent-to-be, here's your mantra: "If I did it when you were a baby, how good could it be?"

The More Things Change, the More They Stay the Same?

Grandparents, here's the inside skinny: Childbirth and childrearing have changed a lot since your day. For example, my mother stayed in the hospital for a week when I was born, eating hearts of palm and getting backrubs from the nurses. I delivered my children via the drive-through window. A few hours after the delivery, I got up to look at the baby. When I returned to my bed, the nurse was making it...for the next patient!

My mother spent her pregnancy hoisting herself out of chairs, eating enough to feed the Ninth Regiment, and wearing clothes designed by Omar the Tent Maker. Terrified that I would gain an ounce more than the prescribed weight, I nibbled on lettuce leaves and didn't look pregnant until my sixth month. I wore only stylish maternity duds and exercised until the day of the delivery. I would have exercised that day, too, but I was busy having the baby.

As was common and proper when I was born, my father showed up for my conception and birth; family legend has it that he later changed a few diapers, but I think that's a myth like the alligators living in the New York City sewers. My husband, in contrast, was involved in every aspect of "our" pregnancy, including labor, delivery, and diapers.

Family Matters

Dr. T. Berry Brazelton and Penelope Leach are two of the best-known new gurus of childcare. Their advice has always struck me as logical and sensible. There's nothing wrong with Dr. Spock's classic *Baby and Child Care*, either. I have a copy from the 1950s and an updated edition that I refer to on many occasions, especially for advice on common childhood illnesses. See, not *everything* about child care has changed!

It's no wonder your daughter-in-law or son-in-law sneers at your advice, grandparents: Your suggestions are likely to appear as out of date as the Hula-Hoop, saddle shoes, and manual typewriters. Don't despair. Read on and I'll show you how we can bridge the gap between the past and the present. Your wisdom won't go to waste; I promise.

Don't Go There
With the birth of your first child, any unresolved conflicts with your parents and in-laws are likely to erupt. Because half of America's grandparents see a grandchild almost every day, there's a lot of opportunity for conflict.

Walk the Walk and Talk the Talk

But first, what kind of grandparent do you want to be? What role do you want to play in the baby's life? What type of grandparent are you expected to be? These questions are crucial because the gap between appearance and reality over the grandparenting issue can cause great problems among in-laws.

Here are the most common types of grandparents. Check the description that you think best suits your personality, lifestyle, and family situation.

_____ 1. I'm Captain Kangaroo, Barney, and the Encyclopedia Brittanica rolled into one. I'd be first picked on *Family Jeopardy*.

_____ 2. I live for my grandchildren. You need my kidneys for Little Billy? Here, take them.

_____ 3. I'd love to spend more time with grandchildren, but there's a garage sale I really want to hit. Besides, I already raised my kids. Give me a break here.

_____ 4. Being with my grandchildren makes me feel like a kid myself.

_____ 5. I spend most of my time with only one of my grandkids because he has special needs.

_____ 6. Do the kids have to make so much noise? Why are they always so wet and smelly?

Score Yourself

➤ If you checked #1, you're a *matriarch* or *patriarch*. You consider yourself a resource, the family library of knowledge, all in one volume.

➤ If you checked #2, being a grandparent is central to your life. You're a *nurturer*, always ready to baby-sit or make a nice tray of baked ziti.

➤ If you checked #3, you're *Grandparent Lite*, what my long-time friend Marla calls "the Five-Minute Grandparent." Your life is full and you enjoy your freedom.

➤ If you checked #4, you're the *Young-at-Heart* grandparent. You're having a ball reliving your childhood with your grandchildren; if they'd told you it would be this much fun, you'd have pushed for the kids to have kids sooner. So enjoy, but try not to pull your groin muscles the next time you bungee jump.

➤ If you checked #5, you're the *Watchdog*, focusing on the interaction of the grandchildren with their parents and the needs of each child. You've decided to turn your attention to the grandchild who needs you the most.

➤ If you checked #6, you're not ready for this close-up, Mr. DeMille.

Don't try to shoehorn yourself into a grandparent role that doesn't suit you, no matter how much pressure you get. Neither you, the grandchildren, or your children are likely to be happy. And don't apologize for being the type of grandparent you are.

Instead, consider ways that you can enrich your role as a grandparent. Perhaps you want to move closer to the grandchildren, attend more of their activities, or take a personal interest in something that interests them.

> **Family Matters**
> According to writer and actor Gore Vidal, one should never have children, only grandchildren.

> **Family Matters**
> If you live far away from one or more sets of grandchildren, consider writing letters or sending videotapes. This can help you create a permanent record as you keep in touch.

Bringing Up Baby

Parents-to-be, nothing changes your life as much as the arrival of a child. Sleep becomes a fond memory. Your home will be blanketed in toys, bottles, toys, diapers, and toys. Suddenly, your life is no longer your own; it belongs to the little wailing creature who has your nose, your spouse's ears, and your mother-in-law's temper.

Just as the arrival of a child changes a marriage, so it changes relationships among in-laws. Sons-in-law and daughters-in-law become fathers and mothers; sisters, sisters-in-law, brothers, and brothers-in-law become aunts and uncles. Your parents and parents-in-law become grandparents. Unfortunately, an operator's manual doesn't come along with the new titles. How should an aunt act? What's the uncle's role supposed to be? The arrival of a baby can stretch these roles to the breaking point, as what one in-law perceives as offering "help" another perceives as "intrusion."

> **Don't Go There**
> First-time mothers, unsure of their own role in the unfolding family drama, are often especially touchy about a mother-in-law or sister-in-law intruding on her territory by showing her how to take care of her baby—even if the advice is sound and well-meaning.

And as roles change, needs and expectations shift more drastically than the San Andreas Fault. Suddenly, everyone is on new ground and the earth's is still quivering.

How do I know this? My insight is born of a wisdom that can only come from blind groping—I have two kids and a slew of in-laws. I am the oldest of three children in my family; my husband is the oldest of three children in his family. Following the law of averages, we married first and had children first. That means we got to be the groundbreakers in shifting the family balance. Let me share some of my experiences and hard-earned understanding with you so when the earth moves in your life, it won't be a result of your mother-in-law fainting when she finally realizes that she's going to be a grandmother.

What's in a Baby Name?

One of the issues that often comes up is the baby's name. As you learned in Chapter 6, names and in-laws are a volatile mix, like Sean Penn and the paparazzi. This is because names carry emotional overtones, indicate religious beliefs, continue cultural customs, and conform to family habits.

Family Matters
Among the most popular names for male babies today are: Andre, Baylor, Brenden, Cody, Conor, Drew, Graham, Griffin, Harley, Jarred, Jessie, Johnathan, Jordan, Joseph, Marc, Nathaniel, Nelson, Quinten, Tye, Tyler, Vernon, Xaviar, Zach, and Zackariah.

Family Matters
Among the most popular names for female babies today are: Adrianna, Alexia, Angeline, Anna, Ashley, Aubrey, Bailey, Bree, Caitlin, Carleigh, Cathryn, Corrina, Darla, Destiny, Faith, Fiona, Goldi, Hailey, Jacklyn, Juliane, Kailey, Kayla, Kyrstin, Leah, Madelin, Madison, Michaela, Rebecca, Robbi, Sabrina, Sadie, Shelby, Tiffany.

For example, in many families, it's customary to name the first male child after the baby's father or grandfather. For a long time, we were the only family on the block whose son was not a junior. Our neighbors, a genial bunch, were totally baffled that we did not want to name our son after his father. To my husband and me, naming our son "Robert Junior" was just another chance to get the mail mixed up.

Religion and culture also add to the mix. My husband's father is Greek, so of course his paternal grandmother Demetra assumed the baby would be named after her husband, Aristedes. My husband's mother, who is not Greek, wanted to give her first child a common American name—Robert. Demetra's English wasn't that strong and she had never heard the name "Robert." "Rabbit!" she shrieked, "what kind of a name is Rabbit!" The family compromised by naming my husband "Robert Aristedes Rozakis."

Megan, a parent-to-be, had this to say about the ethnic baby-naming issue:

"My husband and I are planning to start a family soon. He's 100 percent Italian-American, and I'm Italian-Irish-American. In the interest of representing my Irish heritage, I would like to give one of our future children an Irish first name, like Aoifa for a girl or Declan for a boy. However, I'm not so sure this is going to fly because of the rule we have to follow: My husband's parents must be able to pronounce the name. They are off-the-boat Italians, and some English language words—let alone Gaelic—don't come naturally to them. And forget about words that have a "th" in them. It's just not part of their language. They can't say it; it comes out as "fffff." I think I may be out of luck here—even the luck of the Irish!"

Think you have problems dealing with your in-laws over your baby's name? Pish tosh! You haven't read anything yet.

It's All Relative

Argentina has a law that lets bureaucrats rule against what they deem excessive parental creativity when naming their children. Historians say it has existed in some form since the 1880s, when massive immigration made authorities anxious to preserve the population's homogeneity.

Parents may freely choose their child's name, says the law, with just a few exceptions: You cannot choose names that are "extravagant, ridiculous, contrary to our customs" or that "express or signify political or ideological tendencies." "Foreign" names, moreover, must be "Hispanicized."

Some parents, however, have put up a fight. Recently an Argentine couple intent on naming their baby *Kennedy* took their struggle all the way to the Supreme Court. They lost.

First, Do No Harm

Sometimes your in-laws will be so glad that you're having a baby that they won't care what you call him or her. Other times, however, battles will erupt over names, customs, and culture. How can we resolve these issues? Let's start with comedian Bill Cosby's guidelines for naming a baby:

➤ Always give your child a name that ends in a vowel so that when you yell, the name will carry. Nothing rings out like a good "o," as in Juli-ooooooooo." You just can't do that with "James," "Herman," or "Meredith."

➤ If you must put some consonants in your child's name, try to put them in the middle, where a few "b's or "m's will work (as long as there's a vowel at the end).

> **Don't Go There**
> Here are some baby names to avoid: A. Mistake, Elvis, Dipthong, Bertha, Pugsley, Fester Boyle, Demon Seed, Damien, Hortence, Stimpy, and Dick.

Here are my suggestions for naming your baby:

➤ Start with a name you like because of its sound or connotation.

➤ Make sure it goes with your last name. No *Chanda Leer* or *Seymore Miles*, or *Justin Case* please.

➤ Make a back-up list of equally acceptable baby names in case you change your mind later on. You're done now, if there's no great break with family tradition, heritage, or culture. If there is, read on.

Family Matters
The reason grandparents and grandchildren get along so well is that they have a common enemy.

➤ Share your choices with the family and explain your reasons. It's always better to discuss your name choices before rather than after the birth, when everyone will be busy sobbing, scolding, and sermonizing.

➤ If your in-laws start hyperventilating, have them breath into a paper bag while you get to the root of the issue. Is it just another power struggle? Or is it a perception that your choice of the baby's name is a personal attack? Often, finding the cause can resolve the issue.

➤ If not, see if you can work out a compromise.

➤ If fall else fails: Lie. Microbiologist Charles R. Gerba used this approach. His oldest boy's middle name is *Escherichia*. Gerba told his father-in-law that it was the name of an Old Testament King. What does *Escherichia* mean? It's a type of bacteria.

Let's Get Critical

In the best of all possible worlds, grandparents have their roles on straight, parents accept their in-laws' child-rearing suggestions gracefully, and babies never throw up on your brother-in-law's new suede blazer. Surprise! This is not the best of all possible worlds. Grandparents are bound to overstep their bounds, you'll be ready to strangle your sister-in-law the next time she tells you breast feeding is "dirty," and the baby has uncanny aim with strained peas.

It's especially difficult when a grandparent is overly critical of your child or your parenting style. Here's what Sibohhan told me about her mother-in-law Mildred:

"Last year after living most of our lives in Europe, my husband took a job near his parents in a small, American city. Part of the reason for the move was that our daughters, ages 13 and 7 now, would finally have relatives near. Because money was tight, we had not visited America very often.

My mother-in-law likes my oldest daughter very much and always wants to take her with her and show her off. My daughter is very reluctant to spend any more time with her because she is constantly criticizing her. My mother-in-law also tells my daughter all the things that are wrong with me, her sister, and her father. It is not so much the complaining that troubles my daughter, as the feeling that she gets that she is somehow responsible and that she is expected to fix the problem.

My mother-in-law has never complained about anything to me, only to my child. My efforts to ask her to bring her complaints instead to me have been without success."

Sibohhan's mother-in-law is putting her granddaughter in the middle of a situation that should be worked out between adults. The mother-in-law's behavior is confusing and unfair to the child. Ironically, this is a chance for granddaughter and grandmother to get to know each other better, because they will have to find new things to talk about! Here's how to start the process:

➤ Sibohhan should tell her daughter that she is not responsible for fixing what her grandmother complains about and that she does not need to listen nor comment.

➤ When her grandmother starts in, the child can say, "I'm not the one to tell, Grandmother. Tell Mother or Father." In this situation, let your child know that he or she will probably have to say this over and over again until it sinks in.

➤ Because Sibohhan has already tried talking to her mother-in-law, it's time for hubby to step in. He needs to let his mother know how her granddaughter is affected by her criticisms.

➤ Be firm and clear when you and your spouse talk to your mother-in-law.

Don't Go There
"Before I was married I had three theories about raising children. Now I have three children and no theories." (John Wilmot, the Earl of Rochester, 1647–1680)

Family Matters
Be a supportive in-law by not criticizing. Ditch the negative comments where childrearing is concerned. Instead, show by example.

Jackie had a similar situation with her sister-in-law. In Jackie's situation, the power struggle concerned a specific issue: How to raise a baby. Here's her story. How do you think you'd resolve this situation if you were in Jackie's shoes?

"My sister-in-law, a pediatric nurse who does not have children, thought that my son Chris was not being fed properly. When she started to lecture me on his eating habits and his poor eating history, I tried to tell her that Chris eats a wide range of foods and his last check-up showed that he was healthy.

What really ticked me off, however, was that she had the gall to show up at my house during dinner. I had just gotten him away from all the toys and was quieting him down by reading him a story. He was more interested in the toy train he had picked up than his food. My sister-in-law came prancing into the room and says, 'That's what I mean...The toys go, the book goes, now Chris, you sit down right here, and you eat that supper.' She took the train from Chris, pushed the plate in front of him. He said, 'No, I'm not hungry!' By this time I was furious, though I tried to keep my tone calm. I said, 'I think I can handle this,' because by now, Chris was clearly upset and not ready to eat at all.

She then said, 'I'm a pediatric nurse, and I know that Chris rules the roost, and don't you tell me any differently!' I said, 'I don't have to take that from you!' and bolted from the room. She called after me, but I was so upset that I went for a walk. This happened last weekend and we haven't talked since.

Jackie resents the fact that her sister-in-law is judging her parenting skills and sticking her nose where it doesn't belong. Because the sister-in-law doesn't have children, Jackie also feels she knows nothing about parenting. Worst of all, perhaps, the sister-in-law hijacked the situation and seized control of her nephew.

Because Jackie's sister-in-law is a pediatric nurse, she has definite opinions about the diet, health, and behavior of children. However, she should not give criticism and advice to family members—unless they ask for it. Jackie is doing fine without Nurse Know-it-All.

The sister-in-law was way out-of-line in her behavior. In this instance, Jackie may want to limit her visits with her sister-in-law. In addition, she can confide in someone she is close to, perhaps her mother-in-law, that she needs more positive support from the family.

Tug of War

We all grow up with a set of family rules. Sometimes the rules are clear; other times, they're murkier than the muddy Mississippi. In this case, Marci's in-laws seem anxious to see their grandchildren...but appearances can be deceiving. Here's what Marci told me:

"My husband and our two children moved to the South three years ago. Both sets of grandparents live in New Hampshire. We try to split the time we spend visiting between his parents and my parents, so they both can see the kids. The day after we get back to North Carolina, my mother-in-law is on the phone saying how much she misses us and how she never feels like she spends any time with the kids. They have been to visit us twice in three years, both times coming up early Saturday morning and leaving a day or two later. It seems they're always so busy, yet I get the guilt trip for them not seeing the kids.

I suggested to my in-laws that they keep the kids for a week during the summer. I even offered to drive halfway to meet them. My mother-in-law said, "That's a great idea!" Months have passed, and she still hasn't committed to a date, yet she repeatedly asks me when we're coming to visit. I want to foster a good relationship with my kids and their grandparents, but I don't have the resources to do everything. I feel hurt and jealous when I call home and mother-in-law is baby-sitting my brother-in-law's kids. I hate feeling guilty for moving away. How can I get my in-laws to meet me halfway?"

What's the scoop here? Marci and her husband have broken a family rule and are paying for the error of their ways. The family rule, "Thou shalt not leave home," causes many difficulties for families who move away from their hometown communities in search of a better lifestyle for themselves and their children. Some parents have the attitude that if the hometown was good enough for them to raise their family, it should be good enough for you.

In-laws have to learn to let their adult children be just that—adults who are free to live their own lives and care for their children the way they see fit. Marci's in-laws are having a little trouble making this adjustment. Here's what I suggest:

➤ Keep the lines of communication open.

➤ Continue to ask for support.

➤ Make offers to go halfway.

➤ Be patient.

➤ Try to stop feeling guilty.

We have a right to make our own decisions—it just may take others a while to support them.

Gucci, Gucci, Goo

Then we have the problem of grandparents who get carried away with gifts. Sometimes this is a relatively straightforward issue. Parents may have to tell the deep-pocket in-laws to scale back on their largess, so that there are some toys left in the store for the rest of the kids in the country. After all, does Jena really need 15 identical "Trailer Trash Barbies"?

Other times, however, the situation is more complex than it appears. That's the case with Carly's story:

> "My 18-year-old daughter has been accepting large amounts of money, credit cards, clothes, even cars, from my in-laws, who are well-to-do. I advised her when she went away to college, near her grandparents, that she would find it difficult to earn her own way. We are helping to pay her tuition and are totally against her accepting so much from Grams and Gramps. She has even moved in with them! Grams and Gramps are not speaking to me now because I feel it's wrong to give her so much without any reciprocity on her part. Her twin brother lives at home and is working his way through school. This hurts."

Family Matters
Being able to help a young person get a good start in life, having a grandchild live in their home, and being able to influence him or her can be very important to older in-laws.

Don't Go There
Some grandparents are so thrilled to have their grandchildren play a pivotal role in their lives that they go overboard with the gifts.

If your in-laws spoil the children, don't:

➤ Be judgmental or accusatory.

➤ Say, "You shouldn't do this" or "This is terrible for the children."

Instead:

➤ Look at the long-range effect.

➤ Think, "Is this worth the fight?"

➤ Realize that in most cases, these gestures are being made out of love.

In this situation, it isn't fair that Carly's in-laws give so much to her daughter without giving the same to her son. However, as you've already realized (no doubt the painful way), life isn't always fair. In this case, I'd tell Carly to sit down with her in-laws and discuss the situation with them. If things still don't change, Carly can cut way down on the financial support she is giving her daughter because she is getting so much assistance from her grandparents. Carly can then use the money to help her son more, because he is not receiving such gifts.

NannyGate

More than 32 million children in America have mothers who work outside the home. Whether they work from necessity or choice, they all carry some guilt along with their briefcases. As a result, these families are often most susceptible to criticism. And they are sure to get it—often from their nearest and dearest. Here's what Rhoda, a textile designer, told me.

"After the birth of my daughter Mariah, I stayed home for six weeks. I'm the primary breadwinner because my husband hasn't settled into a career. He works some part-time jobs and takes a few courses. He's not comfortable taking care of the baby, so we hired a nanny from Ireland. She had a one-year work visa. Two years later, we had a son, Devon. Every year we get a new nanny. Some are good, some are not so good, but somehow things get done.

The problem? My in-laws. They constantly condemn me because I won't stay home and 'take care of my children.' My mother-in-law said, 'Why keep having kids if you're not going to bother taking care of them?' Hey, it's *their* son who won't earn a living so I have to work. I'm always so tired and stressed out that the last thing I need is their criticism."

It's All Relative

Women accounted for 59 percent of the labor-force growth between 1985 and 1995.

Unemployment for all women in 1994 was only 6 percent.

In 1984, women held one-third (33.6 percent) of managerial and executive and nearly half (48.5 percent) of the professional occupations. By 1994, they held 48.1 percent of managerial/executive positions and accounted for over half (52.8 percent) of workers employed in professional occupations.

[Source: *1997 World Almanac and Book of Facts* and the Women's Bureau Department of Labor—May, 1995.]

Here are some ways to improve this situation:

➤ Ignore it. Let your in-laws mutter; you're doing the best you can.

➤ Invite your in-laws to baby-sit for you when the nanny is off duty. Use the time to rest, have a date with your husband, take one child on a special outing, or see a friend.

➤ Hire more household help so you're not so exhausted. You can often get high school kids to clean, do yard work, or run errands for reasonable prices.

It's All Relative

Of the approximately 69 million families in the U.S. in 1994, 12 million (18 percent) were maintained by women. In black families, women supported 46 percent; in Hispanic families, it was 24 percent; in white families, 14 percent. The 1994 median income for families maintained by women was $18,236, compared with $27,751 for families maintained by men and $44,751 for married couples. [Source: *1997 World Almanac and Book of Facts*]

The Least You Need to Know

➤ Grandparents may have trouble adjusting to the nineties styles of childbirth and parenting.

➤ Tread gently when choosing a name for your baby because family traditions and customs figure heavily here.

➤ Beware of power plays disguised as differences in parenting methods.

➤ Overly generous grandparents are usually not such a terrible thing.

➤ Working women, don't let your in-laws intimidate you!

Chapter 21

Childfree— By Chance or Choice

In This Chapter

➤ Assess how you feel about children

➤ Decide if you want children, in-law intervention aside

➤ Defend your choice not to have kids

➤ Learn how to deal with the pain of infertility

A mangy looking guy went into a bar and ordered a drink. The bartender said, "No way. I don't think you can pay for it."

The guy said, "You're right. I don't have any money, but if I show you something you haven't seen before, will you give me a drink?" The bartender said, "Deal!" and the guy pulled out a hamster.

The hamster ran to the piano and started playing Gershwin songs. The bartender said, "You're right. I've never seen anything like that before. That hamster is truly good on the piano." The guy downed the drink and asked the bartender for another.

"Money or another miracle or no drink," said the bartender. The guy pulled out a frog. He put the frog on the bar, and the frog started to sing. He had a marvelous voice and great pitch. Another man in the bar offered $300 for the frog. The guy said, "It's a deal." He took the $300 and gave the stranger the frog. The stranger ran out of the bar.

The bartender said, "Are you nuts? You sold a singing frog for $300? It must have been worth millions. You must be crazy."

"Not so," said the guy. "The hamster is also a ventriloquist."

Unfortunately, we all can't get loquacious hamsters to front for us: When it comes to the family, there are times when we have to be willing to speak up for ourselves. In this chapter, you'll learn how to deal with telling your in-laws about your decision to remain childfree, whether by choice or chance.

Don't Kid Me

Some people can't imagine a life *without* children; others can't imagine a life *with* them. "Children are so wonderful," members of the first camp exclaim; "Children are best served cold with a little mustard," the second group insist. Up until now in this book, I've been giving you my own point of view because I'm an impartial expert on in-law relationships. When it comes to kids, however, I'm an expert, but I'm also really biased. That's because I've got two of the best children in the world, my awesome Charles and Samantha.

It's All Relative

In 1995, it cost between $5,490 (low-income families) to $11,320 (high-income families) to raise a child. By the year 2000, the amount is estimated to increase to $7,300–$15,010. Five years later, figure on spending $9,760–$19,340. In the year 2010? You'd better sit down. Then, it will cost between $14,220–$27,620 to raise a child. [Source: *The World Almanac and Book of Facts, 1997*]

In contrast, not everyone is so cheerful about children. Woody Allen claims his parents put a live teddy bear in his crib. Robert Orben says that he takes his children everywhere, but they always find their way back home. Let's see how some other people throughout the ages have reacted to tikes. Along the way, take your KQ (Kid Quotient) by putting a check mark next to each statement you agree with.

_____ 1. A child is a curly, dimpled lunatic. (Ralph Waldo Emerson, 1803–1882)

_____ 2. All children are essentially criminal. (Dennis Diderot, 1713–1784)

____ **3.** Of all the animals, the boy is the most unmanageable. (Plato, 427?-348? BC)

____ **4.** There's nothing wrong with teenagers that reasoning with them won't aggravate. (Anonymous)

____ **5.** I never met a kid I liked. (W.C. Fields, 1880–1946)

____ **6.** Life does not begin at the moment of conception or the moment of birth. It begins when the kids leave home and the dog dies. (Anonymous)

____ **7.** The first half of our lives is ruined by our parents and the second half by our children. (Clarence Darrow, 1857–1938)

____ **8.** Never raise your hand to your children—it leaves your midsection unprotected. (Robert Orben)

____ **9.** No matter how old a mother is, she watches her middle-aged children for signs of improvement. (Florida Scott-Maxwell)

____ **10.** Children are a great comfort in your old age—and they help you reach it faster. (Lionel Kaufman)

____ **11.** Having children is like having a bowling alley installed in your brain. (Martin Mull)

____ **12.** An ugly baby is a very nasty object, and the prettiest is frightful when undressed. (Queen Victoria, 1819–1901)

Score Yourself

10–12 check marks	You must have had a l-o-n-g childhood.
6–9 check marks	Consider raising French poodles instead of kids.
3–5 check marks	Bet you have *a lot* of household help.
0–1 check marks	You must have the one child in America who slept through the night from Day 1.

It's All Relative

How many children are there in America? In 1996, 69.2 million Americans—26 percent—were under age 18. That's a lot of smelly sneakers and sticky fingers.

Straddling the Fence

Okay, so now you know how *you* feel about adding to the world's population, but many young (and not-so-young) couples have yet to take a stand on the kid issue. Often, it's just not something they ever thought about much. The issue can often become central when in-laws get in the act, however. Here's what Kristen told me:

"I've been in a relationship for five years, living together for the last three. We got engaged a year ago, with plans for a wedding in February '98. Recently, my fiancé told me that he does not want to have children, now or possibly ever.

We are attending counseling, and I have undergone serious self-examination to determine if I myself want to have children. There are days when I'm not very sure, and then there are days when I see a baby, and really feel sad thinking I may not experience parenthood.

My in-laws are adding to my confusion. Some, like my mother-in-law and sister-in-law, are really pushing me to have children. Others, like my cousins and father-in-law, tell me I'd be nuts to have kids, especially with a man who has already said that he doesn't want a family."

Family Matters
One of the disadvantages of having children is that they eventually get old enough to give you presents they make at school.

Don't Go There
Your desire to have children, if present now, will most likely increase as you get older. Pay attention to your feelings! Do not negotiate away something as major as parenthood in the future for short-term contentment or avoidance of immediate pain.

Are you in a similar situation? First off, there's no middle ground here. Kids aren't something you can return to the store if you change your mind, like a toaster or foot massager. Once kids arrive, they're yours forever. As a result, there's no wiggle room here. Try these suggestions if you find yourself on the fence about reproduction:

➤ First, count the in-laws out of all negotiations. The question of having children is strictly between husband and wife.

➤ Don't let any family pressure influence your decision.

➤ This is a huge issue, bigger than Bosnia or even Coke vs. Pepsi. If one partner in the relationship does not want children and the other does, reconsider your wedding plans, or at least delay marriage to fully explore your feelings about future parenthood.

➤ See why your partner does or doesn't want children. If the decision is a reaction against bad childhood memories, your spouse may resolve feelings about his or her parents and may have a different view of parenthood. But there is no guarantee that your beloved will choose to be a parent, even if this occurs.

➤ Talk with friends or family who have children of different ages. Ask them if they are satisfied with their decision.

➤ After having gathered information on other people's experiences, discuss the best and worst scenarios of having and not having children together.

➤ Consider what kind of family you would want to have together, and what the important components of family life would be for each of you.

If you are still unsure of your decision, try to delay it. If it's now or never, make it never. Children deserve parents who want them wholeheartedly. I know I'll probably get some heat for this, but as a teacher for more than 25 years and a parent for more than 16, I'll stand by my words. You can direct your attention to young nephews, nieces, cousins, sisters- and brothers-in-law, and friends' kids.

> **Family Matters**
> Review your own childhood for pain that might interfere with your desire or belief in your ability to enjoy or raise children. Determine whether your desire for or against parenthood is based mostly on fear that may prove ungrounded in your relationship, or on realities that you believe will not change substantially over time. This is another place where input from in-laws can be very helpful.

Babes in Toyland

Then we come to another twist on this issue: Couples who have it all and enjoy it wholeheartedly. Tori and Andrew had a luxurious condo, fancy-schmancy wheels, exotic vacations. There was money for some fabulous clothing, jewelry, and stereo equipment, too. And what's so terrible about a little conspicuous consumption, I say? Well, not everyone's in-laws would agree. Tori and Andrew's certainly didn't. Here's what Andrew said:

"When Tori and I got married, we decided that we didn't want children. We both come from large families and always wanted a little more than we had—more clothes, more attention, more toys. We work hard and play hard, and we really enjoy our lives. My in-laws, however, can't get off our case. 'You're so selfish,' they say. They're right; we *are* selfish, and we like it. 'Always thinking of yourself; what about us? Don't we deserve grandchildren from you and Tori?' My brother and sister-in-law have three children and they're really struggling. They try to make us feel guilty about taking a cruise or buying a new TV by saying, 'We'd like to take a

> **Words to the Wise**
> Envy is one of the Seven Deadly Sins. The other six are Pride, Wrath, Lust, Gluttony, Avarice, and Sloth. Bet the devil made you do it.

vacation, but we have to buy the kids school clothes.' The comments are making me so angry that I dread family get-togethers."

No matter how pleased people are with their children, there's bound to be a little envy—it's part of human nature. The situation can be especially acute within families, however, because people are more aware of each other's lifestyles and possessions. The issue of children versus material goods can stir up very strong feelings, as one part of the family struggles with the responsibilities of raising children while in-laws of the same age jet hither and yon with seemingly total freedom.

The Pain of Infertility

The issue of whether to have children takes an entirely different turn when the choice is taken away through infertility. This section isn't going to be very funny, I'm afraid.

First off, *infertility* is defined as the inability to conceive a child after a year of intercourse or the inability to carry a baby to term. It usually has no outward symptoms, yet it affects the lives of millions of Americans in many different ways.

Here are some facts about infertility:

➤ 3–4 million couples in America are infertile—that's one couple out of every seven. Some estimates place the percentage as high as one out of every five couples.

➤ About 25–40 percent of cases are male related; 40–50 percent are female related.

➤ 15–30 percent of all infertility is caused by an STD (sexually transmitted disease). The Alan Guttmacher Institute estimates that between 100,000 and 150,000 women become infertile each year as a result of an STD that has caused pelvic inflammatory disease.

➤ The rate of infertility among couples aged 20–24 has increased from 4 percent in 1965 to 11 percent in 1997. Most of this increase is caused by the after-effects of sexually transmitted diseases.

[Source: American Fertility Society]

It's All Relative

The National Council for Adoption (NCFA) conservatively estimates that there are at least one million infertile and fertile couples who are waiting to adopt children. For every one adoptable infant available, there are at least 40 couples hoping to adopt. Generally, infertile couples receive priority for placement of healthy babies. However, this guideline may be waived for fertile couples when children with special needs or international adoptions are involved.

Empty Arms and Aching Hearts

There's a special kind of hell inhabited by couples who want to have a child, only to remain infertile month after month. Unfortunately, Doreen's story is typical:

> "My husband Bob and I have been trying to get pregnant for a three years now. I've been in infertility treatments for two years now and I've tried everything from drug treatments to artificial inseminations. When I was having all of the tests done in the beginning, I kept hoping they'd find something wrong so it could be just be fixed and I could get on with a normal life of raising kids like everyone else. None of the doctors has been able to find any cause, which is so frustrating.

> My in-laws try to be understanding, but they can't grasp our pain. My mother-in-law keeps asking me whose 'fault' it is. 'All of Bob's sisters are real fertile Myrtles,' she said. 'We never had this problem in *our* family before.' I'm so sick of the advice! My sister-in-law told me to quit my job because it was stressing me; Bob's brother thinks he should wear boxer shorts."

Infertility can test the relationship among in-laws, as family members try to understand and deal with the problem. Even the strongest families can experience difficulty dealing with the issue, because infertility tests many different aspects of a family relationship.

Communication often breaks down at this point, as the couple finds it painful to share the details of their despair. The couple's anguish over their inability to produce a child—as well as their embarrassment over seemingly endless medical procedures—can also keep them from sharing their thoughts with family members. Here's what Stacey said:

Don't Go There
Infertility is a life crisis that has a rippling effect on all areas of a person's life. However, it is normal to feel a sense of failure that can affect your self-esteem and self-image.

> "We have been trying for two and a half years to get pregnant. This year, polyps were found and removed from my uterus, and the next month I

began an aggressive treatment. The first month this did not work. I have been *extremely* depressed, emotional, moody...you name it. I did not experience this so much last month.

I am trying to determine how much of it can be attributed to the hormone treatment and how much may just be depression over infertility. Last month I was very positive because I thought for sure that the treatment would work. This month, I know that even this may not work. My in-laws try to help, but they are depressed over not producing a child who is 'perfect' enough to reproduce."

Coping

When you are experiencing infertility, one of the most difficult challenges is communicating with family and friends about what may be a devastating life crisis. Even the most caring relative or friend may offer a "helpful" suggestion, which will appear wildly insensitive to you. Here are some questions you may encounter—and answers you can use to deal with your in-laws and friends.

➤ Question: "So, when are you going to start a family? You two aren't getting any younger!"

Answer: "We consider ourselves a family now. We love children and especially enjoy our nieces, nephews, and friends' kids. If we decide to expand our family, we'll be sure to let you know."

➤ Question: "When are you going to stop concentrating on your career and start a family?"

Answer: "I don't believe my job and a family are mutually exclusive. My career is advancing, and I'm very proud of my work. When we feel the time is right, we will consider starting our family."

Family Matters
Infertility is a process, and it may mean letting go of initial dreams. Stay informed about the wide range of options available to you. Also, try to connect with others facing similar experiences. The Internet is a great way to do this.

➤ Question: "Well, I guess we'll never be grandparents."

Answer: "We truly hope that someday you will have grandchildren. Whether we have children biologically or through adoption, we look forward to sharing our happiness with you."

➤ Question: "I wish you'd take one of my kids—they drive my absolutely crazy!"

Answer: "Oh thanks, then they'd drive me crazy!"

➤ Question: I've heard about a tremendous new experimental infertility treatment. Why don't you try that?

➤ Answer: "It may sound easy, but infertility treatments are very complicated—not all the new developments apply to every case.

Parents, after your children have explained their infertility to you, give them a rest. Don't demand news of every test, procedure, and medication. Assure them that you may not understand how difficult this must be for them, but you extend your love. In addition, refrain from sharing "helpful" tidbits about getting pregnant, such as Aunt Sherry's use of Vitamin E, surefire sexual positions, and bizarre herbal remedies like powered grasshoppers in mint tea.

As stressful and painful as infertility is, it can also be a chance for families to come together and support each other. An understanding and loving comment can go a long way to help a family member deal with this painful time. In-laws will long remember the kindness done to them at this time.

> **Family Matters**
> "Resolve" is a national non-profit organization that, for more than 20 years, has been helping people deal with infertility by providing information, support, and advocacy through publications, infertility support groups, physical referrals, and a hotline. Their Internet address is **http://www.resolve.org/.**

The Least You Need to Know

➤ Not all couples want to have children. In-laws can find this difficult to accept.

➤ Some couples can't decide whether to have children. In-laws often pressure them to make a decision.

➤ Infertility can be shattering to the entire family.

➤ A little understanding and compassion goes a long way.

Part 5
Circumstance-in-Law

Kentucky: Two men tried to pull the front off a cash machine by running a chain from the machine to the bumper of their pickup truck. Instead of pulling the front panel off the machine, though, they pulled the bumper off their truck. Scared, they left the scene and drove home—with the chain still attached to the machine, their bumper still attached to the chain, and their vehicle's license plate still attached to the bumper.

South Carolina: A man walked into a local police station, dropped a bag of cocaine on the counter, informed the desk sergeant that it was substandard cut, and asked that the person who sold it to him be arrested immediately.

Indiana: A man walked up to a cashier at a grocery store and demanded all the money in the register. When the cashier handed him the loot, he fled—leaving his wallet on the counter.

Virginia: A burglar tried to break into a department store through a skylight. The police nabbed him on the roof. It seems he forgot to wait until the store was closed. His error was reported by some of the many shoppers still in the store.

Things don't always go as we planned. That's because life has a nasty way of kicking us in the face, especially when we're down. To help you deal with these curve balls, I'll wind up this guide with a discussion of some of the serious problems that confront you and your in-laws, including chronic illness, abuse, addiction, aged in-laws, divorce, and widowhood.

A Monkey Wrench in the Works: Ailing In-Laws

In This Chapter

➤ See how family illness brings out the best—and worst—in all of us

➤ Learn how illness affects all your in-law relationships

➤ Find out how to deal with in-laws who suffer from imaginary illnesses

➤ Develop strategies for dealing with ailing in-laws

Let's start with a short history of medicine:

2000 B.C.—Here, eat this root.

1000 A.D.—That root is heathen. Here, say this prayer.

1850 A.D.—That prayer is superstition. Here, drink this potion.

1940 A.D.—That potion is snake oil. Here, swallow this pill.

1985 A.D.—That pill is ineffective. Here, take this antibiotic.

2000 A.D.—That antibiotic is artificial. Here, eat this root.

The Irish have a traditional blessing: "May your relatives stay well and die quickly." This is rarely the case, however. Life throws us many wicked curve balls, and one of the most devious is illness. Few of us escape without a brush with the medical establishment. Any illness is trying, but serious or chronic illness can shred fragile family bonds and strain even the strongest ones. This is true whether the illness affects a young in-law or an older one.

Family Matters
The bacteria found on human skin are roughly the numerical equivalent of all the humans on Earth. So wash your hands!

In this chapter, you'll see how illness can cause people to revert to their traditional roles in the family—which can often increase the stress for everyone involved. Then I'll discuss how illness in the family can drive wedges between family members, especially husbands and wives. Along the way I'll explore the problem of in-laws who use illness to gain attention. Finally, I'll give you strategies for coping with illness and in-laws.

The More Things Change, the More They Stay the Same

When Steve's 75-year-old mother Doris had a heart attack, the family went into crisis mode. Several in-laws did their usual Chicken Little impressions, holding their heads and moaning that the sky was falling. Steve's brother called everyone in the family to get their opinions on the proper course of action. Steve's sister and her husband promptly took off on a vacation; a few cousins did some research and offered empty lip service.

It's All Relative

As of 1990, approximately 45 percent of all single women over age 65 lived in a household with relatives. This included living in a son's or daughter's home. [Source: American Association of Retired Persons]

Melanie, Steve's wife, took charge and moved her mother-in-law into their home. While Steve went off to work all day, Melanie did her best to take care of her mother-in-law. She reminded Doris to take her medicine, made sure that she rested and ate well, and coped with her mother-in-law's isolation and depression.

Meanwhile, Doris did nothing but complain. The food was too greasy, the house was dirty, and Melanie was a cold fish. Melanie understood her mother-in-law's frustration and need to vent, but she had a hard time controlling her temper when the older woman complained that Melanie couldn't hold a candle to Doris's daughter Lesley. Of course, Lesley hadn't called in months. She never visited or sent money. The world would stop spinning on its axis if Lesley offered to give Melanie and Steve a much-needed break from their responsibilities.

Been There, Done That, Got the T-shirt

Family illness brings all the old roles into play. Your in-laws who are good at taking charge, for example, usually step right up to the plate and take care of business. This is what Melanie was doing. She understood that someone had to take care of her mother-in-law right now. Nonetheless, some of the relatives openly complained that Melanie was being bossy, but they were secretly relieved that *they* were off the hook.

Other relatives head for the hills at the first sign of trouble. This is what Lesley was doing. Meanwhile, the troublemakers were busy rehashing old conflicts and the neurotics were trying to milk as much attention as possible from the crisis. How would your in-laws fit into *this* scenario?

Adding to the stress are the different problem-solving strategies people favor. There are two basic approaches: Emotion and reason.

1. *Emotional* people make decisions based on feelings.

2. *Rational* people tend to offer logical, practical solutions.

> **Don't Go There**
> Depression among the elderly is frequently ignored or misdiagnosed as a "natural" reaction to illness and aging. Fortunately, many cases of depression among the elderly can be treated with therapy and medications.

> **Family Matters**
> Ironically, the person who appears to be coping most successfully with the stress of an in-law's illness may in fact be suffering the most pressure. Don't be surprised if this person is the first to crumble when the crisis passes.

Each approach has its advantages and disadvantages, depending on whether you're the "let-it-all-hang-out" or "stiff-upper-lip" sort. Problems arise when these approaches clash in families. The emotional camp is apt to find the rational side of the family cold and unfeeling. The rational group, in contrast, will likely accuse the emotional problem-solvers of being airheads and judge them unable to cope with reality.

Divide and Conquer

Differing patterns of behavior and styles of problem solving often cause schisms among in-laws. Shopworn issues of sibling rivalry are likely to reassert themselves during times of illness, as family members align in the "us" versus "them" patterns of their childhood. For example, if you were always closer to your brother than your sister, you may find yourself siding with bro when your father gets sick—even if you think sis has a more valid approach. Family loyalty is a potent force, like duct tape or gravity.

Don't Go There
Fear is also a big factor with certain family illnesses, especially those that are contagious or genetically transmitted. It's not unusual for other members of the family to fear that they, too, may be taken ill. This can affect the level of care they are willing to give to the ill person.

Illness can drive husbands and wives apart, too. Gene and Kathy experienced this when Gene's brother Marty became ill with AIDS and moved in with them. "When Marty and I argue," Kathy complains, "Gene always takes his brother's side. They act like it's the two of them against the world. I'm left out in the cold. I lose my temper and walk out on them until I can calm down."

Of Myth and Men

Family illness brings out all the dangerous myths that have been passed around for years, like the Christmas fruitcake that's been recycled so often it's almost a member of the family. How many of the following fictions upset the balance in *your* family? Put a check mark next to each statement that has become an issue among your in-laws.

_____ 1. When someone becomes ill, we take care of our own.

_____ 2. It's a woman's role to take care of ill family members.

_____ 3. We don't need any help from outsiders when someone becomes ill.

_____ 4. Everyone will pitch in and do their fair share if one of us takes sick.

_____ 5. Only bad families put their ailing in-laws in a nursing home.

It's tough enough having to deal with a family illness, especially when the sufferer is an older in-law, without having to cope with the guilt that these myths bring. Let's check out the reality.

Myth 1: When Someone Becomes Ill, We Take Care of Our Own

Reality: Sometimes, this *is* possible. Often, however, it's not. You know the stats on working couples. Today's 9-to-5ers don't have the time to bring in the bacon and cook it, much less take care of an ailing in-law. Something's got to give. What gives? *You.*

Ever make up those "Thing To Do Today" lists? I do all the time. Here's a typical one for a typical day:

1. Finish Chapter 22 of manuscript.

2. Call doctor and order mother-in-law's new medicine.

3. Bring medicine to mother-in-law.

4. Pick up kids from school.

5. Take dog to vet for shots.

6. Food shop.

7. Do something about dinner.

8. Iron clothes for tomorrow.

9. Send best friend her birthday card.

10. Have sex. (optional)

What can you do to carve out a little time and space for yourself?

> ➤ Survey the situation. Start by making a list of everyone's needs—including your own. Then put the items in order, from most to least important. Cross out the last third of the list. Yes, out they go. This is war, baby, and we take no prisoners. If the items are really important, they'll end up back on the list higher up. In the meantime, you've got time to take a breath, if not a bath. (What, you want *everything*?)

> ➤ Make time for yourself. "Dream on, Rozakis," you sneer. "I have an ill father-in-law, three kids, a full-time job, and a teething puppy. When would I have time for myself?" Of course you don't have the time. That's why you have to *make* the time.

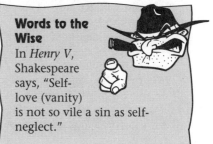

Don't Go There
Increasingly, scientists are noting the link between stress and illness. In addition to driving you crazy, your family can make you sick as well, depending on your capacity to deal with stress. Take care of yourself or you won't be able to take care of others.

My mother-in-law lived with us for a while after she had surgery. At the time, I was teaching full-time in a high school, adjuncting part-time in a university, attending graduate school, and coaching the debate club, pep team, and senior class. In addition to being in pain, my mother-in-law was very depressed and isolated. For a while, I had to carry out nursing tasks such as catherization, for which I had never been trained. No sweat; I was Superwoman. Ha! I knew it was time to take a break when I backed into a stopped school bus, broadside. Fortunately, no one was hurt, but my car was in the shop for a week. It took my ego a whole lot longer to recover.

Words to the Wise
In *Henry V*, Shakespeare says, "Self-love (vanity) is not so vile a sin as self-neglect."

When you make your list of things you have to do, be sure to include a sliver of time for yourself. Allow half an hour to work in the garden, make a phone call to a friend, read the newspaper. Soak in a bubble bath; go for a walk with a friend.

Stretch yourself too thin and you'll run yourself right into the ground. Then you won't be of any use to anyone.

Myth 2: It's a Woman's Role to Take Care of Ill Family Members

Reality: In times of family crisis, such as illness, in most families, it *is* the women rather than the men who most often shoulder the burden. There are many reasons for this, including:

➤ It fulfills their need to feel powerful and needed.

➤ It's not viewed as a burden, but as a duty.

➤ It's a way of repaying a debt for care they may have received in the past.

➤ It feels as if there isn't a choice under the pressure of family.

Are you likely to become the family caretaker if an in-law becomes ill? Take the following quiz to see. Check each statement that applies to you.

_____ 1. My mother-in-law has no daughters.

_____ 2. I'm married to the oldest son in the family.

_____ 3. I live geographically close to my in-laws.

_____ 4. My sisters-in-law live far away or work demanding full-time jobs.

_____ 5. I'm the kid who can't say "no."

Family Matters
ElderCare Web is a great source of information about helping older in-laws (**http://www.elder web.com/**). There are links to health, lifestyles, aging, social, financial, legal, and regional concerns. Also try GoldenAge .Net at **http://elo.mediasrv .swt.edu/goldenage/ commercial.html**. It contains information on housing, long-term care, products, services, and health.

Score Yourself

5 check marks	Prepare the guest room; company's coming.
4–3 check marks	It may be time to call the self-esteem fairy.
2–1 check marks	Don't tread on me.
0 check marks	Were you a man in your first life?

Just say no. This is the hardest lesson to learn. Many women have been raised to be all things to all people. And as glamorous as it sounds when Whitney Houston sings about it, enough is enough. Fight back! Take on what you can handle, not what you believe others think you should do.

Myth 3: We Don't Need Any Help from Outsiders When Someone Becomes Ill

Reality: Yes, you do. We all do. You simply can't do everything yourself—and you shouldn't have to. Have someone share the burden. Many religious organizations have agencies that provide services for the elderly. See if the Catholic Charities or the Jewish Family Service can send someone to your in-laws' house to read to them, prepare simple meals, or do chores. These resources are supplemental to your efforts; they won't replace you, but they *can* give you the few extra hours you need each week to regroup.

Myth 4: Everyone Will Pitch In and Do Their Fair Share If One of Us Takes Sick

Reality: When pigs fly. Never assume that your spouse knows that you're feeling overwhelmed by responsibilities as well as emotions. Your spouse may not understand the extent of the burden you've been carrying— especially if you make it look easy. Ditto for the rest of the family. Communicate your needs and be sure to take theirs into account.

Family Matters
ANSWERS is a magazine for adult children of aging parents. Write or call: *ANSWERS*, P.O. Box 9889, Birmingham, AL 35220–0889 (800) 750–2199.

Myth 5: Only Bad Families Put Their Ailing In-Laws in a Nursing Home

Reality: As you've learned from this book (and from personal experience), we do the best we can. Sometimes, however, families are unable to take care of their in-laws. Sometimes, it's the nature of their illness. Certain illnesses may require more nursing care than unskilled relatives can handle. Other times, the caregivers are experiencing their own stress: Divorce, money issues, problems with abuse, even their own illness. In these situations, families turn to residential care.

Can't Win for Trying

What do you do when a family member is very seriously ill...and unexpectedly gets better? That's what happened in Danny's family.

Danny's mother was diagnosed with terminal cancer; she was expected to last less than a year. The entire family pulled together and jumped into action. Danny's sister moved up her wedding date so Mom could attend; another sibling and his wife decided to have a baby before Mom shuffled off this mortal coil. One relative sold a business and moved closer to home. Amazingly, the cancer went into remission. That was five years ago. The family has been redefined based on Mom's illness.

"'I get yelled at if I don't call Mom every day,'" Danny said. 'We're expected to be at her beck and call. If we don't drop everything and do what she wants, she says, 'I'd be better off dead. No one wants a sick old lady around. I've outstayed my welcome on Earth.' The family is divided on the issue. Some of the in-laws have set aside their lives to make Mom happy; the others are going about their business."

The martyrs are smug; the selfish are guilty. This really is a no-win situation.

It's All Relative

Here are some statements you don't want to hear during surgery:

"Better save that. We'll need it for the autopsy."

"Hand me that...uh...that uh...that thingy there."

"Oh no! Where's my Rolex?"

"Ya know, there's big money in kidneys and this guy's got two of 'em."

"Could you stop that thing from beating? It's throwing off my concentration."

"Darn! Page 47 of the manual is missing."

"Don't worry. I think it's sharp enough."

The "G" Spot

Why do they get away with it? They hit the "G" spot—guilt. The stresses of realigning the family to accommodate a seriously ill in-law can upset even the sturdiest apple cart. People feel guilt that because both adults are working full-time to support the family, nobody is home to take care of an ailing in-law. Are you living half-way across the globe from your ailing in-law? Expect to feel guilt over that, too. We all have other priorities that must be met before we help the extended family. The result? More guilt. Here's Amanda's story:

> "I'm an only daughter, age 50, and married. In addition to working full time, I do my mother-in-law's shopping and balance her checkbook. Yet I'm always haunted by the gnawing feeling that I ought to be doing more. Because I love my ailing, 80-year-old mother-in-law very much and because I am appreciative of her many sacrifices in my behalf, I would like to return my mother-in-law's good deeds. My mother-in-law does not demand this of me: I demand it of myself."

Amanda is one of many devoted daughters and sons who believes in the myth of return of total care. When Amanda was a child, her mother died of a long-term illness—and Amanda has always felt guilty about not being able to help her mom. Therefore, she's determined to help her mother-in-law. Also, Amanda reasons that she's raised three children herself and knows how to be a good caretaker. What Amanda doesn't stop to consider is that she is older with less available physical and emotional stamina. Amanda also doesn't stop to consider that raising her three children was dramatically different from caring for her mother-in-law, who will become increasingly dependent and require more and more care. Without realizing these stark realities, Amanda is caught in a no-win situation where guilt tears her apart. Is it any wonder Amanda is always feeling guilty and depressed?

Guilt, Begone!

That old catch phrase, "How can one mother take care of ten children but ten children cannot take care of one mother?" no longer washes in a society where children are saddled with unprecedented responsibilities and are older themselves. If you are truly doing all you can to help your ailing in-law, then your guilt is self-punishing. Don't buy into guilt trips, either. If you feel stuck, get help, either from a support group for children of aging parents or a mental health professional.

I have yet to meet an emotionally healthy parent who wants her child to become ill while caring for her. Most parents, in fact, want their children to "have it better" than they. Most parents, too, are willing to listen to children's expressions of their life needs, provided their children approach them with respect and without rancor.

Don't Go There
Beware of giving care from obligation. Care should come from love, which is what most parents and in-laws want anyway.

The In-Law Who Cries Wolf

Every family has one: The in-law who claims to suffer from every ailment under the sun but manages to muster enough strength to do exactly what he or she wants. Never one to miss a wedding, graduation, or funeral, this in-law nevertheless spends an extraordinary amount of time moaning on the sofa, demanding mugs of soup and heaps of attention. The rest of the family must dance attendance on the *hypochondriac* or risk being called "cold," "uncaring," or—worst of all—"selfish."

These professional sickos are also experts on every illness under the sun. Got a headache? Sally Sick is sure to diagnose a brain tumor. Stomach ache? No

Words to the Wise
A *hypochondriac* is a person who worries or talks excessively about his or her health.

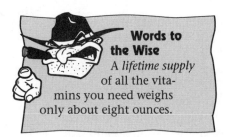

doubt it's intestinal parasites, elephantiasis, or beriberi. Doc in the Box has the answer to everything—and whatever you've got, he or she has far worse. Think your head hurts? Think again. *Her* head feels like all Seven Dwarfs are tapping away with their pick-axes. Think you've got a bad case of the flu? That's nothing. Your in-law the hypochondriac had a case of the flu so bad they wrote him up in the *New England Journal of Medicine*. Want to see the article? He has it right here.

Here's what Fred told me about his sister-in-law, the long-suffering Nicole:

> "Nicole always has bizarre stomach pains, which she blames on the food she's being served. She's sure it hasn't been cooked or refrigerated properly. In addition, she claims to be allergic to everything ever grown or made. As a result, she carries around enough medicine to stock her own drug store. Since she swears she has heart palpitations, she carries a stethoscope so she can check her heart. Last week, she walked into my in-laws' house and started sneezing. 'Has there been a cat in here?' she demanded. 'About 10 years ago,' my father-in-law replied. 'I knew it!" she exclaimed, 'You can't imagine how sensitive I am to cats. You'd better have the rugs cleaned before I come over again.'
>
> Every one of Nicole's illnesses, real or imagined, is an event, and we all have to share in her pain—every single detail of it. Nicole is so tiresome that no one wants to be around her any more."

Don't get sucked into this sicko's scene. Give polite attention, but keep a healthy distance from the manipulation. Beware: Somewhere along the line, the family hypochondriac will probably get genuinely ill and you'll probably have to step in. But until then, save yourself.

It Ain't Easy

Parenting a parent or an in-law isn't a cakewalk, no matter how much love and compassion exist within the family. That's because caring for an older person takes very different skills and fosters different emotions than taking care of a young child. After all, you expect your two-year old to be balky or obstinate, but not your mother-in-law.

Besides, if we did simply become our parents' parents when they became old, then caring for them would be a snap. We'd simply fit them into our lives as we wanted, and treat them as kids. They'd get a schedule and discipline. We wouldn't agonize over decisions we'd make on their behalf, feel guilty when we had to say no to them, or experience the heartbreak of their dependence. The truth is that however infirm our parents and in-laws become, they forever remain our parents and in-laws. Here are some parting suggestions:

➤ Understand that long-term illness is very stressful on *everyone*.

➤ Recognize that people have different ways to approach problems.

➤ Accept that different approaches may be equally valid, even though they don't suit your personal style.

➤ Make allowances for these differences.

➤ Keep your sense of humor. You'll need it.

Don't Go There
The expectations of ailing family members and the guilt resulting from them are a major cause of arguments and feuds at a time when support is most needed.

The Least You Need to Know

➤ Family illness is very stressful on *everyone*.

➤ Stress and responsibilities caused by the illness can divide a family.

➤ Don't be afraid to ask for help and be sure to make time for yourself.

➤ Resist guilt, no matter how heavily it's laid on.

➤ Keep your sense of humor. It will serve you well.

Chapter 23

Here's to You, Mrs. Robinson

In This Chapter

➤ Learn about abuse within families

➤ Discover what to do if your in-law is a "funny" uncle...or aunt

➤ Find out more about physical abuse

➤ See the scars emotional abuse can leave

➤ Explore the issue of child neglect

➤ See how an in-law's substance abuse can shatter a family

➤ Learn when to butt in and when to shut up

In the first of several similar incidents reported to the press, Jonathan Prevette, a first-grader from Lexington, North Carolina, was removed from class and kept out of an ice-cream party for kids with perfect attendance records. His crime? He kissed a first-grade girl on the cheek. School authorities, deluged by phone calls, defended their actions, citing a rule against "unwelcome touching." They also pointed out, contrary to public perception, that Jonathan had not been accused of sexual harassment as such. As pundits everywhere debated the case, Jonathan emerged as a national celebrity, with his picture in the newspapers. Of course, he appeared on CNN and NBC's *Today* show.

There's no question that we've gone a little haywire over the notion of sexual harassment. But the hysteria over sexual harassment masks a very real problem with sexual abuse in the workplace, in schools, and even in social situations—a problem that also extends to families as well.

Abuse is wrenching any time it occurs, but it's especially tragic when the betrayal is caused by those you love and trust. That's what this chapter is all about. You'll learn how to recognize sexual misconduct, physical abuse, emotional terror, and other forms of brutality among in-laws. Most important, you'll learn how to deal with these situations.

There Goes the Neighborhood

It's easy to spot an abuser, isn't it? They're the smarmy men in greasy raincoats. They keep their hands in their pockets and read dirty magazines. They say things like, "Hey, little girl, want a lollipop?"

Unfortunately, abusers rarely wear name tags that say things like "Hello My Name is Jack the Pervert." You can't judge a book by its cover—and you can't judge an abuser by his or her age, gender, or appearance. Abusers take many forms, from the apparently jolly grandparents to the distracted parents. Seemingly gentle uncles and witty sisters-in-law can be abusers as well. In part, that's because there are different types of abuse. Here are the five types most often found among in-laws:

➤ Sexual abuse

➤ Physical abuse

➤ Child neglect

➤ Emotional abuse

➤ Substance abuse

Don't Go There
Sometimes, the victim will deliberately provoke the abuser to speed the explosion. This action gets the worst over quickly and allows a period of calm before the next crisis. However, the provocation allows the abuser to claim that the victim "caused" the explosion, when that is not true at all.

Heart of Darkness

It may be difficult to recognize an abuser, but it's easy to recognize the cycle of abuse. First, the abuser feels pressure. As the tension builds, the abuser becomes more and more tightly wound. Because he or she is unable to deal with the pressure, it spills over to the family. Perhaps it takes the form of critical comments or some shoves and slaps.

As the pressure builds, the abuser looks for reasons to vent his or her frustrations. Finally, the abuser reaches critical mass and explodes. After the incident, the abuser is ashamed and embarrassed. The abuser often showers the victim with gifts and promises never to lose control again. Unless there is intervention, the cycle starts again....

Sex, Lies, and In-Laws

How much do you know about sexual abuse within families? Take this simple quiz to see.

1. Child abuse is over-reported in the United States.

   True   False

2. Sexual molestation of children is usually a single, violent incident.

   True   False

3. Sexual molestation of children usually begins in adolescence.

   True   False

4. Sexual contact with a child is illegal even if the child consents.

   True   False

5. Child sexual abuse doesn't occur unless an adult forces a child to have intercourse.

   True   False

6. A large majority of child victims are molested by a family member or another person known to the child.

   True   False

7. Non-violent sexual abuse or coercion is less traumatic than aggressive or violent abuse.

   True   False

8. Many offenders were molested themselves as children.

   True   False

Family Matters
For additional information about child abuse, you can contact:

The National Child Abuse Coalition
733 15th Street, NW
Suite 938 Washington, DC 20005
(202) 347-3666

9. Most sex offenders are heterosexual males.

    True   False

10. Children can be psychologically harmed by the reaction of significant adults upon disclosure.

    True   False

Bonus: Child abuse happens at about the same rate in all kinds of neighborhoods and in all parts of the world.

    True   False

Score Yourself

1. False	6. True
2. False	7. False
3. False	8. True
4. True	9. True
5. False	10. True
Bonus: True	

Secrets and Lies: Sexual Abuse

Words to the Wise

According to the Child Abuse Prevention and Treatment Act (Public Law 100-294), sexual abuse is "the use, employment, persuasion, inducement, enticement or coercion of any child to engage in, or assist any other person to engage in, any sexually explicit conduct (or any simulation of such conduct) for the purpose of producing any visual depiction of such conduct, or rape, molestation, prostitution, or other form of sexual exploitation of children, or incest with children."

An acquaintance told me this story about her past:

"When I was six years old I was molested by my sister's husband. We all trusted him because he was a relative. Ten years later, it still hurts. I can't go a day without crying. I'm always thinking about it. Sometimes I wish I hadn't told, but when I revealed the truth, other family members came forward to say "Uncle Ed" had sexually molested them as well."

It is very threatening to our concept of "family" and the image we hold of our in-laws to confront the possibility that a member of the family may be suffering sexual abuse, much less at the hands of an in-law.

Sexual abuse can be obvious or subtle. Rape and molestation are overt acts of sexual abuse; lewd comments are far less obvious. Whatever form it takes, sexual abuse is against the law.

Nonetheless, more than 150,000 children were the reported victims of sexual abuse in 1995, the most current statistics available from the National Center for Child Abuse and Neglect. This represents a 300 percent rise in sexual abuse of children since 1980. For every reported case of sexual abuse, an estimated five more cases go unreported.

What makes these numbers even more terrible is that in more than half these cases, the abuser was a member of the child's family, a "caring" father, mother, stepparent, grandparent, uncle, aunt, brother, sister, cousin, or other in-law. No one argues that sexual abuse is wrong—but no one wants to admit that it can happen in anyone's family, even our own.

> **Don't Go There**
> According to the National Center for Child Abuse and Neglect, 77 percent of the perpetrators were the victims' parents, and 12 percent were other relatives.

Connect the Dots

How should you deal with sexual abuse within the family? Here's the advice I got from my acquaintance who's had personal experience. It dovetails with my own suggestions:

> "If a child comes to you and tells you they were abused, you have to take action. Don't worry if the child is lying; they most likely aren't. I know if my parents had any doubt in their minds when I told them it would have killed me. Do everything you can to help that child—and other children. No one deserves to go through what I've gone through, and what many other survivors have gone through. I will never be the same."

It's especially difficult to detect sexual abuse and help the victim because the abuser is often a parent or a relative, their most trusted protectors. Children may not recognize sexual abuse when it happens or even know it's wrong. Nonetheless, children rarely lie about being victims of sexual abuse, even though they may be too confused or frightened to talk directly about it.

Pay close attention to any children or in-laws whose behavior suddenly shifts. Be alert for physical and behavioral changes that might signal sexual abuse. Physical signs *may* include:

➤ Bedwetting

➤ Loss of appetite

➤ Nightmares

➤ Complaints of pain or irritation around the genital area

➤ Venereal disease

Behavioral symptoms *may* include:

➤ Refusing to go to school or to be alone

➤ Increased anxiety or immature behavior

➤ Artwork that depicts strange sexual overtones and a change in attitude toward an in-law, neighbor, or baby-sitter

If you suspect that an in-law is sexually abusing a vulnerable member of your family, such as a child, a handicapped person, or an elderly person, report your suspicions to the police or a child protection agency. Seek counseling for the victim from a community mental health or sexual abuse treatment program.

J'Accuse!

But what if you accuse your in-law and you're wrong? Once you accuse a family member of sexual abuse, your relationship to that person will change forever. To make sure your suspicions are correct, follow these steps:

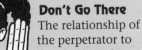

Don't Go There
The relationship of the perpetrator to the victim varies depending on the type of abuse. Non-parents and parent substitutes account for about half the cases of sexual abuse. Neglect and physical abuse, in contrast, are most often perpetrated by a natural parent.

1. Gather your evidence.

2. Talk to your children about touches that are appropriate and ones that make them feel uneasy.

3. Pay attention to the nonverbal signals in any relationship between a child and a family member that makes you uncomfortable.

4. Talk to the child and gain his or her trust.

5. Let the child know that you're someone to rely on. Stress that they can always talk to you when someone's been touching them in a way that makes them feel uncomfortable.

Six Degrees of Separation

Your in-laws' past experiences with sexual abuse colors their attitude toward normal sexual relationships. When there has been a history of sexual abuse within a family, everyone is affected—even newcomers to the family. A long-time acquaintance I'll call Ginny shared her experiences:

"I'm a 38-year-old incest survivor. I've had over 10 years of therapy and I've healed a lot. However, it is still so hard to be with my family members. I broke off all contact for almost seven years. Now they've contacted me and want to attempt a relationship. I'm scared, threatened, angry, and stressed out. I don't want to go back to being manipulated, and especially I don't want to put my children at risk. I hate my family and love them at the same time. My parents are getting old, and part of me feels sorry for them. My kids want grandparents."

Kids are entitled to grandparents—but even more, they are entitled to safety. Never leave vulnerable family members alone with an in-law (or anyone) who has a history of sexual abuse. Family members who reestablish contact with sexually abusive parents or in-laws must above all else protect their children. When dealing with sexual predators, a few moments can change a person's life forever, so always err on the side of caution.

It's All Relative

A 1995 study of homeless people found that many of them had a history of sexual or physical abuse as children. Preventing child abuse can help reduce juvenile delinquency, runaways, childhood drug and alcohol addiction, and teenage prostitution.

Sometimes Love Hurts: Physical Abuse

We all know what "discipline" means…or do we? Perhaps your mother-in-law believes in "sparing the rod and spoiling the child," but you're opposed to anyone ever striking your child. "When he was a child, I sent your husband to his room without his dinner and look how well he turned out!" your father-in-law thunders. To you, depriving your child of food is cruel and abusive. Who's right? What's appropriate punishment—and what's abuse? Where's the line between love and abuse?

Adrienne's family had a problem with physical abuse. She came to me for advice. Here's what she said:

> "My four-year old daughter adores her aunt, my sister-in-law. The trouble is, my sister-in-law doesn't have an interest in kids, has no kids of her own, and has told me that she would hit my daughter if she ever misbehaved. Recently my daughter pulled on my sister-in-law's arm, and my sister-in-law pulled my daughter's arm right back, dragging her along, saying 'How do you like having someone pulling *your* arm?'

> Shocked, I separated them and walked my daughter away from my sister-in-law. My daughter is confused. I feel I should have somehow physically protected my daughter. Besides, I'm very angry at my sister-in-law. She disappeared into a crowd, causing my brother to go search for her. Then she got down on her knees to apologize to my daughter, creating an even bigger scene. My husband felt we should have seen it coming and separated the two, but my sister-in-law nearly always welcomes our daughter to play.

Don't Go There

False charges of abuse are becoming increasingly common in bitter child custody battles. About six percent of unsubstantiated child-abuse reports are false accusations.

Words to the Wise

Physical abuse is characterized by inflicting physical injury by punching, beating, kicking, biting, burning, or otherwise harming a child. Although the injury is not an accident, the parent may not have intended to hurt the child. The injury may have resulted from physical punishment that is inappropriate to the child's age.

Family Matters

As a result of the Child Abuse Amendments of 1984 (P.L. 98-457), withholding of medically indicated treatment for an infant's life-threatening conditions is also classified as child abuse.

We have a very small family. If we don't allow our daughter to be with her aunt—or if we confront my sister-in-law about her behavior—we could cause big problems. Maybe I should only consider my daughter's safety and security and to heck with this woman my brother married."

A vulnerable person's safety and security *always* come first. Do all that you can to protect a child or vulnerable adult from abuse. Here's how:

➤ Take abuse seriously. Even one slap can set the stage for a pattern of increasingly violent abuse.

➤ Never leave your child or a vulnerable adult with someone you don't trust completely—even if that person is an in-law.

➤ Always be alert to when your intervention is needed.

➤ Don't hesitate to intervene if you think an in-law's behavior in any way puts your child or a vulnerable adult at risk.

This Hurts Me More Than It Hurts You?

In America alone, five children die every day of abuse or neglect. All told, 3,102,000 children were reported being abused or neglected in the U.S. in 1995. Here are some other statistics about child abuse to curl your hair—and turn your stomach.

➤ More children under age four die from abuse or neglect than from falls, choking on food, suffocation, drowning, residential fires, and motor vehicle accidents.

➤ Overall, the total number of reports of child abuse and neglect nationwide increased 49 percent since 1986 [source: National Committee to Prevent Child Abuse].

➤ The number of actual child abuse and neglect cases nearly doubled between 1986 and 1993, according to the Third National Incidence Study of Child Abuse and Neglect [1996, U.S. Department of Health and Human Services].

➤ In a 1995 Gallup poll of parents, reports of physical abuse were about 16 times higher than the number of reports officially recorded.

➤ Substance abuse and economic stress are the two most frequently cited problems in families reported for child maltreatment.

Older, Wiser—and More Vulnerable

Don't assume that physical abuse in families always occurs between adults and small children. Reports of domestic abuse against the elderly increased 150 percent from 1986 to 1996—from 117,000 cases to 292,000 according to the National Center on Elder Abuse. And hundreds of thousands more instances go unreported, they noted (*Newsday*, November 15, 1997).

The problem will likely get worse as American society ages. Such abuse often goes unreported because an in-law is the abuser and the elderly person is reluctant to say anything. Often, the victim is dependent on their abuser, the in-law who is taking care of them. Usually, physical abuse is the symptom and financial abuse is the motivation.

A Dollar Late and a Day Short

About a decade ago, a New York City toll collector observed a woman covered with bruises in the rear of a car. The collector radioed the New York State police, who stopped the car. The woman's husband, an attorney, explained to police that the bruises were accidental, and he was released. A week later, the woman was dead from a beating inflicted by her husband.

Many women are hit once or twice and then leave an abusive relationship. Unfortunately, others stay—sometimes until it's too late to escape. If you have an in-law who is involved in recurring physical abuse, he or she must get treatment. If an in-law is doing the beating, you need to intervene. Confront the person and explain that such behavior is not acceptable. Another member of the family may have to step in as well. Don't hesitate to get the help you need to stop the violence.

Don't Go There
Victims of physical abuse often have been intimidated and will usually support the abuser's version of how their injuries occurred to avoid further injury. After years of maltreatment, they may be convinced that the abuse was just punishment because they were bad. This can make it especially difficult to correct the situation.

Don't Go There
There are relatively few case of wives abusing their husbands or male partner. In some cases, it turns out that the female partners are finally striking back. However, there *are* cases of women beating men, so all such reports cannot be dismissed. They *must* be investigated by the authorities.

Home Alone: Neglect

Here's what Corrine told me about her family situation:

> "My sister-in-law (she and my brother are divorced) is neglecting my four-year-old nephew and a second baby that she had with another man. The children are not fed or clothed properly. Last week, I found the four-year-old alone in the apartment minding the baby! My sister-in-law said she had to 'run out and get a few things' and felt safe leaving my nephew baby-sitting. My sister-in-law has gotten into trouble with the law for drugs and criminal activity. I want to turn her in to the authorities, but I'm afraid of what will happen to the kids."

Child neglect is characterized by failure to provide for the child's basic needs. Neglect can be physical, educational, or emotional. A child of any age, sex, race, religion, and socio-economic background can fall victim to child neglect. A large number of neglected children are never reported to the authorities who can help them and their families.

Family Matters
Willful neglect is likely to trigger Child Protective Services intervention. A parent who is unable to provide the necessities of life due to poverty may, instead, seek assistance from agencies that provide financial assistance, health services, housing, or other basic services.

When are you justified in reporting your in-laws to child protective services for child neglect? It's important to realize that child neglect is rarely stopped without intervention. The U.S. Advisory Board reported that near-fatal abuse and neglect each year leaves "18,000 permanently disabled children, tens of thousands of victims overwhelmed by lifelong psychological trauma, thousands of traumatized siblings and family members, and thousands of near-death survivors who, as adults, continue to bear the physical and psychological scars. Some may turn to crime or domestic violence or become abusers themselves."

Most horrifying of all, most children continued to live with their abusers. Nearly nine out of every ten perpetrators of child maltreatment investigated are either the child's parent or other relative. Only five percent of all children reported for maltreatment were removed from their homes.

Consider the following recommendations:

Family Matters
For additional information, you can contact:

Child Welfare League of America
440 First Street, NW
Suite 310
Washington, DC 20001–2085
(202) 638–2952

1. The child's safety comes first. Always keep this in mind.

2. Don't wait for another in-law to step in and resolve the situation. In-laws are often very unwilling to shake the family tree.

3. Talk to an attorney to find out how the law works. Once child protective services are notified, they must respond to the situation.

4. Call your child welfare office if you think a child is being neglected.

5. Child abuse and neglect are a community concern. No one agency or professional alone can prevent and treat the problem; rather, all concerned citizens must work together to effectively identify, prevent, and treat child abuse and neglect.

Shut Up, Stupid: Emotional Abuse

The great American poet Robert Frost, no stranger to inflicting emotional abuse on his in-laws, wrote a powerful little poem called "Fire and Ice." In it, he questions whether the world will end in fire (passion) or ice (hate). He concludes:

> I think I know enough of hate
> To say that for destruction ice
> Is also great
> And would suffice.

Emotional abuse is far more subtle than sexual abuse, physical abuse, or neglect, but it can leave wounds that are just as deep. However, it can be difficult to determine whether an in-law is being emotionally abused because we all respond to verbal jabs differently.

How can you tell if an in-law is being emotionally abused—or if an in-law is an emotional abuser?

See how your in-law—or the person you may think is being abused by the in-law—responds to critical comments. Is the person emotionally shattered? Humiliated? Often, someone who has been emotionally abused repeatedly will become dependent on the abuser. If you suspect emotional abuse, you may want to intervene by demonstrating appropriate patterns of behavior. If the abuse continues, therapy might be required to break the cycle of maltreatment.

Family Matters

The link between substance abuse and child abuse has strengthened over the years. Parental abuse of alcohol and use of other drugs has been identified as a major factor contributing to child maltreatment and death. It is estimated that nearly 10 million children under the age of 18 are adversely affected by the substance abuse of their parents.

Words to the Wise

Emotional abuse includes acts that cause serious behavioral, cognitive, emotional, or mental disorders. For example, the parents may use bizarre punishments, such as torture or confinement of a child in a dark closet. For less severe acts, such as habitual scapegoating, belittling, or rejection, demonstrable harm to the child is often required for authorities to intervene.

Better Living Through Chemistry: Substance Abuse

For years, the neighborhood watched the unfolding story of Kim and John. John drank like a fish and the couple finally divorced. It wasn't until Kim and I served on a district committee together that I understood what had happened. Here's what Kim told me:

> "I knew that John liked to drink when I married him, but I thought it wouldn't be a big problem. Well, I was right and I was wrong. The booze wasn't the real issue; it was my in-laws. A few months into our marriage, John started getting verbally abusive when he drank too much. Every time I told him I didn't have to take it from him, he ran home to Mommy and Daddy. He would sleep over his parents' house and they would all have a few drinks together. My in-laws told me that I was overreacting: After all, John worked hard, so why couldn't he relax with a few beers after dinner? I called my sister-in-law, John's sister, but she had distanced herself from the family and didn't want to get involved. At that point, I decided that I couldn't stand up to my in-laws and my husband, so I just got out."

Sometimes, your in-laws will intervene on your behalf. This was the case with a man I'll call Marc, who had a problem with drug use. The family pulled together and got him the help he needed. Other times, however, the newcomer to the family can find it very difficult—if not impossible—to break long-standing substance abuse problems. The newcomer may even join his or her in-laws in substance abuse to become accepted by the family.

If you see substance abuse among your in-laws and do not speak up, you are facilitating the abuse. This harms not only your family, but also a far wider group, as the substance abuser drives a car when drunk or operates heavy machinery stoned.

Love Me Tender

The following worksheet can help you determine if sexual, physical, emotional, or substance abuse is occurring among your in-laws. Answer "yes" or "no" to each question. Even a handful of "yes" answers can indicate a pattern of abuse.

_____ 1. Do I see signs of sexual abuse, such as complaints of pain or irritation around a child's genital area, increased anxiety, or artwork that depicts strange sexual overtones?

_____ 2. Do I see signs of physical abuse on or from my in-law, such as black eyes or unexplained bruises?

_____ 3. Do I see signs of neglect, such as dirty clothing or hair, on an in-law's child?

_____ 4. Do I see signs of emotional abuse among my in-laws, such as habitual scapegoating, belittling, or rejection?

_____ 5. Is an in-law missing work or school for unexplained reasons?

_____ 6. Has the person become withdrawn and depressed?

_____ 7. Does this person seem frightened of being left alone with a particular in-law?

_____ 8. Do my in-laws require alcohol or drugs to enjoy themselves?

_____ 9. What are my reasons for getting involved? Am I genuinely concerned or do I have a desire to achieve revenge on this in-law for a previous run-in?

_____10. What will happen if I don't get involved? Can I live with these consequences?

For more information, you can contact:

The National Clearinghouse on Child Abuse and Neglect Information
P.O. Box 1182
Washington, D.C. 20013–1182
(800) FYI–3366

Child Help USA
6463 Independence Avenue
Woodland Hills, CA 91367
(800) 4–A–CHILD or (800) 422–4453

This group provides comprehensive crisis for adult and child victims of child abuse and neglect, offenders, and parents who are fearful that they will abuse or who want information on how to be effective parents.

National Committee to Prevent Child Abuse
332 South Michigan Avenue
Suite 1600
Chicago, IL 60604–4357
(312) 663–3520 (800) 835–2671

This group has 68 local chapters in all 50 states. They provide information and statistics on child abuse and maintain an extensive publications list.

National Council on Child Abuse and Family Violence
1155 Connecticut Avenue, NW
Suite 400
Washington, DC 20036
(202) 429–6695

or

> 6033 W. Century Boulevard
> Suite 400 Los Angeles, CA 90045
> (800) 222–2000

This group provides services to increase public awareness and education and to strengthen professional and organizational development in family violence prevention and treatment programs.

> The National Crime Prevention Council
> 1700 K Street, NW, 2nd Floor
> Washington, DC 20006
> (202) 466–6272

They provide personal safety curricula, including child abuse and neglect prevention for school children and model prevention programs for adolescents. Educational materials for parents, children, and community groups are available.

> Parents Anonymous
> 675 West Foothill Boulevard
> Suite 220
> Claremont, CA 91711
> (909) 621–6184

This group has 1,200 chapters nationwide. Each state has different program components in this professionally facilitated self-help group.

The Least You Need to Know

➤ Abuse takes five main forms: Sexual abuse, physical abuse, child neglect, emotional abuse, and substance abuse.

➤ If you suspect that an in-law is sexually abusing a member of your family, report it to the police or a child protection agency.

➤ Take physical abuse seriously. Even one slap can set the stage for a pattern of increasingly violent abuse.

➤ Emotional abuse isn't as overt as other types of abuse, but it can leave equally deep scars.

➤ If you see substance abuse among your in-laws and do not speak up, you are facilitating the abuse.

The March of Time: When In-Laws Age

A juggler, driving to his next performance, was stopped by the police. "What are those knives doing in your car?" asked the officer.

"I juggle them in my act."

"Oh yeah?" says the cop. "Let's see you do it."

So the juggler starts tossing and juggling the knives.

A guy driving by sees this and says, "Wow, am I glad I quit drinking. Look at the test they're making you do now!"

Few things test your character like elderly in-laws—and taking care of them may make juggling knives seem like a snap. America is graying. People are living longer, so it is more likely than not that you will have the responsibility at one point in your life of taking care of an elderly parent, sibling, in-law, or other relative. If you don't actually have the day-to-day responsibility for their care, you'll likely have to make decisions about your in-laws' medical needs and living arrangements.

In this chapter, you'll learn some startling facts about the changing face of America. Then I'll help you survey your in-laws to discover their needs as they age. Next, I'll show you how technology can help you ensure your in-laws' safety. We'll take a brief guilt trip as we explore some of the issues that can arise as in-laws age. You'll learn how to write new scripts to adjust to changing conditions.

Age Before Beauty

The United States is moving from a youth-oriented culture to a nation of middle-aged and older adults. That's because people are living longer. Let me dazzle you with some numbers:

➤ In 1920, the average life expectancy for men was 53.6 years; for women, 54.6 years. By 1970, the average man could expect to make it to 70.8; the average woman, 74.7. In 1997, the average man was still alive (and maybe even kicking) at 75.8; on average, women were living until age 78.9.

➤ By the year 2000, the average life expectancy in the U.S. is expected to top 80 years.

➤ Since 1982, the number of people in the U.S. over age 65 has exceeded those under the age of 18.

➤ The *over* 55-population is multiplying three times faster than the rest of the population.

➤ People age 85 and older make up the fastest-growing segment of the population in the U.S. During the past 30 years, the U.S. population grew 39 percent—but the ranks of those age 85 and older jumped an astonishing 232 percent.

➤ By the year 2000, 65 percent of all U.S. citizens will be over 65 years old. There will be six million people over age 85.

➤ By the year 2030, there will be 70 million Americans over age 65, according to The National Center for Elder Abuse.

➤ In 1990, the oldest person on the U.S. Social Security rolls was an 136-year-old man named Charlie Smith. (That's one way to squeeze the last drop from the government!)

[Source: *The 1997 World Almanac and Book of Facts*]

It's All Relative

Housing for the elderly is expected to be the primary focus of the construction industry over the next two decades. Even now, special types of housing are springing up across the country to accommodate the needs of seniors. Different types of assisted-care facilities provide varying degrees of care to seniors.

Are *you* feeling old? If not, consider this:

➤ The people who are starting college this fall across the nation were born in 1980. The Iranian hostage crisis occurred before they were conceived.

➤ They have no memory of a time before MTV.

➤ Cyndi Lauper, Boy George, the Pretenders, the Kinks, the Sex Pistols are all old music they have heard of, if they have heard of it at all.

➤ Black Monday 1987 is as significant to them as the Great Depression.

➤ Their world has always included AIDS, but not polio and certainly not smallpox.

➤ As far as they know, stamps have always cost about 32 cents.

➤ From their earliest years, a camera was something you used once and threw away.

Don't Go There
Old age is the only disease you don't look forward to being cured of.

➤ Most of them have probably never seen a nun in a traditional habit, even if they went to Catholic schools.

Live Long and Prosper?

Late one Saturday at an Idaho racetrack, a custodian came upon an elderly man sitting calmly in a wheelchair. He was wearing a brand-new sweatsuit, blue slippers, and a baseball cap inscribed "Proud to be an American." A typewritten note had been pinned to his jacket. It identified the old man as "John King," a retired farmer suffering from Alzheimer's disease.

In reality, the man was John Kingery. A former auto worker from Portland, Oregon, he was 82 years old. His daughter had apparently removed him from an Oregon nursing home and driven him 300 miles east, where she had left him.

Family Matters
Death is just a distant rumor to the young.

Such "granny dumping" is on the rise. While no exact figures are available on this appalling situation, hospitals estimate between 100,000 to 200,000 elderly people are left on hospital doorsteps every year.

Good Help Is Hard to Find

My friend Sheila has three sons. She heaved a sigh of relief when one of her sons finally got married. At the wedding, she pointed to the bride and said, "That's my insurance policy. You know that I never had a daughter. Now that I have a daughter-in-law, I know that I'll be taken care of in my old age."

Family Matters
Women are more likely to be cast into the caretaking role than men, especially when it comes to their in-laws.

Unfortunately, having a daughter or daughter-in-law is no guarantee that you'll be taken care of when you're old. As life expectancy has increased and the health of senior citizens has improved, programs for the elderly have become a growing concern. Adding together living parents, parents-in-law, step-parents, and step-parents in-law, the average American has more parents than children. Further, only one in ten person over age 65 is able to be totally independent.

The care of elderly parents is a significant concern for most of us—and for good reason. Who hasn't seen a situation where a son or daughter-in-law resented having to care for his or her in-laws?

Help Me, Rhonda

Fortunately, most of our elderly relatives can live on their own far longer than in previous generations. And I'm not just talking about 75-year-old granny on safari in the Congo or the 84-year-old Ironman who runs the Boston Marathon. In many cases, all our elderly in-laws need is some judicious help.

It's All Relative

Scientists suspect that mood plays a significant role in our immune system. Preliminary studies have shown that when we're happy, we're better able to fight off infection. The inverse is also true: When we're depressed, we have a harder time fighting off illness and recovering from it. Ergo, a strong network of friends and in-laws helps people stay healthy.

When his grandfather was alive, my husband used to help with the chores around his house. Actually the term "house" is somewhat misleading: Grandpa owned a decaying

17-room mansion that could have served as the model for the Bates Motel in *Psycho*. The house tilted like a drunken derelict; the plumbing and electricity were balky at best. Even if he had been in the very best of health, Grandpa couldn't have managed that monstrosity.

Fortunately, your elderly in-laws are not likely to own a crumbling mansion, but that doesn't mean they don't need a hand in their condo here or there. Consider these ideas to make life easier for your elderly in-laws:

➤ Offer to do the shopping and run some errands. The bundles are heavy; the sidewalks can be slippery.

➤ Slow down. I can't keep up with myself; how can I expect my 85-year-old father-in-law to?

➤ Provide physical help. Rake the leaves, clean the gutters, clean the carpet.

➤ Spend time together. Go out for a cup of cappuccino, take a walk around the lake, hit the mall on a rainy day. We all need company, especially people who may have difficulty getting around because of age.

➤ Consider getting your older in-laws a low-maintenance pet such as a cat or small dog. Scientific studies suggest that pets help people recover from illness faster.

➤ Travel together.

➤ Stay in touch. Write, call, e-mail.

Family Matters
The Information Superhighway is an inexpensive and fun way to stay in touch. It's easy, too. If my proudly techno-phobic mother can send e-mail, *anyone* can send e-mail.

Elder Care

Thorny problems arise when families are called on to take care of an elderly in-law. The issues are rarely insurmountable, but I'd be playing with your head if I said they're a breeze. Emotional as well as economic issues come into play as the traditional parent-child roles shift.

If you find yourself in this situation, start by taking stock of everyone's needs, wishes, and resources. You can use the following worksheet to help you plan for the future with your in-laws.

Family Matters
Obviously, the best way to cope with the issue of aging in-laws is to discuss the situation before it becomes a crisis. Ideally, find out what everyone wants and how to make it happen. Hey, I can dream, can't I?

1. Who are my elderly in-laws? _____
   _____

2. What are their needs at the current time?
   _____
   _____

3. What are their needs going to be a year from now? In five years?
   _____
   _____

4. How will their needs change in the future? _____
   _____

5. What family help is available now? _____
   _____

6. What family help might become available in the future?
   _____

7. What resources do we have now?
   Financial _____
   Social _____
   Religious _____
   Psychological _____
   Other _____

8. How might our resources change in the next five years?
   (For example, anticipated college expenses, our own retirement plans, etc.)
   _____
   _____

9. What type of care would our in-laws prefer? (Example: living in an apartment with a housekeeper, living in our home)
   _____
   _____

10. How do their plans fit with our needs and situation?
    _____

11. How can we provide this care? _____
    _____

12. If not, what compromise can we reach? _____
    _____

The basic rule is simple: Treat elderly in-laws with dignity and respect. For that to happen, however, there has to be communication. Try the following five ideas to help you work with your in-laws to make their golden years shine.

1. Communicate clearly with everyone in the family as you make decisions about aging in-laws. This is not the time to play the Lone Ranger, even if you are (a) the oldest, (b) the smartest, or Mom always loved you best.

Don't Go There
According to composer Arnold Schopenhauer, the closing years of life are like the end of a masquerade party, when the masks are dropped.

2. Be willing to make decisions. As long as your in-laws are able, they should make their own choices about care. But the time may come when you will have to step in. It's likely that you'll have to intervene for your in-laws' safety and the safety of others. For example, an elderly in-law may think he is able to drive a car when he's as blind as Mr. Magoo and twice as stubborn. Get the menace off the road, even if you have to be the meanie. Similarly, your elderly in-law may want to live alone, but it may no longer be safe or wise.

Family Matters
Many public agencies, service groups, and religious institutions offer assistance to caregivers of the elderly. The Methodist Church in my community, for instance, has a full-daycare program for elderly people who are in reasonably good health.

3. Ask for help. No martyrs need apply, cupcake. Start with the rest of the family. If they can't give mucho money or tons of time to help in the care of your elderly in-laws, get them to give a little here and a little there. If you have a very small family, you may not have any relatives who can help you care for aging in-laws. In that case, ask friends, neighbors, co-workers, and public agencies for assistance. You don't have to be a piggy about it, but you won't be any good to anyone if you've collapsed from the strain.

4. Be willing to make some personal sacrifices. "No pain, no gain" doesn't only apply to washboard abs. Be prepared to sacrifice some space, time, money, and privacy. It won't be easy, but were you such a peach as a toddler? And I'll bet your spouse had his moments, too.

5. If an elderly in-law comes to live with you, work out space arrangements and areas of responsibility. As long as your in-law is well, encourage him or her to remain independent.

Help Is Just a Call Away

Technology isn't a substitute for human contact, but gadgets and gizmos *can* help you give better care to your elderly in-laws. One of the most affordable and practical concepts is a personal emergency response system.

A personal emergency response system allows a person living at home to signal for emergency assistance by pushing a button. The button activates a communicator located in the home. It immediately sends an emergency signal over a telephone line to a 24-hour monitoring center. The monitoring center determines the nature of the emergency and sends the appropriate help which is usually an immediate family member or in-law, neighbor, ambulance, or police.

It's All Relative

Developed by Dr. Andrew Dibner at Duke University in 1973, personal response systems now serve about 350,000 individuals in North America. The industry leader, Lifeline Systems, distributes its service directly from calls to (800) LIFELINE and through more than 2,000 healthcare providers in the United States and Canada.

Don't Go There

While many people feel more secure and independent with a personal emergency response system, others won't use the system because they think they will lose their independence. Some live on a fixed income and cannot afford the system. Others deny being frail and having need for the device. Consider your in-law's image before ordering a personal emergency response system.

Personal emergency response systems were initially developed to allow aging, disabled, and ill persons to live independently at home with remote access to 24-hour assistance. Today, personal emergency response systems are also used by people of all ages, including active seniors with no prior medical conditions.

Personal emergency response systems:

➤ Give elderly people an increased feeling of independence, security, and peace of mind.

➤ Relieve the anxiety caregivers experience when they cannot physically be with their parents.

➤ Decrease the number of long-term care days and hospital admissions.

Caveat Emptor

Selecting a personal emergency response system can be confusing. About 30 companies in the United States currently offer these systems. About seven companies control the total market. Quality, service, and price can vary greatly. The following steps may be useful in evaluating the systems.

Don't Go There
Don't accept factory returns for repair or replacement. The equipment is like the cable box on your television. You pay for the service, not the equipment.

1. Find a local equipment provider that guarantees service of equipment within 24 hours. "Service" means replace or repair locally.

2. Ask your local provider to identify the system's manufacturer. Determine how long the manufacturer has been in business and how many customers use its system.

3. Get references from subscribers and healthcare organizations. Ask for references from your in-laws' doctor, your local council on aging, your hospital, the Better Business Bureau, or the state attorney general's office to make sure the company is legitimate.

4. Before you sign any agreements, the system should be installed in your in-laws' house and tested. Test everything: Hook the system to the telephone line, turn it on, arm it, disarm it, set it off, and reset it. Adjust the volume control up and down and change the batteries. Your in-laws must be able to perform all of the operating tasks on their own.

5. Find out who will monitor the signals when your in-law pushes the help button. The personal response system should be monitored by certified professionals at a central location or by a reputable health care organization.

6. Monitors should be senior-oriented, caring, and social in nature. Most calls will be for non-urgent reasons. When an emergency occurs, you want a center that will stay on the line until emergency personnel arrive.

7. Consider whether your in-law needs national versus local emergency monitoring. If the company is senior-oriented and has a national monitoring center using trained professionals 24 hours a day, a call could be answered more efficiently from across the country than by a local monitoring station without round-the-clock professional service. Computer technology allows national monitoring facilities, no matter where they are located, to respond quickly and efficiently to emergency signals.

8. Ask who will respond to the help signal. Some services automatically send an ambulance, regardless of the emergency. If the ambulance isn't needed, it must be paid for anyway. A better choice would be a monitoring center that will send

Family Matters
"After age 70 it's patch, patch, patch," the late actor Jimmy Stewart claimed.

different "responders," depending on the situation. Often, the responder can be a relative or neighbor. In critical emergencies, immediate response can come from an ambulance, law enforcement official, or the fire department. You and your in-law can maintain a list of immediate responders in the monitoring center's database.

9. Ask if the system offers maximum protection. Some systems have additional safety features such as a speaker phone to let the monitoring center know exactly what has happened. These companies and others offer a variety of advanced features and are improving their systems all the time. Interview each company to find out about their state-of-the-art features.

10. Ask if the system comes with an optional smoke detector alarm. It will automatically signal that the fire department should be notified.

Money Matters

Some providers do not sell any part of the system. Rather, they rent the help button and the communicator box. Others sell or lease the system and charge a monthly monitoring fee. Rental and monitoring costs between $25 and $45 per month. Purchase prices range from $200 to $2,000. Installation visits can cost from $50 to $150.

A research study conducted at MIT concluded that systems costing $150 to $350 worked as well as systems selling for 20 times that amount.

Don't Go There
When you call for information, the company should tell you over the phone how much their system costs. If they will not quote prices over the phone, the company may attempt high-pressure tactics in person.

For further information, you can contact:

Communi-Call
9765 Clairemont Mesa Blvd.
San Diego, CA 92124
(800) 447-6467

Emergency Response Systems (ERS)
577 West Century Blvd., Suite 1701
Los Angeles, CA 90045
(800) 833-2000

Home Technology Systems
340 CyCare Plaza
P.O. Box 598
Dubuque, IA 52001
(800) 922-3555

Lifeline Systems
One Arsenal Marketplace
Watertown, MA 02172
(800) 451-0525

Attention Must be Paid!

Check out the following cautionary tale:

> Louise needed minor surgery. Her daughter-in-law Tanya offered to drive her to the doctor, wait during the procedure, and take her home. Tanya was gracious and kind and she often helped Louise. However, Louise insisted that her son Jay had to take her to the doctor. When Jay, a lawyer, explained that he had to be in court that day, Louise got even more insistent. "You never do anything for me," she screamed. "If you can't take me, I'll just hire a car service!" Jay was baffled; his wife Tanya was more than willing to take his mother to the doctor. What was going on here?

There's no question that Louise is being irrational here. Her daughter-in-law was perfectly willing to take her to the doctor; her son has a busy work day. In addition, the medical procedure was very minor, so why did everyone have to jump to attention? There's often a hidden agenda with an in-law's escalating needs and demands. Let's look at it from Louise's point of view.

Imagine that you're an elderly woman. Your son-the-hot-shot-professional is becoming more and more preoccupied with his career. Your daughter-in-law is a dream. Although she has several kids and a part-time job in hubby's office, she nevertheless makes time to drive you to the doctor, take you to lunch, and pick up the designer bean sprouts you need for your salad. Even though you love your daughter-in-law, she's not your son. She's not the one you endured 48 hours of labor for, the one who made you a vase in the fourth grade, the one who has your sense of humor. What to do?

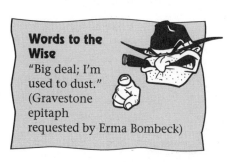

Words to the Wise
"Big deal; I'm used to dust." (Gravestone epitaph requested by Erma Bombeck)

Gradually, you intensify your needs and demands. Unconsciously, you hope your daughter-in-law will be so annoyed with you that she'll throw up her hands in disgust and your son will be forced to step in.

Louise's needs are very real, but her tactics are ineffective. Better she should have told her son how much she appreciates his wife's kindness but she has a need to be with him. On their end, the younger set have to be more aware of the needs of their parents and in-laws. It's brutally hard to watch a parent or in-law become dependent as they age, especially if they are alone. The elderly often feel vulnerable, especially in times of stress. They often want their flesh-and-blood to be with them, no matter how close they feel to their in-laws. They need sympathy and empathy, in addition to attention.

Days of Whine and Poses

Don, age 57, is an only child who is riddled with guilt. His mother knows exactly which of Don's guilt buttons to push. Aware that a large part of Don's self esteem rests on being a "good son," she barrages him with demands to visit and call. Hearty and of sound mind, 86-year-old Edna constantly jabs Don with just the right words to produce guilt: "If you loved me, you would visit more often; you're always having such a good time, how can you forget your mother who is all alone and old; you owe me so much after all I did for you; I see what other children do for their parents and it is more than you do for me."

Don't Go There
Some wines get better with age. So do some in-laws. Other wines, in contrast, turn to vinegar as they get older. Ditto with in-laws.

Such calculated salvos do the trick each time, catapulting Don into instant filial duty, often at the expense of his own family and health. Is it any wonder then that in the five years since his father died, Don has developed a host of his own minor medical conditions? Is it any wonder, likewise, that Don's wife, Lynne, is in a fury over the time Don spends visiting and worrying over his mother?

Crank Case

Life is like a kaleidoscope. The same pieces remain in the picture, but they shift positions and form a new pattern. Even though the new pattern is not radically different from the old one, it is altered enough to require a second look...and maybe a third.

It is the same with your relationship to your in-laws as everyone ages. People usually do not change to great extremes, but with maturation they will usually shift and readjust their positions to some degree. Unfortunately, some people lack the ability to change. As a result, when they grow older, they become more of what they basically are—crotchety, critical, narrow-minded, selfish, and dissatisfied.

Don't Go There
Most people grow and mature as they get older. Others just get older! It may be hard to believe that 10 or 20 years from now your point of view on many issues will change drastically—but it's even more frightening if your opinions don't change.

Don't be blown away if your in-laws get more selfish and demanding as they mature; after all, old age isn't for sissies. Often, the situation can be improved with a little communication and concern.

You have a choice: You can choose to follow in the patterns of the past or take new roads. Even if your in-laws are getting difficult as they age, take the time to create the kind of family you want—before it's too late. Reach out to perform the little kindness, forgive the slight, mend the breach.

The Least You Need to Know

➤ America is aging. By the year 2000, 65 percent of all U.S. citizens will be over 65 years old.

➤ As a result, many of us will become caretakers for our elderly in-laws.

➤ Start by taking stock of everyone's needs, wishes, and resources.

➤ Communicate clearly with everyone in the family as you make decisions about aging in-laws.

➤ A personal emergency response system can give an elderly person greater independence.

➤ Our elderly in-laws need sympathy and empathy in addition to care.

Chapter 25

The Relatives Formerly Known as "In-Laws"

In This Chapter

➤ Discover the stages people go through when a couple dissolves through death or divorce

➤ Find out what to call your former in-laws

➤ Learn how to make drastic life changes less painful for all your in-laws— and yourself

A man was zooming home late one afternoon, way above the speed limit. Sure enough, a police car picked up his scent. The man thought, "I can outrun this guy," and floors it. The cars were racing down the highway—60, 70, 80, 90 miles per hour. Finally, as his speedometer passed 100, the guy figured, "What the hell," and gave up. He pulled over to the curb.

The police officer got out of his cruiser and approached the car. The officer leaned down and said, "Listen, mister, I've had a really lousy day, and I just want to go home. Give me a good excuse and I'll let you go."

The man thought for a moment and said, "Three weeks ago, my wife ran off with a police officer. When I saw your cruiser in my rear view mirror, I thought that you were the officer and that you were trying to give her back to me."

The officer didn't give the man a ticket.

With the divorce rate zooming faster than the man in this story, chances are we're all going to end up with an ex-in-law or two...or three or four or five. How we relate to our *former* in-laws is even less clearly defined than how we relate to our *current* in-laws. Not to worry; Rozakis to the rescue! In this chapter, you'll learn how divorce and death change the in-law landscape. Along the way, I'll give you tips for handling these difficult issues. You'll get the tools you need to maintain and enrich your relationships with your in-laws through the years.

In Love and War

Whether you love your in-laws or hate them, over time they become part of the scenery, like the dishwasher or the TV. Suddenly or slowly, the scenery starts to change. Then one day, the couple divorces or one partner dies, and you have an ex-law. A divorce is the legal dissolution of the marriage, but it doesn't have any impact on the emotional bonds that have been formed. The same is true about death, except that it's a whole lot more final. No matter how you felt about your in-laws, divorce or death shatters everyone's emotional landscape.

When divorce dissolves a couple, the spouse gets a divorce and all the closure that comes with lawyers, litigation, and lavish bills. There's no sense of closure for the rest of the family, however. What happens to your brother-in-law after the divorce? Without the "law," there's no brother. A divorce breaks up a marriage, but not the feelings that have been forged between in-laws over the years.

Words to the Wise

Clans of long ago that wanted to get rid of their unwanted in-laws without killing them use to burn their houses down—hence the expression "to get fired." (I could make this stuff up?)

Family Matters

According to the National Center for Health Statistics, most divorces occur within the first 10 years of marriage. The median duration of marriage for divorcing couples in 1995 was 7.2 years. *That's* why they call it the "Seven Year Itch."

When death dissolves a couple, the spouse often has a ritualized period of mourning designed to assuage the pain. There's no similar ritual for the in-laws, however. They're the supporting players in this tragedy, expected to help the widow or widower. Who helps *them* deal with their pain and sense of loss? Death can dissolve a marriage, but not the feelings that have been forged between in-laws over the years.

Now and Zen

An older couple met their demise in an auto accident and were transported to Heaven. As they were waiting to be processed, they began to look all around at their setting for eternity.

The wife was amazed at the beauty, the peace, and the contentment she felt and commented over and over about what a nice place Heaven was and how fortunate she felt to be there.

The husband sneered, "If it weren't for you and your damned oat-bran muffins and health food crap, we'd have been here 15 years ago."

The aftermath of a death or a divorce follows a pattern. Nearly everyone involved in the situation follows these steps:

1. **Denial**

   The bereaved family member, divorcing couple, and their in-laws are likely to think, "This can't be happening to me! This can't be happening to this family."

2. **Anger**

   Unfortunately, anger over death or divorce is usually indiscriminate; anyone within firing range is apt to be the target of errant hostility. Keep a low profile during this stage.

3. **Acceptance**

   Finally, the individuals accept the situation and begin to make plans for the future.

Circle the Wagons

Paradoxically, death and divorce can have a silver lining, because they allow all the in-laws to rally round, united by their common pain. Of course, adversity also allows family members to engage in covert or open hostilities. It all depends on individual agendas and family history. Unfortunately, the people least able to duck are often in firing range.

How can you help make drastic life transitions less painful for all involved? Here are some ideas.

➤ Keep important decisions private until you're ready to alert the media; i.e., a couples' initial decision to divorce should be kept between them until they are ready to make it public to the family. Remember, a divorce isn't a class action suit, no matter what your in-laws may think.

➤ Remember that discretion is the better part of valor. As an in-law, keep your mouth shut. Of course you knew all along that your sister's ex-husband was a louse. It's no secret that your brother's deceased wife was a tramp. Since everyone knows it, why add fuel to the fire by commenting on it? Loose lips sink ships...and friendship among in-laws.

> **Don't Go There**
>
> How long does it take a person to grieve over death or divorce? No one can set a time limit on sorrow, but if you notice prolonged sadness or sharp changes in personality, it may be time to call in some professional help.

> **Family Matters**
>
> As they deal with their feelings over death or divorce, family members are also likely to bargain ("I'll be good if you can just make this go away") and grieve. Be patient and allow your in-law time to follow all three stages in the healing process.

Family Matters
Here's another good reason to keep your own counsel: You never know if your divorcing in-laws will reconcile. If they do and you've bad-mouthed one of them, who do you think is going to end up in the dog house? Better stay on Fido's good side if you're going to be a blabbermouth.

Don't Go There
Be especially careful not to criticize a dead in-law. Death elevates even the worst scoundrel to instant sainthood. And every family has a few reprobates.

Don't Go There
There are times, unfortunately, when it just won't be possible to stay in touch with a former in-law. This can occur when abuse was involved, for example.

➤ Be supportive, but don't take sides. It's sweet to side with your blood relative against the infidel in-law, but beware—your former in-law may be in the right here. How can you guard your flank against later attack? Listen but don't comment. Here are appropriate responses: "Uh huh," "Ummm," "Oh!" and the ever-popular "You don't say!"

➤ Know your in-laws. Unless you've spent your time with your head in the oven, you know which buttons are likely to set off a family explosion. Here's a simple solution to common in-law problems when it comes to divorce and death: Don't push the hot buttons.

➤ Be patient. It can take years to work out a divorce or get over the death of a loved one. Keep the family together and try to minimize the damage.

Make New Friends But Keep the Old?

Divorce can be difficult for the in-laws whenever it takes place, but it is often especially traumatic when a marriage of many years breaks up. Here's Mike's story:

"My sister and her husband were married for 25 years when they decided to get a divorce earlier this year. We all knew that things hadn't been going well between them, but since they had been married for so long, we all just figured that they'd be married forever. I really like my brother-in-law—sometimes more than I like my sister. I thought he liked me, too. We spent a lot of time together over the years, but when I called to talk to him after the divorce, he never returned my call. I tried a few more times, but he never got back to me. I guess I made the mistake of thinking he was a friend."

Mike is overreacting here. After a divorce—especially one that severs a long-term marriage—it can often take time for the feelings to settle. Sometimes, the best strategy is to give the former in-law some time to cool off before trying to resume a relationship.

The Devil and the Deep Blue Sea

Adrienne had been very close to her in-laws. When she divorced their son Paul, however, she was frozen out of the picture. "It took me a long time to stop crying," she told me. Adrienne's in-laws decided to choose sides...and Adrienne wasn't picked.

It's likely that someone in the family will try to force you into choosing sides when your blood relative and an in-law divorce. Here's what a friend told me about her family's situation:

> "When my sister Su divorced her husband Bruce, she laid it right on the line: Any friend of Bruce's was no friend of hers. If I even spoke to Bruce, she threatened never to speak to me again. I really liked Bruce, but if I wanted to keep my sister, Bruce had to go. I'm hoping that she'll cool down and I can be friends with Bruce again, but I know it will take a long time for the bitterness to die down."

But just because your relative didn't get along with his or her spouse is no reason for you to sever your connection with your former in-law. Your kin is likely to feel that you're being disloyal if you keep up the friendship. Tough nougies. The decision to remain friends with a former in-law is yours.

Kids are an especially important reason to maintain a friendship with an ex-in-law. A loving grandparent, uncle, or aunt is very important to any child, but especially to one whose parents are divorcing. Loving relatives give a child continuity and a sense of stability.

Family Matters
In divorce proceedings, Middle Eastern men usually assume they are the most appropriate parent to have custody over the children. The father's opinion will usually prevail, because he is considered superior to his wife within this culture.

Party Animals

Then we come to the issue of family functions. How do you decide whether to invite former in-laws to family functions such as weddings, graduations, and holidays? This gets us to the ultimatum portion of our show. Here are the most common threats you can expect to have showered on your head if your in-laws have parted on less than amicable terms.

"If you invite my former spouse to the party...

➤ I'm not coming!"

➤ I'll never speak to you again!"

➤ you're no parent (sister, brother, aunt, cousin, etc.) of mine!"

➤ you'll never hear the end of it!"

➤ you'll be sorry!"

Family Matters
Everyone needs a couple of dull friends. I mean *really* dull—the kind who make it seem exciting to watch linoleum curl. Boring friends make a great buffer at charged family events because you can sit them next to any feuding in-laws; like a black hole, they suck the anger out of everyone by virtue of their very dullness. We call our couple "The Blands," and they sure do come in handy.

Family Matters
You really don't owe anyone an explanation of your in-laws' status vis-à-vis each other and the rest of the family. If you don't feel comfortable with any of these solutions, just use the person's name in the introduction. Let the guest puzzle out the relationship. It will keep them busy and leave all the cocktail weenies for you.

So what can you do if your blood relative says "I'm not coming to the wedding/bar mitzvah/communion/graduation party if you invite my former husband, he-should-rot-in-hell?" It's your party; you can invite who you want to. Try these ideas:

➤ Invite everyone. Let them duke it out.

➤ If they all decide to come to the event and you know there will be fireworks, sit the feuding ex-laws in opposite corners of the room. Divide the room with a demilitarized zone of neutral guests. Neighbors, friends, and colleagues make a good DMZ.

➤ Worst case scenario: Hold two events. This may not be possible, however, and it's usually a last-ditch move in any case.

The Name Game, Redux

In Chapter 6, you grappled with the issue of what to call your prospective in-laws. Did you think *that* was difficult? That was just a warm-up, baby. Try figuring out what to call your *former* in-laws.

How do you introduce an ex-grandparent-in-law? How do you refer to a former son-in-law? Father-in-law? Sister-in-law?

"I don't want to be called an 'ex' anything," someone in my family once told me. "'Ex' means you've been wiped off the board." Here are three ways you can smooth these stormy waters:

1. **Ask former in-laws what they want to be called.**

   Talking about the name issue right up front allows everyone to air their feelings and knocks stress down to manageable levels.

2. **Follow the leader.**

   This only works is there's been a previous divorce or death in the family. When you're renaming in-laws, one size *does not* fit all, so beware.

3. **Use your noggin.**

   Here are some logical ways to introduce your ex-in-laws to people who aren't savvy to the current family shuffle:

➤ "Here are my former in-laws, Ozzie and Harriet."

➤ "Let me introduce my father's seventh wife, Elizabeth Taylor."

➤ "This is Richard Dick, my child's father."

➤ "Have you met my mother-in-law's husband, Alfonse?"

Life in the Fast Lane

If you had asked me to define "family" when I was a child, I would have said, "A family is a mommy, daddy, sisters, brothers, grandparents, and a cat or two." Without doubt, I was a clever child.

There's no doubt that the "family" has changed drastically in the past generation. In 1997, for example, nearly 20 percent of children under the age of 18 years were involved in divorce. Many children are living in what we now call "nontraditional families." Mother's Day and Father's Day have taken on a whole new meaning as Heather has Two Daddies and We're All Free to Be You and Me.

The changing face of families around the globe means that we have to deal with a redefinition of "in-laws." Today, we increasingly have to accommodate former as well as present in-laws. How do people adjust to the new realities? Here are some ways:

> **Words to the Wise**
>
> What's a *family*? Here's the best definition I've heard: "A family are the people you live with and love." Feel free to fiddle with this definition all you like. Just don't call, write, or e-mail with your suggestions.

Dazed and Confused

Against all signs to the contrary, some women figure that they'll marry Prince Charming and live happily ever after. Conversely, some men figure they've got their hands on Betty Crocker and all's right with the world. Think again. Here's what an acquaintance told me about her current in-law situation:

> "Recently, my live-in and I decided to separate for a time. We have a three-month-old daughter, and I also have a three-and-half-year-old daughter from a previous relationship. While my intent was to solidify the relationship and commit to marriage, it's looking less likely as time passes. Should I try to foster the relationship between my former in-laws and my oldest daughter? Her biological father has never taken part in her life, and recently she has been referring to my younger daughter's grandparents as her own."

This is really an issue that the adults must explore together. How committed is the biological father to maintaining a relationship with his daughter? How committed is the lover to maintaining a relationship with his former girlfriend's daughter? How do the grandparents feel about taking on two grandchildren? Are they willing be an involved part of her life?

Here's a variation on the theme:

> "My husband and I have been separated for six months and my nine-year-old son has had a hard time with this situation. My in-laws have given my son mixed signals about how much they want to be involved in his life—and mine. We are trying to plan for the upcoming Thanksgiving and Christmas holidays. These were always very family-oriented holidays in the past. Should we do something completely different? How much should we change the routines and activities that we did in the past?"

Don't Go There
Children need to feel safe, knowing there are adults they can count on. If an in-law can't make a firm commitment to children from former relationships, the in-law may be better off out of the picture.

If former in-laws aren't willing to maintain the family traditions, it's time to develop new customs with your children. Holidays are usually the most difficult to bear after divorce or death ends a marriage, so go slowly.

Power to the People

It's not uncommon for former in-laws to use children as pawns to manipulate the situation. Here's what Mary Ellen told me:

> "My ex-brother-in-law wants to sign my children up for martial arts lessons twice a week. Some of these time slots interfere with their dinner time. I am all for the children spending time with their favorite uncle and participating in martial arts. However, he refuses to feed them dinner, insisting it is my responsibility. I feel if he takes them during this time, he needs to provide dinner.

> To complicate matters further, he only takes three of my four children—only the boys. My youngest, a daughter, is not included and her heart is breaking. I would like to limit lessons to twice a month, have him provide dinner if the lesson interferes with their dinner, and have him include his niece, too."

What we have here are issues of power and control. Uncle Kung Fu Fighter doesn't seem malicious, just dopey. Drop the power struggle and get on the same side for the sake of the kids.

Splitsville

Some in-laws break off their friendships. The stress of the divorce proves too great on the relationship. This is what happened with Irma and her mother-in-law Maria. Irma had depended on her mother-in-law for back-up childcare; Maria had been generous with money as well as time. The two women had a solid, affectionate relationship. Here's what Irma told me:

> "When Julio and I decided to get divorced, my mother-in-law was a great sounding board. I told her all about Julio's unwillingness to do his fair share around the house and how tight he was with money. Maria understood all my problems, because her husband, my father-in-law, was just as rigid and cheap. As it became apparent that Julio and I were going to divorce, however, Maria started to clam up. She saw that her son was in pain, too, and she resented me for my share of the problems. Ultimately, she took her son's side in the divorce."

Sad as it may seem, some in-laws just can't remain friends after death or divorce, as you can see in Irma's story. Although, it isn't out of the realm of reality for some to become even closer friends. The friendship deepens after their trial by fire; they may have liked the in-law better than the blood relative all along.

Picture Perfect

Nothing says lovin' like something from the oven, and nothing says "Holiday Madness" like family pictures. It's that time again. Perhaps you all trek down to the local department store photography studio to stand on a line that stretches from here to eternity. Maybe you pull out all the stops and hire a professional photographer to come to your house. Whether you go budget or blow a wad, the family photo is always an adventure.

Is your daughter the Princess screaming because you won't let her wear her nose ring in the picture? Has your son Buster dyed his hair spruce green? No doubt the baby has gotten into the peanut butter and is now hugging the dog.

Are we having fun yet? Wait…we have to decide *who* gets to be a part of the picture. Here's what my friend Sandy asked me:

> "This year for the holidays, my family has decided to have a portrait taken. My married sister doesn't want my fiancé in the portrait. She claims my fiancé could end up out of the picture before the picture is even developed. Who belongs in the picture?"

Then we have Belva's story:

> "Several years ago, we had a family portrait taken that included our parents, my husband and myself, my two married sisters and their husbands and children, and my unmarried sister. Well, both of my brothers-in-law have since become ex-brothers-in-law. We make family jokes about using 'sticky notes' as cover-ups, or covering the face of each ex with his replacement. Maybe we should just get a marker and X their faces out?"

Get the picture? To keep peace in the family, try these ideas when it comes to family pictures:

➤ Play it safe: Always have photographs taken of your parents by themselves and with their children.

➤ Display the new photograph, but don't destroy the old one. Keep the photograph with the exes in your album. All the exes are part of your family history, if not its future. (But then again, you never know.)

Last Licks

All change is hard. After an eternity of doing things a specific way and interacting with in-laws in set patterns, death or divorce pulls the rug out from under us. After any traumatic change, all the in-laws find themselves adrift, bobbing on the ocean of life without any bearings. No matter how much we want to resist, the situation has changed. We have to learn new ways of dealing with each other if we are to survive.

Try these ideas:

1. Don't expect the situation to resolve itself in a McMoment. Meaningful change comes as slowly as continental drift.

Don't Go There
Billy Graham has described heaven as a family reunion that never ends. What must hell possibly be like? Home videos of the same reunion?

2. Ask for assistance. It's a sign of strength, not weakness.

3. Consider seeking help from someone outside the family, such as a friend, religious advisor, or professional counselor.

4. Realize that with change comes growth. It might not seem possible when the family is going through the crisis, but positive things can come from loss. After the crisis, you may emerge as a stronger person with a much greater appreciation of your in-laws.

The Least You Need to Know

➤ Losing an in-law through death or divorce is among the most stressful things that can happen to a person.

➤ After a loss, in-laws follow predictable patterns of grieving, from denial to anger to acceptance.

➤ Families have to readjust to make room for the new reality. Be discrete and supportive, but don't take sides.

➤ Change can bring growth and even happiness as in-laws come together to support each other.

➤ Your in-laws may not be perfect, but they're yours.

Index

T-U-V

W-Z